Family
Caregiving

Volume 186 Sage Library of Social Research

RECENT VOLUMES IN . . .
SAGE LIBRARY OF SOCIAL RESEARCH

Family Caregiving

Autonomous and Paternalistic Decision Making

Victor G. Cicirelli

Sage Library of Social Research 186

SAGE PUBLICATIONS
The International Professional Publishers
Newbury Park   London   New Delhi

For information address:

SAGE Publications, Inc.
2455 Teller Road
Newbury Park, California 91320

SAGE Publications Ltd.
6 Bonhill Street
London EC2A 4PU
United Kingdom

SAGE Publications India Pvt. Ltd.
M-32 Market
Greater Kailash I
New Delhi 110 048 India

Printed in the United States of America

Library of Congress Cataloging-in-Publication Data

Cicirelli, Victor G.
    Family Caregiving : autonomous and paternalistic decision making /
Victor G. Cicirelli
        p.   cm. — (Sage library of social research ; v. 186)
    Includes bibliographical references and index.
    ISBN 0-8039-3906-X. — ISBN 0-8039-3907-8 (pbk.)
    1. Aging parents—United States—Family Relationships. 2. Aging
parents—Care—United States—Decision making. 3. Autonomy
(Psychology) in old age—United States. 4. Parent and adult child—
United States. I. Title. II. Series.
HQ1062.6.C53   1991
306.874—dc20   91-11256
                                                                                CIP

HQ
1063.6
.C53
1992

FIRST PRINTING, 1992

Sage Production Editor: Diane S. Foster

Contents

Preface

Personal autonomy is a central and complex value of our society. In long-term care, family members and professional caregivers influence the exercise of personal autonomy in the lives of older adults who have physical or cognitive disabilities. Autonomy may be either enhanced or diminished through the actions of those providing care. Even for well-intended family and professional caregivers, the task of caring for an older adult who has impairments without controlling that person is delicate and complicated.

This book examines these issues. It is a result of a project sponsored within the Retirement Research Foundation's (RRF) Personal Autonomy in Long Term Care Initiative, a 4-year, $2 million, 28-project grant program focusing on ethical issues in autonomy and decision making for older adults who have frailty and impairments. Despite consensus that elderly individuals receiving long-term care services in the home or in an institution have a right to maximum self-determination and dignity, there is often an erosion of personal autonomy as others make a variety of decisions for them. In addition to fundamental legal and ethical considerations, this erosion may lead to negative effects in the health and well-being of these older adults. Mindful of the crucial importance of autonomy issues in long-term care, the Foundation established its initiative as an interdisciplinary forum that involved health professionals, human service professionals, lawyers, social scientists, and humanists. The projects funded within the initiative had as their core the realities of the lives of older persons in long-term care, emphasized everyday ethical issues as opposed to life-and-death issues, and focused upon practical issues that would in some way improve the quality of life of elderly individuals in long-term care.

Victor Cicirelli's project examined and developed an instrument to measure beliefs in respect for autonomy and paternalism in family caregiving situations, fulfilling these initiative criteria. It also added some unique contributions. It was the only project to operationalize autonomy-related constructs to the point of instrument development. The instruments, included in the Appendix of this book, will be important tools for a variety of researchers and practitioners. Other projects in the initiative focused on autonomy issues in formal care involving professionals and paraprofessionals in institutional, guardianship, and medical home-care settings. Because family members comprise the major support system through which formal care plans are implemented and provide the bulk of informal care, it was important for the initiative to give attention to autonomy and paternalism in informal family care dealing with problems of everyday living. Also, personal autonomy involves psychological, as well as physical, dimensions. An older adult in long-term care could be paralyzed from a stroke and quite immobile yet have considerable personal autonomy by making meaningful decisions that are implemented by others. It was important for the psychological level of autonomy to be considered in some depth. This initiative project examined the autonomous or paternalistic decision-making behaviors that family caregivers and care receivers actually display and explored possibly related antecedents. Because one important antecedent was thought to be beliefs in respect for autonomy and paternalism, instruments were developed to assess such beliefs.

The strengths of this book in presenting and discussing these contributions are considerable. It provides a valuable and comprehensive review of the literatures of both family caregiving and applied ethics with regard to autonomy issues, synthesizing the two in original and helpful ways. The research reported is itself an exemplar of the marriage of applied ethics and the social sciences. A need exists for more basic descriptive data within ethical analysis. Facts cannot resolve value questions, but empirical research can help frame the analysis of difficult issues. In turn, descriptive research should focus on key ethical issues. The results reported in this volume will be informative and reinforcing to both ethicists and psychosocial researchers.

The book fills a major gap in the literature regarding autonomy issues. It provides information about how families are involved in decision making for long-term-care older adults, how perceptions and preferences of family members may differ from those of older persons, and provides important initial thoughts on how resulting conflicts best can be resolved. It highlights that the preferences of older adults receiving care are diverse, including preferences regarding autonomy and paternalism. It would be paradoxical, ironic, and unfortunate if family and professional care providers insisted that all older adults receiving care had to be autonomous! The book also emphasizes that family caregiver and older adult perceptions and preferences may differ markedly. These differences may result from inadequate communication or from different values and world views. Finally, the book provides strong evidence that lack of education, negative attitudes toward elders, and an authoritarian family tradition can influence the frequency of paternalistic decision making.

In summary, this book provides a wealth of information, ideas, and concrete tools of interest and use to both researchers and practitioners. It is an important milestone in the examination of autonomy issues in the informal family caregiving of older adults.

—Brian F. Hofland

Acknowledgments

To note all the influences that led to the preparation of this volume would be a formidable task, with some forces coming early in my career. More recently, my interest in the topic of autonomy and paternalism in family caregiving was kindled by personal dilemmas that arose in the process of caring for my own frail elderly parents and those of my wife as we struggled with the ethical question of whether we had the right to intervene.

Professionally, the excellent 1985 issue of *Generations* helped clarify many of the ethical issues involved in caregiving and led up to the research giving rise to this book.

First, I want to express my thanks and appreciation to The Retirement Research Foundation for their support of my research in this area as part of their Personal Autonomy in Long Term Care Initiative, a large and well-organized 4-year grant program focused on the topic of autonomy in long-term care. (My project came in the second phase of this program.)

Special thanks go to Brian Hofland, Vice-President of the Foundation, who conceived and guided the entire autonomy research effort. His vision, organizational skills, and keen intellectual interest in the topic helped make my own research work a rewarding experience. Thanks also go to Debra David of San Jose State University, who served as monitor for my research project. Her readiness to help and insightful comments were always welcome. Also, I must mention the periodic grantee meetings organized by Brian Hofland that brought together all the researchers working on the autonomy in long-term care initiative. Although nearly all of these projects dealt with autonomy in formal long-term care, while mine dealt with informal family care, I want to express my appreciation to these fellow grantees (too many to list here) for their stimulating ideas and critical comments.

I am particularly indebted to Bart Collopy of Fordham University for his fine conceptual analysis of autonomy and paternalism in relation to the frail elderly and for his generosity in granting me permission to adapt some of his case study vignettes for research use and to reproduce them in the Appendix to this volume.

In addition, I want to acknowledge an intellectual debt to those colleagues who also have been exploring ethical issues surrounding decision making in family long-term care of the elderly: Dallas High of the University of Kentucky, Amy Horowitz of the Lighthouse and Fordham University, and Clara Pratt of Oregon State University. Their work helped immensely in clarifying issues and concepts in this emerging area.

Next, I want to thank Della Wellman, Phyllis Shipman, and Elva James of the Area IV Council on Aging and Dena Targ of the Purdue University Extension Service for their help in identifying adult child caregivers and their elderly parents as possible study participants.

Above all, I am deeply grateful for the cooperation of several hundred elderly parents and adult children who unselfishly gave their time and energies to share information about their lives, their feelings, and their beliefs with all of us.

Finally, I must thank my hardworking research assistants, who carried out the field interviews with me: Margaret

Woltjer, who also assisted with the management of the interviewing task, Michele Killough, Shari Spence, Victoria Sprague, and Laura Tarr. Without their care and diligence in eliciting good interview data, this work would have been impossible.

—Victor G. Cicirelli

PART ONE

Background Information

ONE

Autonomy and Paternalism in Long-Term Care

The number of elderly people is increasing and will continue to increase well into the 21st century, with the most dramatic growth occurring in the number of those over age 85. Unfortunately, a vigorous life has not automatically or necessarily accompanied a longer life; instead, during an extended time period, people decline physically and mentally, suffer pain and various other symptoms, and deal with a multiplicity of chronic illnesses. Most of the aged spend a longer time being dependent upon others than in earlier generations. Caregiving exists primarily to manage the chronic illnesses of these impaired and frail elderly, satisfying their needs for everyday living within a long-term care system.

A serious concern by many researchers and practitioners is that long-term care may limit unduly the autonomy of older people by fostering the practice of paternalism to an unnecessary degree. By its very nature, long-term care may inadvertently present obstacles that must be overcome to ensure the elderly individual's exercise of autonomy.

IMPORTANCE OF AUTONOMY
IN LONG-TERM CARE

Culturally, self-reliance or independence has always been one of the professed values of American society. Psychologically, much research indicates that feeling in control of one's own destiny has a strong impact on one's health, morale, and self-esteem (Hofland, 1988). Ethically, autonomy of the individual has been an important value throughout Western civilization. For Aristotle (1925) and Kant (1964), to be human is to think for oneself. Similarly, Mill (1926) felt that no one should interfere with a person's freedom so long as society was not harmed in any way.

Unfortunately, the individual's right to autonomy does not always receive parallel affirmation and protection by governments. Hofland (1988) has pointed out that historically the Fourteenth Amendment to the United States Constitution gave the federal government primary responsibility for guaranteeing individual rights. In the 1960s and 1970s, great concern by many people initiated social reform movements that led a sympathetic Supreme Court to reject various laws that violated the civil rights of many vulnerable groups, including blacks and other racial minorities, women, the mentally retarded, illegitimate children, and the poor. The impaired and frail elderly represent an emerging minority group whose rights may be threatened as they make use of certain forms of long-term care that may limit their freedom. Social reform must continue with the enactment of whatever laws are necessary to protect the rights of this minority group.

Before proceeding, it seems important to review the long-term care system to identify the conditions that might limit autonomy and promote unnecessary paternalism.

LONG-TERM CARE

Although various definitions of long-term care appear in the literature, Kane and Kane (1982) have defined it as a range of services addressing the health, personal care, and social needs of individuals who lack some capacity for self-care. This definition would seem to apply both to impaired individuals who lack some functional capacity and to the frail elderly, i.e., those who are too weak and fragile to provide all the care necessary for themselves. Ideally, long-term care involves a continuum of programs and services that fit the needs of the elderly population, depending upon their stage of dependency. Also, it should include a set of programs and services linked together in a coordinated fashion to meet the physical, emotional, social, and financial needs of its elderly clients at a given moment in time.

The long-term care system may be divided into the categories of formal and informal care.

Formal Care

Formal long-term care is care sponsored by such public organizations as government agencies (federal, state, local), community organizations, and proprietary organizations. It includes such programs and services as Medicare, Medicaid, Social Security, Meals-on-Wheels, transportation services, nursing homes, adult day care, hospice care, home health services, home care, community senior centers, respite care, counseling, legal services, and so on.

As important as they are, these programs and services have many problems (Gilliland & Havir, 1990; Gubrium, 1991; White, 1989). If high-quality programs are offered by private organizations for profit, they are usually too expensive and, therefore, inaccessible to the majority of the elderly. Financial budgets for government-sponsored programs appear to be limited in the foreseeable future. The consequences of such budget limitations are that available programs and services are restricted in number and limited to certain localities. In addition, the workers needed to perform various services are insufficient in number and are often poorly trained or unqualified; the turnover rate is high due to low salaries and poor working conditions.

Furthermore, coordinated systems of formal care have not materialized to the degree that had been hoped. Much fragmentation and duplication of effort occurs, with insufficient connections between various organizations, personnel, programs, and services. Then too, even when programs or services are available, families may not know about them or reject the idea of using them. Finally, evaluation programs to determine the effectiveness of existing programs and services are relatively rare although they are needed as a basis for making continued improvements. Given the present condition of the national economy, the philosophy of limited government participation, and the priority given to other social problems, formal long-term care does not seem able to fulfill its potential.

Concern for Autonomy in Formal Care

Exacerbated by the problems outlined above, a serious concern exists regarding limitations of autonomy and unnecessary paternalism in formal care. For example, nursing home staffs may employ unnecessary paternalism in making decisions for patients because it is expedient to do so under crowded conditions or to keep an institution functioning on a limited budget. Also, untrained aides may not appreciate the elderly person's need for autonomy.

Another aspect of paternalism remains to be considered; that is, the tradition in medical ethics that manifests itself in formal care. According to Hofland (1988), the dominant framework of moral responsibility within the Hippocratic tradition is the beneficence model. The moral principle of beneficence directs the physician to promote and protect the best interest of the patient by seeking the greater balance of good over harm in treatment and care. But since the physician defines the patient's best interest, this model is strongly paternalistic. The traditional paternalism of health care is further enhanced by the highly technical nature of modern medicine and the fear that debilitated and ill patients will make mistakes if left to their own decisions. Hofland goes on to state that personal autonomy concerns are not indigenous to medicine, but emerged in other areas after World War II as concerns about the need for informed consent to treatment and the freedom to decide to participate in research. These advances occurred primarily in acute-care settings where the situation was rather clear-cut. To implement informed consent in long-term care for which chronic illness is the norm requires a much more difficult assessment of the situation. By definition, the chronic illness is not curable; resulting long-term care needs may be multi-dimensional, including physical, social, and psychological needs. Even within the realm of physical or medical needs the possibility of alternative methods of treatment exists, as well as negative side effects. It is easy for medical personnel to be paternalistic in this context because they may claim to know what is best for the elderly person with no other authority to challenge them.

Informal Care

Informal long-term care may be defined as the assistance provided at no public cost by family (or similar primary groups) to an individual whose needs must be met to remain in the community and to avoid institutionalization (Tennstedt & McKinlay, 1989). These needs include personal care, instrumental activities of daily living (e.g., transportation, shopping), skilled health care (e.g., dressing changes, injections), and emotional or affective care.

According to Tennstedt and McKinlay (1989), the vast majority of long-term care to the elderly is provided informally and privately, at no public cost. They concluded that when impairment increases, the corresponding increase in informal services is greater than any increase in formal services.

In general, when people become old and frail, it is their family members who help them most, especially their spouses and adult children. After the widowhood of a parent, the adult children tend to become the primary caregivers (Brody, 1978; Cantor, 1975, 1985; Cicirelli, 1980, 1981; Horowitz & Dobrof, 1982; Troll, 1971). Indeed, parent caring is so widespread a phenomenon that Brody (1985) termed it a "normative family stress." The proportion of bedfast and housebound elderly being helped at home is twice that cared for in institutions (Shanas, 1979). Further, some 62% of all medical and personal care to elderly in the community comes from family members (Brody, 1978). When other types of help are considered as well, an estimated two thirds of the elderly receive help from their adult children (Cantor, 1975, 1985). In a study focusing upon elderly who required assistance with personal care or daily activities (Noelker & Townsend, 1987), 92% of daughters and 62% of sons interviewed were caregivers.

Although estimates of the numbers involved vary from study to study, it is clear that family members still provide the brunt of help to the elderly for ordinary daily living, as well as for extraordinary help involving illness, disability, impairment, and immobility. These findings are based upon numerous field studies, including surveys, observations, interviews, and case studies. Samples used in some of the studies were small, nonrepresentative, and nonrandom, while other studies involved large, representative, random samples obtained in such major national surveys as the National Health Interview Survey and the Long Term Care Survey (Doty, 1986; Stone, Cafferata, & Sangl, 1987). The results all converge to the conclusion that the majority of elderly depend upon help from adult children and other family members more than help from any other source. Thus the phenomenon of adult children's help to elderly parents is well documented in the literature.

Many problems and issues remain to be resolved regarding the family caregiving portion of the long-term care continuum (Biegel & Blum, 1990; Kahana & Young, 1990; Raveis, Siegel, & Sudit, 1990; Schulz, 1990). The need exists: (a) to define clearly the meaning of a family caregiver so that the definition can be standardized for research and reimbursement of some sort; (b) to formulate an adequate classification system of services provided so that delivery systems can be organized according to types of services needed; (c) to understand the sources of sustained motivation of caregivers in order to better provide support and incentives; (d) to further clarify the causes of caregiver burden that occur under different conditions in order to deal with it more effectively; (e) to determine the limits and potential of sons' participation in caregiving, as well as the most effective combination of brothers and sisters in a sibling helping network, in order to reduce gender differences in caregiving; (f) to more clearly distinguish neglect from normal caregiving in order to rehabilitate or replace family caregivers without sufficient commitment to provide care; (g) to better understand the process of caregiving over time in order to identify more effective points of intervention; (h) to determine subcultural differences in family caregiving in order to deal more effectively with the kinds of families expected in a 21st century world, and (i) to determine the effectiveness of caregiving and the satisfaction of receivers in order to determine how well their needs are met.

Concern for Limited Autonomy in Informal Care

The above issues and problems with informal care may involve questions of limited autonomy and unnecessary paternalism in some way. For example, the term *caregivers* may be defined in a way that shows a bias toward paternalism. Regarding caregivers' motives, if sustained motivation to provide care is primarily selfish rather than altruistic, then premature paternalism may occur, especially under stress. The use of more sons for caregiving in the future may have a negative side effect if men tend to be more paternalistic than women. Studies of subcultural differences in caregiving may reveal greater tendencies toward paternalism in certain groups, identifying a need to protect the rights of these elderly. Presently, no answers exist to the above issues and problems, but one should be aware that any resolution may involve positive or negative implications in regard to maintaining or limiting autonomy.

DIFFERENCES BETWEEN
FORMAL AND INFORMAL CARE

Formal care may be subdivided into institutional and community-based care, while informal care may be categorized into care provided by family and nonfamily (friends, neighbors, volunteers).

Determining whether an individual receives formal or informal care is not always easy or clear-cut. Some elderly persons take part in a formal care program (e.g., day care), shift to family care, then back to formal care, and so on. Also, informal care may be carried out in a formal care setting and vice versa, making it difficult at times to determine what is formal or informal caregiving (Kane, Illston, Eustis, & Kane, 1990). Although formal care professionals are paid for the services they provide, family members are also paid for helping elderly parents in some states. This financial support makes it still more difficult to maintain the distinction between formal and informal caregiving.

Nevertheless, certain differences do seem to exist between the two types of care. In formal care, greater expert knowledge is needed to deal with more serious health or financial problems or difficulties in everyday living. Second, the relationship between caregiver and care receiver may involve strangers or no commitment beyond implementing a specific treatment of some kind.

In contrast, family care involves help based upon more general knowledge with the emphasis on everyday problems of living and health or financial problems of low to moderate severity. More important, special relationships already exist between family members prior to a caregiving relationship, acting to influence that relationship. Therefore, autonomy and paternalism may have different meanings in the two types of caregiving situations.

Much of the autonomy literature is concerned with the conditions under which autonomy is limited. The topic is viewed usually from an ethical perspective (in terms of what ought to be) and applied to formal long-term caregiving. This view is certainly important, but one should also be concerned with a psychological perspective (in terms of how people behave) and an application to informal care.

In recent years, efforts have been made to maintain and promote autonomous behavior in impaired and frail elderly, but such efforts have taken place primarily in formal care settings, for example, interventions to promote the autonomy of the elderly in nursing homes (Cassel, 1988; Hofland, 1988; Kane et al., 1990). Little similar research has taken place in the area of informal or family care.

DYADIC FAMILY CAREGIVING RELATIONSHIPS

According to Wetle (1985), care of the chronically impaired individual raises difficult issues for the family. As the dependency of the elderly person increases, changes occur in the patterns of interaction between family members, leading to changing interpersonal relationships reflecting concomitant shifts in power and role status. More important, family members struggle with balancing the autonomous wishes of the frail or impaired elderly against the concerns for his or her personal safety (implying paternalistic actions). Such family concerns seem to be more common than perhaps realized. In a study by Pratt, Schmall, and Wright (1987), family caregivers of dementia patients were preoccupied with many ethical issues, including autonomy versus paternalism while providing care. Such ethical issues may be more salient for the family members giving the major portion of the elders' care than for others.

In family caregiving of the elderly, a primary caregiver tends to be predominant, with lesser amounts of help from secondary caregivers. If married, the spouse tends to be the primary caregiver for as long as possible. Among the frail or impaired elderly, however, the largest group consists of widows cared for by adult children, mainly by daughters. (Obviously, other caregiver-care receiver dyads exist, such as mother-son or aunt-nephew, but these are not the norm.)

Since family caregiving is the core of long-term care for impaired and frail elderly, and daughters helping elderly mothers is the modal form of family care, then the focus should be on the autonomy of the mother and the possible paternalism of the daughter within a family caregiving dyad. In many cases autonomy may not be maintained and paternalism may be implemented prematurely.

Objectives of the Book

This book deals with one part of the long-term care system— the family. The first objective is to determine the relative occurrence of autonomy and paternalism in the dyadic family caregiving relationship. A second objective is to determine the antecedents of such autonomous and paternalistic behavior. Obviously, many possible antecedent variables may be involved. The focus, however, is on the contextual and personal-social characteristics of the family caregiver and care receiver themselves. To what extent do the characteristics of the caregiver and care receiver directly (and indirectly through their dyadic interactions or relationships) influence the maintenance or enhancement of the care receiver's autonomy? To what extent do such characteristics influence paternalism? External obstacles, such as regimentation in institutions or in family routines, or internal obstacles, such as deficits in intellectual capacity, are known to limit autonomy, but what has not been considered in existing research are the personal-social characteristics of the individuals themselves.

Within this dyadic context, one must consider also the congruence of the views of both members of the dyad as important, as well as the views of each member separately. Furthermore, to consider the family context in greater depth, one must consider the adult child not only in relation to the elderly parent but also in relation to siblings. In this sense, one is going beyond the dyadic relationship to the larger family system to determine family influences on autonomy and paternalism in the caregiving situation.

Finally, as others have stated (Callahan, 1984; Moody, 1985), autonomy is an important value but should not become an obsession. Given such a viewpoint, this book is concerned with determining the occurrence of autonomy and paternalism in family caregiving and with understanding their causes in order to make changes, if desired. Rather than blindly insisting that autonomy should always be given priority, one should seek to understand when it is appropriate and when it is not. Are there times when paternalism may be more helpful in a family caregiving setting, either as a means to promoting autonomy in the long run or as an end in itself? Are there times when the autonomy of the elderly individual should take precedence? Are there times when shared autonomy or paternalism is more important than either one alone? Or are there times when the good of the family outweighs the importance of the autonomy of the elderly individual?

In some ways, the questions of autonomy and paternalism within long-term family caregiving are more complicated than in long-term formal care. It is hoped that this book will contribute to answering some of the questions at the psychological or behavioral level.

Meaning of Autonomy and Paternalism

As indicated in Chapter 1, decision making affecting the elderly, whether autonomous or paternalistic, may be a common denominator underlying other issues in family caregiving. Consequently, it is important that the meaning of autonomy and paternalism be clarified as much as possible.

AUTONOMY

Autonomy is not an easy concept to define. It has been seen as synonymous, overlapping, or otherwise confused with such various other terms as *self-determination, self-rule, self-governance, self-efficacy, personal control, independence, liberty,* and so on (Collopy, 1988; Dworkin, 1988). It has been conceived from perspectives ranging from political to legal to moral and to individual autonomy. Given this confusion, it is difficult to define autonomy to everyone's satisfaction. My definition of personal autonomy assumes a psychological perspective.

For an individual, *personal autonomy* means having the capacity to make and execute deliberated decisions to satisfy needs and attain goals in a manner consistent with one's values.

Some important components of this definition need further elaboration.

Deliberated Decision

Although distinctions can be made, the terms *decision, choice,* and *judgment* will be used interchangeably in this book. To make a *decision* is to make a selection between two or more alternatives; the decision may involve selecting needs, values, and goals, or the means (behaviors or specific courses of action) to satisfy or attain them.

Deliberation means reflection, thoughtfulness, analysis, or logical reasoning when the decision-making process is carried out. It would seem relevant to summarize the steps involved in decision making to help clarify the role of deliberation even though the following may be somewhat idealized or too prescriptive.

First, a need to make a decision must exist. One may conceive of decision making as a type of problem solving (Huber, 1989). For a problem to exist, a need must exist for a new course of action (a former action may no longer be appropriate to meet the demands of a new situation), and the individual must recognize the existence of the need for a decision to solve the problem.

Second, the individual must have in mind objectives or goals to be achieved by the decision making; this may involve reflection to clarify the goals relative to the problem situation.

Third, alternatives must be identified or generated. An individual easily may settle for too few alternatives to make possible an intelligent decision.

Fourth, the implications, consequences, or possible outcomes of each alternative must be considered. Some alternatives may have few potential outcomes, while others may have many; the individual cannot make an intelligent decision without knowing whether these potential outcomes are negative or positive. In an example given by von Winterfeldt and Edwards (1986), a person might consider two alternatives in relation to a health ailment; to have surgery or not to have surgery. This may seem to be a simple decision between two alternatives, one leading to restored health and the other to continued suffering. Further reflection may indicate several possible consequences of the surgery: restored health, no change, complications resulting in being worse off than before, or not surviving the surgery. On the other hand, not having the surgery could lead to continued suffering, a spontaneous cure, a possible cure through drugs or other means, or becoming more seriously ill. To generate and examine these possible outcomes requires reasoning, knowledge, and maturity.

Fifth, the individual must determine the relative merits of each alternative in terms of its positive and negative consequences, the probability of occurrence, and the subjective value or worth of each consequence to the individual.

Sixth, the individual must select the best alternative from the set of alternatives evaluated.

In general, deliberated decision making is a reasoning process whereby a problem is identified, alternatives are stated or generated, the relative merits of the alternatives are evaluated, and an alternative is selected based upon formulated criteria that take all the above factors into consideration.

Problems vary on a continuum from those that are simple or trivial and that have little effect on our lives (e.g., selecting a red rather than a blue sweater to wear) to those that are more serious and complex and that affect the core of our identity and challenge our decision-making skills. Decisions of the latter type have serious consequences for the individual. To determine the trade-offs between alternatives may require a high level of information input, analysis, and reasoning. Some complex problems may involve processing so much information regarding many alternatives that existing decision-making skills and strategies may not be adequate to allow one to be completely logical. Therefore, a distinction must be made between deliberation and rationality. Rationality is the use of total logic in one's analysis of alternatives, selecting the one that maximizes benefit and minimizes cost to the individual. *Deliberation* is an attempt to be rational; it involves degrees of rationality. Deliberated decision making as a degree of rational decision making stands in contrast, however, to making decisions based upon impulse, habit, intuition, imitation of others, peer pressure, anxiety or fear, norms of society, prejudice, manipulation by others, and so on. Still, deliberated decision making (in contrast to purely rational decision making) leaves room for emotions or needs to influence selection of alternatives and also allows the use of heuristic shortcuts in thinking.

In this book, autonomy is regarded as including both deliberated decision making and executional decision making (Collopy, 1986, 1988). To *execute* is to implement or carry out a course of action based upon a deliberated decision. It may involve verbal or physical behavior of some kind to accomplish the task directly or to enlist the service of others. Personal autonomy is both decisional and executional.

Capacity

Capacity or *decisional capacity* refers to the individual's ability to make deliberated decisions. The term *decisional capacity* is now preferred to the term *competence,* which has more specific connotations in the legal profession (Cassel, 1988; Dubler, 1990; High, 1987). In this book, *decisional capacity* is used to refer to cognitive functioning that includes reasoning, memory, attention, decision-making skills and strategies, comprehension of information, various other mental abilities, background knowledge relative to a task, and emotional maturity. All of the above factors are part of decisional capacity. For example, an extremely rigid or highly anxious person will have less decisional capacity to make deliberated decisions that lead to successful outcomes than someone who is not. This book includes values and goals as aspects of personal autonomy that are separate from decisional capacity although others do not (e.g., Dubler, 1990).

Assessing decisional capacity is a difficult task (Cassel, 1988; Dubler, 1990; High, 1987), especially when one must consider all of the above components and weigh their importance relative to the context of the task. Also, decisional capacity may fluctuate daily or periodically in older people with illness-induced deficits. Thus a person may have decisional capacity at some times ("windows of lucidity") and not others or relative to certain decisions and not others.

In general, people cannot be fully informed if they lack background knowledge beyond incoming information, and they cannot voluntarily consent to a decision if they have inadequate reasoning ability or defects in other components of decisional capacity. Stanley, Stanley, Guido, and Garvin (1988) summarize six criteria for assessing decisional capacity that are worth reflection. The first criterion is the ability to actually make a decision; a person without decisional capacity may not even attempt to make a decision. The second criterion is the ability to comprehend the information relevant to the task. The third criterion is the quality of reasoning—the quality of the deliberative decision-making process. The fourth criterion is the comprehension of the consequences of the decision. The fifth criterion is the reasonableness of the outcome of the decision making—whether it is congruent with what a reasonable person would have done. The sixth criterion is the inference of incompetence based upon such status characteristics as age (e.g., age under 16), mental illness (e.g., Alzheimer's disease), and so on.

Each criterion has potential value, and all are helpful in assessing an individual's decisional capacity relative to a given decisional task.

Needs, Goals, and Values

Deliberated decisions and their execution are a way to deal with problems or challenges in order to achieve satisfaction of needs or attainment of goals. The manner in which this is done is usually consistent with one's values. For example, one may decide to eat lunch at noon but consistent with one's values, the lunch is paid for rather than stolen.

This aspect of personal autonomy has led to much confusion, as many terms have been substituted for *needs, goals,* and *values.* In the literature, one frequently finds such terms as *aspiration levels, wishes, desires, purposes, intentions, fulfilling a life plan, self-realization, commitment,* and so on.

Most of these terms refer to motivation and are different ways of labeling motives in the individual, and to standards (values, principles) by which the individual lives. Regardless of the terms, motives and standards initiate, guide or regulate, and direct the making and executing of deliberated decisions toward certain outcomes. For personal autonomy to exist, however, these motives and standards must be intrinsic to the individual; living by them must be rewarding in itself, not a means of pleasing someone else. Regardless of any socialization or early conditioning, one is able to reflect on the motives or standards that drive oneself. In time, one may reject them or identify with them, i.e., internalize or accept them as one's own genuine motives and standards by which to live. Thus one has the ability to escape decision making that is determined by socialization or conditioning (Dworkin, 1988; Young, 1986). One may even desire not to desire something. For example, one may desire alcohol and also desire not to want it. Having both desires simultaneously may lead eventually to gaining freedom from the use of alcohol. This is another instance of being able to change one's motives rather than being driven or directed by internal unconscious drives or external forces from society. Deliberated decision making is not only a means to satisfy needs and attain goals but also to select the needs and goals themselves and to alter them over time.

As an individual, one has the potential to be one's "own person." One can be free from internal constraints and live according to one's own life plan. This ability is self-determination, controlling one's destiny, or being responsible for one's life.

EXERCISE OF AUTONOMY

The exercise of autonomy by an individual is the actual making and executing of deliberated decisions to satisfy needs or to attain goals in a manner consistent with values. This distinction is necessary as personal autonomy may exist in the individual—that individual has the capacity for autonomy but it is not being exercised. Internal constraints may exist (e.g., an individual may not care to make decisions), or external constraints may exist (e.g., opportunities to make decisions do not exist in the environment because of rigid rules).

By making the distinction between the existence of personal autonomy and its exercise, one can think in terms of individual differences. Individuals may vary in terms of decisional capacity, as well as in external opportunities for making decisions, leading to different degrees of the exercise of autonomy.

RESPECT FOR AUTONOMY

To have respect for autonomy is to honor or accept the exercise of personal autonomy by others. It is only at this point that ethics enter the picture. Personal autonomy and its exercise exist as a fact of human nature. Taking that as a starting point, various authors have stated that it is a moral duty or principle to recognize the right of others to be autonomous. Aristotle (1925) considered man's unique attribute to be the ability to reason. For Kant (1964), reasoning, through which we can all discover universal moral principles, is intrinsic to man's nature. For Kant and others, to be rational is to be human. One should respect personal autonomy because it is essential for the individual's personhood; without it, one cannot rise above the animal level.

Such views overlap somewhat with the humanistic and existential traditions. From a motivational standpoint, the individual has a basic tendency to want to develop to the fullest (Maslow, 1967; Rogers, 1963). In other words, people not only have the need to use their unique reasoning abilities but do so in the service of their unique need to continually fulfill a basic tendency for growth over time. Thus the individual not only has the capacity for deliberated decision making, but also a fundamental need to exercise it as an end in itself: "I have the capability to make and execute deliberated decisions and I must exercise this capacity to be free, and true to my human nature." In the process of doing so, the individual makes decisions to select more specific needs and goals and the means to satisfy them. By such reasoning, individuals must be treated as ends in themselves, that is, allowed to be self-ruling or autonomous.

In practice, one can show respect for personal autonomy in two general ways: by refraining from external interference with an individual making and executing decisions, and by promoting or enhancing that individual's decision making. These behaviors have been called negative and positive autonomy (Collopy, 1988; Dworkin, 1988). Respect for autonomy, however, does not seem to be autonomy itself as much as a way of relating to the autonomy of others.

Mill (1926) wanted no external constraints upon personal autonomy. He defended the moral principle of respect for autonomy on the utilitarian grounds that it furthers human welfare and happiness. External interference consists of physical restrictions from the environment, a lack of accessibility of resources, or conflicts with the interests or views of powerful others, the norms of society, and the rules of institutions. Such external constraints should be eliminated or reduced to a minimum so that individuals can chart their own destinies. This definition is usually what is meant by freedom, independence, or liberty, especially when applied at the political level. On the individual level, one can practice noninterference by simply allowing individuals to spontaneously make and execute their own decisions.

Promoting autonomy goes beyond noninterference; it includes attempts to improve people's decisional capacity and attempts to motivate them to exercise personal autonomy. For example, to promote elders' autonomy, one might help identify available alternatives; provide training programs to develop decision-making skills; provide information needed for adequate decision making; help clarify needs, goals, and values; provide counseling to alleviate emotional disturbances; help develop higher levels of aspiration; provide opportunities to participate directly in diagnosis, treatment, and management of illnesses; eliminate stereotypes of elderly people as incompetent; and so on. In such ways individuals can be helped to gain confidence in their own decision making.

From an environmental perspective, one may also promote autonomy. One may make resources available so that older people can more easily and effectively execute decisions, for example, providing ramps, escalators, or walkers to promote needed mobility. One may help negotiate compromises with powerful others or modify institutional rules so that execution of decisions can be implemented without penalty or punishment.

Freedom from internal and external constraints is essential for the exercise of autonomy. This does not, however, mean freedom of the will in the sense that decisions are made spontaneously without any antecedent causes. Freedom from internal constraints means that in deliberated decision making the final selection of an alternative is not hampered by one or more defective components of one's decisional capacity. The individual is free from mental retardation, lack of sufficient knowledge, emotional disturbance, alien needs and goals, and so on. The individual is free from external constraints to the extent that no external interference exists. To be free is to be effective in making and executing decisions; it does not mean spontaneously generating decisions with no antecedent causes. The latter condition, if it existed, would not guarantee personal autonomy but would produce someone totally unpredictable and perhaps without commitment.

Finally, there is a distinction between personal autonomy and personal control. It is important to clarify this distinction because autonomy and control are so often equated in the literature. Personal control is an expected relationship between behavior and consequences. One expects certain behavior to lead to or cause the attainment of certain rewards. The emphasis on personal autonomy is the freedom from internal constraints to make and execute decisions regardless of the consequences. This is not to deny the desire for certain consequences or possible rewards, but the latter are secondary. In other words, personal control is concerned with a causal relationship between behavior and reward, while personal autonomy is concerned with being the cause of one's decisions regardless of the consequences. Personal control is not necessary for personal autonomy, and personal control does not assure personal autonomy. For example, one might decide between two negative outcomes, such as committing suicide and living with the pain of a terminal disease for six months. In both cases, there is little expectation of reward; there is only freedom to decide between two events, with death the ultimate outcome. The desired outcome of continued life is beyond the individual's control in both cases; that is, control of decision making is not necessarily control of desired outcome. Another example is the case in which one may simply want to make a choice and act accordingly when the uncertainty of the consequences is extremely high (making control impossible), but nonetheless one feels the conscious sense of freedom to make such a decision.

The important reason for this distinction is that individuals may not always need to be in control of events as much as they need to decide for themselves or be in control of their decision making, even if the outcome is harmful or a disaster. To the extent that control and autonomy overlap, this is a bonus; if one must be sacrificed for the other, then personal autonomy should have priority even with potential risks of great uncertainty, disaster, or no ultimate reward. In both cases, individuals may feel in control of their destiny in a generic sense, as indicated in Chapter 1.

DILEMMAS IN THE EXERCISE OF
PERSONAL AUTONOMY

With respect to the dependent elderly, Collopy (1986, 1988) has done an excellent job in discussing risks, dilemmas, and contradictions in the exercise of personal autonomy and also has suggested resolutions. It is important for further clarification of the concept of autonomy to summarize his views and possibly to suggest further resolutions.

Collopy (1986, 1988) distinguished between decisional and executional autonomy—between the making and executing of decisions. The problem is that, when executional autonomy is lost (e.g., through a stroke, loss of voice through cancer, paralysis through an accident, surgical loss of legs due to diabetes), one might conclude that the autonomy of the individual has been destroyed. One cannot really state that the individual is still totally autonomous without executional autonomy. On the other hand, if one accepts partial autonomy (i.e., decisional autonomy only), then we have an individual who can make decisions but cannot execute them. Collopy's solution is to provide aid to such individuals in carrying out their decisions. In this way, partial autonomy is preserved and premature paternalism is avoided.

Collopy (1986, 1988) also made a distinction between direct autonomy and delegated autonomy. Direct autonomy is the type that has been discussed previously and defined as personal autonomy. Eventually, however, many elderly people will decline in their decisional capacity to make deliberated decisions with successful or nonharmful outcomes. Some of their decision making may be delegated to others. When this happens, should we still consider these individuals as having personal autonomy? They no longer can behave in a manner that fits the definition of personal autonomy. On the other hand, they may not be sufficiently helpless to warrant paternalism. Collopy, in effect, stated that we should still recognize partial autonomy even when a certain amount of decision making must be delegated. He suggested that some norms or acceptable procedures be established for deciding what authority or decisions the elderly person still can make and what can be delegated. In other words, delegated autonomy does not eliminate autonomy, for autonomy can still be represented by the decisions that the elderly person retains.

Collopy (1986, 1988) distinguished situations in which an individual has decisional capacity and those in which decisional incapacity exists. In the latter case, personal autonomy would be lost. There is great danger in assessing an individual as decisionally incapacitated, however, because assessment of capacity is so difficult at the present time. Second, when decisions are in conflict with institutional goals, professional expectations, or societal norms, the individual may be judged falsely as being incompetent. Collopy strongly urged that as thorough an assessment of decisional capacity as possible be carried out. It is important to avoid global and superficial assessments. Instead, one should assess capacity relevant to the context or task at hand and avoid judging individuals as incompetent simply because their decisions are different from what others might make under the same circumstances. It is important to assess the decisional outcome from the standpoint of the individual's own needs, goals, and values.

In an elaboration of the concept of autonomy, Collopy (1986, 1988) discussed authentic versus inauthentic individuals. Authentic individuals make and execute deliberated decisions that are consistent with their true or genuine values, needs, and goals. Inauthentic individuals make decisions leading to outcomes that are motivated by fear, obsessions, pleasing others, and so on. Collopy suggested that the problem here is misjudging some individuals as exercising autonomy because only the criteria of decisional capacity are being used to assess them. One also should use the criterion of authenticity. Collopy felt that we should understand and document older people's previous history for evidence of consistency regarding their needs, values, and goals so that their present decisions can be assessed against such a standard (above and beyond any assessment of decisional capacity) to determine the existence and exercise of personal autonomy.

Collopy (1986, 1988) also made a distinction between immediate and long-range autonomy; that is, giving priority to the right of the individual to have personal autonomy in immediate or ongoing situations versus giving priority to actions that preserve the individual's personal autonomy in the long run. It is possible that individuals will make decisions in the short run (e.g., taking drugs) that may destroy their personal autonomy in the long run. On the other hand, others may intervene paternalistically to force individuals to make certain decisions now that will enhance their autonomy in the long run. Should one respect the personal autonomy of the individual in the immediate situation regardless of the long-run consequences, or should one ignore the individual's present rights and intervene temporarily with the goal of maintaining autonomy in the future? Collopy recognized the difficulty of the problem and recommended that caregivers try to implement a balance by respecting some short-run autonomy but also maintaining autonomy in the long run insofar as possible. This recommendation may be more difficult to carry out in practice than it appears.

Finally, Collopy (1986, 1988) referred to negative and positive autonomy. Negative autonomy means respecting autonomy by noninterference; that is, allowing others to exercise their autonomy spontaneously. The problem is, however, that negative autonomy may encourage a laissez-faire attitude that promotes making no attempt to help the elderly when they might need it.

Positive autonomy means actively attempting to enhance the autonomy of others. To do so, however, may lead to an overzealous attitude whereby one interferes with the rights of others in the name of trying to promote their exercise of autonomy. Collopy suggested giving priority to noninterference but cautiously going beyond this to explore ways to enhance autonomy without taking over the decision making of the individual.

PATERNALISM

Paternalism in caregiving sometimes has a negative connotation but actually represents an important ethical position. Paternalism does not imply an uncaring, selfish, or exploitative attempt to deal with dependent people. Rather, paternalism is intervention in the making and executing of another person's decisions for the welfare of that person. In paternalism, one blocks another's decision, substituting one's own decision and its execution for that of the other person.

In paternalism, the expert or person in authority (a) is concerned with the welfare or happiness of the dependent person, (b) knows best what decisions and courses of action are most beneficial and least harmful to the dependent person, and (c) has the moral right to go beyond reasoning or persuasion to force the dependent person to accept certain decisions and courses of action (Gert & Culver, 1979; Halper, 1980). The interventionist also may use force, deception, threat, misinformation, manipulation, or other strong means in the process of intervening in the decision.

One can respect paternalism and accept it as a highly ethical position if one gives priority to welfare of the individual over freedom of choice, and one is convinced that one knows what is best to maximize benefits and minimize harm to the individual.

Gert and Culver (1979) indicate that many times paternalism is justified because a dependent person may make a decision for which the probability and magnitude of harm is quite great, even when the person is informed and acts voluntarily. Second, harmful outcomes may be almost sure to occur when the person is definitely incapacitated. Defects may exist in reasoning, ignorance, false beliefs, emotional disturbances, and so on.

Paternalism, however, may be justified from the other side of the coin. It may not be so much a question of avoiding or reducing harm as much as maximizing benefit. Interventionists who are experts or who have authority in an organization may be able to provide greater benefit to the individual regardless of the latter's level of capability.

Although paternalism has been criticized much in recent years, it is far from dead. It may not be labeled explicitly, but paternalism regularly occurs in such areas as medicine, social services, education, and the family. (It must be emphasized that intervening in the decision of others to exploit or dominate them is not paternalism; it is not justified from any ethical position. Paternalism is an ethical position because one cares about the welfare of the other person and is interested sincerely in that person's welfare.)

AUTONOMY VERSUS PATERNALISM

So far, some basic ideas regarding autonomy and paternalism have been presented. In the case of autonomy, one wants to exercise one's own freedom of choice regardless of the consequences. One wants to control one's own destiny, and if harmful decisions are made, one will be responsible and suffer the consequences.

In paternalism, on the other hand, one's welfare is viewed as more important than one's freedom to choose, and if intervention of others is necessary to promote one's welfare, so be it, regardless of freedom of choice.

Obviously, such opposing viewpoints can lead to conflict. It can be a battle of the "rugged individualist" versus the "benevolent dictator."

There are problems and limitations associated with the exercise of both autonomy and paternalism, suggesting that each may be more appropriate under different conditions. If one conceived of respect for autonomy and paternalism only in their extreme forms, one could not apply both approaches simultaneously. It would be a contradiction to allow the elderly complete exercise of their autonomy and simultaneously make all the decisions for them. If arguments for autonomy won out, however, the victory would be temporary. When older people's decisional and executional capacities did decline, no one would help such individuals out of respect for their autonomy, leaving them isolated and helpless. On the other hand, if arguments for paternalism initially prevailed, older people might have to submit to the decisions of others before, as well as during, any declines in decisional and executional capacity. Paternalism might be premature, eliminating any possibilities of the elderly making their own decisions. Such decisions would likely lead to resentment, low morale, loss of self-esteem, and perhaps the facilitation of further physical decline (Hofland, 1988).

Fortunately those authors who are proponents of strong autonomy and paternalism also recognize the central importance of the level of the elder's decisional and executional capacity as a justification for their viewpoints. They recognize that there are degrees of decline in capacity, which makes it difficult to continue to respect strong autonomy for those who have lost a significant degree of their capacity. It also becomes difficult to justify strong paternalism for those who retain some degree of capacity.

To avoid the conflict between caregiver paternalism and caregiver respect for autonomy, one may expand the concepts of paternalism and autonomy so that both may be applied in limited fashion as the elderly person's capacity declines during long-term care of an elderly family member.

The recent work of various ethicists (Collopy, 1986, 1988; Dworkin, 1988; Gillon, 1985; Young, 1986) has provided the basis for expanding the concept of autonomy to include various subtypes. Cicirelli (1989) has further suggested that such subtypes form a roughly ordinal progression based upon the degree of participation by others in the individual's decision making. Thus strong autonomy would become the highest point on such a scale, labeled *direct autonomy*. Here, one depends upon one's existing information and capacity to make and execute decisions for oneself. This point would be followed by *consultive autonomy*, for which one consults with others to obtain information and opinions relative to a decision but makes the final decision oneself. The next point is *joint autonomy,* for which one shares one's decision making with another, arriving at a decision together. Next is *delegated autonomy,* for which one freely transfers some of one's decision making to another person and abides by the decisions that the latter makes in one's behalf. Finally, there is *surrogate autonomy,* for which one is no longer capable of making decisions on one's own, but the caregiver attempts to make the decision in the way that one would if able.

Direct and surrogate autonomies represent the opposite ends of the scale, with no participation by others at one end and total participation at the other end. Consultive, joint, delegated, and surrogate autonomies represent varying degrees of participation by another person. (Such a scale is theoretically feasible in that the points on the scale are mutually exclusive in terms of the degree of participation they represent. In the real world, older individuals may exercise consultive, joint, and delegated autonomies on different tasks. In other words, the dimension of "degree of participation in decision making by others" is a dimension that may lead to a valid scale of mutually exclusive points relevant to a specific task. Or an individual could shift sequentially from the exercise of one degree of autonomy to the next on the same task over time.)

Correspondingly, one may conceive of various subtypes of paternalism, although the ordinality of the various subgroups is less clear than in the case of autonomy.

In *direct paternalism,* the expert or person in authority forces a decision or its execution upon another person, regardless of the latter's informed and voluntary choice. One may conceive of *indirect paternalism,* in which the expert or person in authority uses deception or manipulation to impose decisions and/or their execution upon another person. In *benevolent paternalism,* the expert or person in authority interacts and participates in a decision with the dependent person to explain what is best (as the dependent person may be living in ignorance or with false beliefs) and the necessity for imposing the decision. In *moderate paternalism,* the expert or person in authority intervenes only to prevent harm. Further, one may conceive of *weak paternalism,* in which the expert or person in authority intervenes only when there is mental deterioration. Finally, one may conceive of *default paternalism,* in which the dependent person is capable of making informed and free choices but is totally indifferent to doing so; since decisions must be made, the expert or person in authority must make them.

Partial autonomy is preserved in the face of declining decisional capacity by allowing another person to participate in the decision making in varying degrees. Paternalism is tempered when some decisional capacity remains by decreasing the amount of force used to impose a decision upon another person or by decreasing the instances in which paternalism is applied.

When various degrees of autonomy and paternalism are recognized, a direct opposition no longer exists between autonomy and paternalism, that is, between allowing older people to make all their own decisions and forcing decisions upon them with no consideration of an alternative.

Delegated autonomy is confused sometimes with paternalism because both involve someone making decisions for another person. In delegated autonomy, the elderly person accepts decisions made by others who have been previously delegated to make such decisions, whereas in paternalism, others make decisions for the elderly person without prior delegation and with expected submission to the decision. In paternalism, the intervener may use force, threat, deception, manipulation, and so on. The elderly person may resist, argue, complain, or otherwise express dissatisfaction (overt or covert) with the intervener's decision, finally submitting because there is no choice in the situation or because he or she wants the needed caregiving to continue.

Most important, consultive, joint, and delegated autonomies, as well as benevolent paternalism, all involve some degree of reciprocal communication and interaction with another person. Autonomy and paternalism are thus no longer the province of lone individuals, either elderly people making their own decisions or caregivers making decisions for them.

THREE

Autonomy and Paternalism in Family Decision Making

As discussed in Chapter 1, informal family care is the core of the long-term care system, and the relationship between caregivers and care receivers may be quite different from that in formal caregiving.

In formal care, knowledge of experts is needed to deal with more serious health and financial problems, difficulties in institutional living, and complex ethical issues that surround terminal illness. Also, the relationship between caregiver and care receiver may involve strangers and no commitment beyond a specific treatment or continuing management of some chronic condition.

In informal family caregiving, by contrast, help involves general knowledge of family members to deal with less serious health and financial problems, and concern with problems and ethical issues that are involved in everyday living. More important, special relationships already exist between family members prior to a caregiving relationship and act to influence not only the nature of caregiving but the degree of autonomy-related and paternalistic decision making carried out in the caregiving situation. Thus although concern for personal autonomy of elderly individuals is important, its significance (and that of paternalism) may have a different meaning within the context of family decision making.

Individuals do not always make decisions alone, but make them together with others either in dyads or groups. Years ago, Erich Fromm (1941) theorized that man needs freedom or autonomy but simultaneously needs escape from the loneliness that such freedom can bring. Fromm's answer to this dilemma was that an individual can find security and companionship either by submitting or conforming to a paternalistic society or by uniting with others in a collegiate manner to share work, love, and, presumably, decision making.

A family may be considered a group in which group decision making occurs. More important, the family also can be considered a system, each family member's behavior influencing the behavior of every other family member. A reciprocal interaction occurs between the individuals in a family so that other family members influence the exercise of autonomy by elderly parents, and the elderly parents influence other family members' exercise of paternalism.

Jecker (1990) presented various interesting arguments as to the necessity and moral justification for other family members' involvement in the elderly parent's autonomous decision making. First, in regard to the elderly person's illnesses, family members may be involved in helping resolve in-hospital patient management problems (e.g., dealing with the person's morale while in the hospital). Family members themselves are affected greatly by the elderly person's illness. As reported by Jecker, Livingston (1987) maintained that the elderly person's illness may mean an added financial strain for family members, force a change in housing or life-style, or carry a stigma that may become attached to family members as well as to the elderly person. Family members may even react to an elderly person's illness by developing their own emotional problems. In a more positive vein, an adult son or daughter often will be in a position to bridge communication gaps between parents and health professionals, facilitate exchange of information, convey explanations parents will understand, negotiate treatments, and offer emotional support in dealing with medical problems, treatments, and consequences (Roscowe, 1981). The implication is that the adult children become incorporated into the elderly parents' decision-making process, which in turn may enhance the quality of that process.

Jecker (1990) also argued for family involvement in the elderly person's autonomous decision making from another point of view, elaborating on Rhoden's views (1988) that the family is the context within which a person first develops his or her values and decision-making skills. Developmentally, parents help form their children's values and autonomous decision-making skills, so there is a commonality and acceptance of each other's views. Brody (1978) stated that the family is a place where its members can try out ideas and values on each other to help clarify their thinking. The family as a facilitator and the dialogue possible (Gadow, 1980a, 1980b) make family involvement inevitable in the elderly person's decision making.

Jecker (1990) justified family involvement in autonomous decision making from a moral viewpoint. Within a family, intimacy between its members develops, and this intimacy serves as the basis of the moral authority for facilitating or limiting the elderly parent's autonomy. For example, many times when an elderly parent has not delegated decision making via a durable power of attorney or made explicit his or her desires either verbally or in writing (e.g., a living will), someone will make a surrogate decision for the elderly parent based upon "best interests,"—an objective weighing of the benefits and costs of a particular course of action. Jecker argued, however, that the type of decision ethically justifiable in this way is surrogate autonomy, that is, making the decision for the elderly parent based upon what can be inferred to be the values or wishes of the elderly parent. Intimacy with parents gives adult children special knowledge and insights into their parents' values and wishes, so such surrogate autonomy becomes morally acceptable and quite feasible.

Another aspect of the moral viewpoint must be considered, however. Direct autonomy is an important value, but its promotion can be carried too far, leading to selfish decisions in which individuals think only of fulfilling their own wishes without considering others. The elderly parent has a special moral relationship to other family members. If fulfilling the elderly person's wishes comes at the expense of other family members, especially where resources are limited, then the family as an autonomous unit has the right to restrict or limit the elderly person's individual autonomous decisions. Just as a society claims the right to distribute its resources for the common good (Wetle, 1985), the family has the right to do likewise. Autonomy is an important value in American society, but the intimacy and commitment of family members to each other should lead to respect for the autonomy of all family members, the concern for the common good of the family, and the appropriate distribution of its resources without burdening any one member at the expense of that person's autonomy. In short, Jecker's (1990) thesis is that family involvement is morally necessary to facilitate the elderly parent's autonomous decision making, to protect the elderly parent through surrogate autonomy when necessary, and to limit the parent's individual autonomy for the common good of the family autonomy should this become necessary.

This position has further implications. Most individuals do not create themselves entirely through the exercise of direct autonomy or by making their decisions alone, but individuals tend to create each other through some form of partial autonomy. (This process also may apply to paternalism in that someone else does not make decisions for an individual in an isolated fashion.) It seems that most of the time more than one person is involved in the making and executing of decisions. People exist and develop within a context of interrelationships with others. Whether family caregivers respect autonomous decisions made by elderly parents or whether they act paternalistically, some degree of interaction and involvement exists with the elderly parent.

As psychologists, our focus is usually on the individual, and we seem preoccupied with situations in which individuals act alone. But interest is increasing in the study of interaction and communication between individuals. Recognition of a quality of behavior that Goodnow (1990) has labeled "shared activity" is also increasing. She states that it refers to most human activity. Without realizing it, we constantly are doing something with others or sharing with them.

This approach applies to shared decision making. Joint autonomy not only preserves some degree of autonomy but, as Jecker (1990) indicated, also limits selfish autonomy for the common good of the family. In this sense, joint autonomy may emerge as a higher ethical ideal than direct autonomy. Consultive and delegated autonomies also involve interaction with others, but in joint autonomy the involvement and mutual investment in the decisional outcome are nearer equal. When paternalism can no longer be avoided, perhaps some form of paternalism would be most acceptable when at least discussion occurs and an attempt is being made at communicating an understanding of why a decision is best or why an elderly parent should conform or submit to a caregiver's decision.

EXISTING LITERATURE

Although research studies dealing with autonomy and paternalism within the family caregiving situation are limited in number, the existing studies will be reviewed here.

High (High, 1988; High & Turner, 1987) carried out an exploratory study of 40 men and women ranging in age from 67 to 91. In-depth interviews were done to determine how health care decisions were to be made for them in the event they became incapacitated and could not make their own decisions. Most of these people had no interest in making a living will, arranging for durable power of attorney, or even completing an informal written directive revealing their wishes as to what or how decisions should be made regarding their health care in the future.

Instead, they expected that family members would make such care decisions for them. In most cases, no discussion of these matters had taken place with family members (at most, a casual conversation); these older people simply felt that a tacit understanding existed between them and their family members. It was assumed that family members would accept the responsibility and make appropriate decisions if it became necessary. Although High's interviewees expressed a hierarchical preference (i.e., preferring a spouse to make the decisions, then adult children, and so on), a greater preference was shown for having all family members discuss together what was to be done, iron out any disagreements or conflicts, and then make decisions accordingly. High (High, 1988; High & Turner, 1987) labels this kind of family decision making "family autonomy," in which the family as a unit makes decisions regarding the frail, elderly parent. It is as if what goes on in the family is "no one else's business." High's argument is that since the family knows more about the elderly parents and their values than anyone else, family members should make such decisions for the parents. The family members as a group may decide in the way they think the elderly would want, or they may decide in terms of what they think is best for the elderly parent. This is expected family surrogate autonomy. It seems to be based upon a trusting relationship with family members more than loyalty, closeness, affection, or moral commitment. High feels, however, that the expression of family autonomy itself is the primary reason the elderly depend upon family members for future surrogate decision making.

Pratt et al. (1987) carried out a study with 116 caregivers of dementia patients to determine their ethical concerns. One of these concerns was preservation of the dementia patients' autonomy after they become incapacitated. Various caregivers were relieved when the patients made their wishes known after diagnosis and before they became too mentally deteriorated to make decisions for themselves. Thus it was important to these caregivers that they were able to establish the patients' future wishes early in the disease process. Ethically, they could feel more at ease in implementing surrogate autonomy. Most important, the study demonstrates that surrogate autonomy, when time is taken to plan for the future, is not necessarily the sole decision of the caregiver. Interaction exists between the caregiver and care receiver in which surrogate autonomy emerges based upon mutual influence.

In another study, Pratt (Pratt, Jones, Shin, & Walker, 1989) examined perceptions of decisional autonomy and decision-making processes among 64 elderly, single mothers and their caregiving daughters. Although the mothers were highly involved in decisions affecting their lives, ranging from daily care to major health decisions, daughters were also very much involved in helping them make such decisions. Daughters were particularly influential over major health, financial, and housing decisions. According to Pratt, mothers usually had the final say, however. The decision making resembled consultive autonomy. Most interesting, the daughters' influence was great because they knew their mothers' values and preferences. Clearly, having information about a parent's values and preferences is important as a basis for consultive autonomy, as well as surrogate autonomy. Also, Pratt found that as mothers declined in capacity or lost confidence in their ability to make decisions, daughters' influence in decision making became greater. It is not clear from Pratt's study whether this process involved a shift from consultive autonomy to joint or delegated autonomy.

Keith (1983) examined patterns of assistance among very old parents and childless persons. Analysis of interviews with 551 older men and women indicated that parental status was less important than marital status in determining whether individuals received help from others in the tasks of daily living. There was, however, one area in which parents received substantially more assistance than childless persons. Elderly parents received more advice or help in making decisions; 37% of the parents receiving help in making decisions, compared with 12% of the childless. Of those who received advice, 88% of the parents received it from children, while the childless most frequently obtained advice from siblings (46%). Since the focus of the study was not on decision making per se, Keith did not attempt to determine whether consultive, joint, or delegated autonomy was involved. Most important here is the fact that adult children do get involved in their elderly parents' decision making.

According to Horowitz (Horowitz & Reinhardt, 1988; Horowitz, Silverstone, & Reinhardt, in press), long-term care begins and is maintained within the family system. Issues and dilemmas concerning the autonomy of a disabled relative inevitably arise within the context of family interactions long before, and continue long after, formal providers are involved in care. Horowitz carried out an exploratory study with 28 older persons and 15 of their family caregivers ranging in age from 42 to 81. The older persons were asked about recent decisions in six areas, including health care, housing, social activities, finances, diet, and vacation plans. The elderly reported 66 specific decisions, and in more than three fourths of them they consulted with family members. In general, decisions were made by "mutual flexibility" or by the elderly having the last word. Most important, conflict surrounding the decision making was minimal. Either there was consultive autonomy or what may be interpreted as joint autonomy (mutual flexibility) in which the elderly or their caregivers gave in or modified their views.

An additional aspect of the Horowitz work (Horowitz & Reinhardt, 1988; Horowitz et al., in press) focused primarily upon the older person's attitudes towards autonomy rather than upon actual decision making. Interviewees were asked for their reactions to a series of vignettes describing family situations involving autonomy issues. The result was that family members exhibited much greater sensitivity to autonomy issues in later life than did their older relatives, who were more concerned with the health and safety of the older people in the vignettes. In fact, the elders felt that the needs for health and safety would override any rights to self-determination and personal choice. Perhaps the most important finding of this study was the involvement of the family in the elderly person's decision making. According to Horowitz, the availability of family help is the elderly's greatest resource. This resource may be used for decision making in the form of consultive, joint, or delegated autonomy.

Coulton, Dunkle, Chow, Haug, and Vielhaber (1988) examined the decision making of 314 patients regarding post-hospital care to determine the multiple dimensions involved in such decision making. A confirmatory factor analysis revealed that one of six factors related to effective decision making was the support and involvement of family members during the decision-making process. The patients studied by Coulton et al. felt that their family supported and accepted their decisions for posthospital care. Along with other factors, family involvement was important to their decision making.

Townsend and Poulshock (1986) studied 101 pairs of impaired elderly parents and their adult children, comparing the reports of each regarding the elder's caregiving and decision-making support networks. In regard to decision making, consensus was shown that fewer people made decisions about the elder's care arrangements than provided care. The decision makers were most likely to be immediate family members—spouses and adult children. Although the adult children felt very much involved in the elderly parents' decision making, they felt that parents had the final say. Much of the time the elders agreed, but in many cases they reported that the spouse had the final say. It seems clear that consultive autonomy predominates in decisions involving the elderly and their adult children (and to some extent with spouses, if living). For the married couples, however, some evidence of delegated autonomy and possibly joint autonomy also was clear. In the case of widows, children (more than any other relative) had the most influence on decision making, but again, both children and widows indicated that the widows had the final say.

A few studies suggest that paternalism also occurs in a family context involving a reciprocal process between elderly parents and their adult children. Steinmetz and Amsden (1983) studied family caregivers' experience of stress and burden, finding that some caregivers manifested abusive approaches in the caregiving relationship. For example, since 16% of the elders refused food and 13% refused medication, 4% of the adult children resorted to forcing food and 14% used force to medicate an elder. Physical restraint of the elderly parent was used by 8% of the caregivers, and physical force was threatened by 4% of the caregivers. Much conflict existed between family caregivers and the elderly parents; techniques used by the elderly to deal with such conflict included pouting, withdrawing, manipulating, crying, imposing guilt, and so on. Although this study does not deal with ethical issues per se, it is relevant here as the differences in behavior between parents and children imply some form of paternalism. Obviously, conflict existed, and the adult children were attempting to enforce behavior that they judged to be best for the elderly parents.

Cicirelli (1981) showed that one of the most frequent sources of conflict between adult children and elderly parents involved the adult child's attempt to exert control over the elderly parent's health behavior and behavior in other areas. Such conflicts centering around attempted control of the elderly parents' activities were reported by approximately 40% of all adult children. Again, a general paternalistic stance is taken by adult children in dealing with elderly parents. Most important, the behavior of the elderly parents indicated their involvement in the conflict situation; paternalistic decision making by adult children was partly a reciprocal reaction to the parent's behavior rather than being initiated solely by the caregiver.

THE PARENT-CHILD DYAD

Many of the existing studies bearing on caregiving decision making dealt with the family as a group. A family may be conceived also as an aggregation of dyadic relationships formed from a series of dyadic interactions (Hinde, 1989). This book follows Hinde's position in studying a caregiving dyad. The primary concern is with the relationship between a family caregiver (adult child) and a care receiver (elderly parent).

According to Feinman and Lewis (1984), the disadvantage of working at the dyadic level is that explanatory power is limited, since the dyadic relationship is influenced by the relationships of each member with other family members. There are, however, certain advantages as well. First, the primary mode of caregiving is a dyadic one (studies indicate that in most cases an elderly family member has a primary caregiver), and what happens at this level should be understood. Many times, this dyadic unit is relatively isolated from other family members and their influence is low. Second, it is easier to collect, analyze, and interpret data pertaining to dyads than to larger systems. This ease is important when research time and resources are limited. Third, the study of dyads may be perceived as a first step in understanding triads, tetrads, and, ultimately, the entire family system. If the present work is considered as a first step to understanding decision making in family caregiving, then it seems appropriate to restrict the focus of the study to the caregiving dyad.

In most family caregiving situations, a primary caregiver usually helps an elderly family member (Horowitz & Dobrof, 1982; Johnson, 1983; Stoller & Earl, 1983; Tennstedt & McKinlay, 1989). Secondary caregivers tend to be few in number and to provide much less care on only an intermittent basis (Tennstedt & McKinlay, 1989). To attempt to study reciprocal influences in the entire family during caregiving was beyond the resources of the present investigation. With this limitation in mind, it was felt best to focus on the dyadic family caregiving relationship between the adult child who was the primary caregiver and the elderly parent. (Obviously, spouses are also important caregivers, but over a long enough time period one spouse outlives the other. Thus family caregiving for the frail elderly usually involves adult children and elderly parents.)

Therefore the basic theme of this chapter is that neither the adult child nor the elderly parent in the dyad makes decisions alone very frequently. The adult child would rarely use direct paternalism, and the elderly parent would rarely use direct autonomy. In other words, within a dyadic relationship, one would expect the adult child to influence the parent's exercise of autonomy, resulting in various combinations of consultive, joint, and delegated autonomies. On the other hand, one would expect the elderly parent to influence the adult child's use of indirect, benevolent, and weak paternalism. Each member of the dyad is expected to be involved in the decision making of the other in a dyadic relationship in which mutual interactions and influence occur.

PART TWO

Beliefs as Antecedents of Autonomy and Paternalism

Beliefs and Dyadic Family Caregiving Decision Making

Although the family is a social system, the study of decision making regarding care for elderly family members often can be reduced to the study of decision making in dyadic family relationships. Families may be conceptualized in terms of subsystems, many of which are dyadic units (Hinde, 1989). Such dyadic units may arise in the attempt to satisfy mutual needs and concerns not necessarily common to the family as a whole (e.g., young sisters' discussion of their romances and means of dealing with boyfriends may be a topic that is of little concern to brothers or parents). The norms, values, and beliefs of the family as a whole probably will influence the dyadic relationship but only after being reinterpreted to some extent to fit the needs of the dyad.

Since a family member usually is acting as a primary caregiver to an elderly parent, the domain of caregiving and care receiving is relatively exclusive to this dyad. Obviously, the degree of chronic illness of the elderly parent and the caregiver's burden may have a negative effect upon the whole family, with the latter in turn influencing the type and amount of caregiving provided; these effects will be minimal, compared with the reciprocal effects between the individuals in the dyadic relationship. In some families, of course, caregiving responsibilities and decision making may be divided more evenly. Understanding caregiving within the dyadic unit is a first step in comprehending total family decision making in regard to caregiving.

DECISION MAKING

Individuals make decisions alone, in groups, and in dyads. It seems important first to make comparisons between these three approaches in order to clarify family caregiving decision making.

Individual Decision Making

Studies in this area are concerned with understanding the processes of decision making. Different processes may be involved, depending upon whether decisions are made primarily by intuition, impulse, peer pressure, or the like. Most researchers are concerned, however, with rational decision making, investigating either the extent to which it occurs or the way it ought to occur for maximum benefit and minimum cost to the decision maker.

According to Jaccard, Brinberg, and Dittus (1989), an individual's rational decision making is made up of many components, such as the recognition of the problem, the identification of the goal (the purpose of the decision), the generation or selection of alternatives, the evaluation of potential alternative solutions, the pursuit of information for further alternatives, the identification of the properties of each alternative, the comparison of properties of the alternatives until preferences are formed, and the formulation of the final decision. Jaccard et al. also suggest that one might study how the individual implements the decision and any postdecision evaluation of the success of its outcome.

Individuals do not always make rational decisions or even partially rational decisions, but to the extent that the rational decision can ultimately be understood, the psychologist can make prescriptions of what ought to be done or set standards to assess degrees of rational decision making.

Group Decision Making

Group decision making involves three or more individuals. In this case, the decision-making process shifts from the micro level within the individual to the macro level between individuals. One must consider more than the individual decision-making process. One must consider the group dynamics, or how the interpersonal relationships of all the individuals involved influence the decision-making process.

Some small group studies, however, are based upon a rationalistic model of decision making. It is held that even if groups do not behave rationally, their performances may be compared to some baseline of rational decision making considered to be optimal (Steiner, 1972).

According to Sillars and Kalblesch (1989), effective group decision making for certain tasks involves many of the following elements: (a) arranging for a separate time and place to discuss decisions, (b) gathering information systematically, (c) organizing discussions leading to the generation of alternatives, (d) maintaining open channels of communication, (e) tolerating and even encouraging conflict regarding alternatives, and (f) continuing to evaluate alternatives while implementing the decision.

In general, groups have short attention spans. They may shift to unrelated topics to get sidetracked, members may lose focus regarding the topic at hand, different members may feel under pressure to attain different goals, members may need periodic redefinition of the problem to avoid confusion, different members may be working on different components of the problem simultaneously and so their efforts are not synchronized, or influence may become concentrated in a few members (Poole & Billingsley, 1989).

Group decision making may be relatively formal in order to coordinate members' efforts to deal with the task at hand; it is basically different from individual decision making in that the interpersonal relationships between group members become part of the decision-making process. These interpersonal relationships must be understood and utilized for effective decision making.

Dyadic Decision Making

Although similarities exist, dyadic decision making is different from both individual and group decision making in that, if one member of the dyad withdraws, the dyad no longer exists. This possibility puts pressure on the dyad members to manage and maintain their relationship.

Dyadic decision making has been regarded as consisting of two types of decisions: (a) task-oriented decisions, or decisions that deal with the task at hand; and (b) relational-oriented decisions, or decisions that deal with the relationship itself.

Relationship concerns appear to emerge even when the dyad is making decisions regarding a task. According to Poole and Billingsley (1989), the members of the dyad may smooth over differences, make token agreements, show incomplete sharing of information about the problem, and do little problem solving to maintain the relationship. Or, as Poole and Billingsley indicate, they may develop a relationship of great intimacy and openness to overcome relational threats posed by the process of making a task-oriented decision; thus, the possibilities of disagreement are minimized by creating a mutually shared perspective. In other words, there may be more concern for decisions that couples make about their own relationship than concern for decisions about external tasks facing the dyad (Kenny & Acitelli, 1989).

Dyadic Family Decision Making

In dyadic family decision making, the dyadic unit is viewed as a subsystem of the family system. Thus, although the dyadic family unit first involves a unitary relationship between two people, the dyad will be influenced by the norms, values, and beliefs of the total family system. Second, family members typically do not make decisions alone. Reciprocal interactions occur throughout the family and within each dyadic unit. Thus in a caregiving relationship, an elderly mother rarely would utilize direct autonomy, and an adult daughter or other family caregiver rarely would utilize direct paternalism. More often, within the family decision-making relationship, decision making would be shared in some way. Third, when the help is given by a younger family member to an older one, the cohort or generation difference between members of the pair may increase barriers to adequate communication.

Dyadic Family Caregiving Decision Making

Dyadic family caregiving decision making has some unique characteristics. First, such decision making usually is concerned with the care of an aging family member (mother, father, etc.). This care involves varying degrees of dependency or need for help by the elderly family member. In other words, an imbalance exists in any equity exchange between caregiver and care receiver. This fundamental fact of dependency is the basis for the existence of helping or caregiving by another family member. Second, not only does a long history of relationships between members of aging families exist, but in later life a long history of caregiving and care receiving within a dyadic family unit also may exist.

These two characteristics of the family situation have three implications for decision making:

1. Structural factors or characteristics of the individuals in the dyad may be more important in predicting decision

making than process. In a context of historical relationships and caregiving relationships, process may become habitual, causing few unpredictable changes over time. Expected decision behavior may flow more from the resources of the caregiver and care receiver than from process. Thus to predict decision behavior, one might be more concerned with developing a structural theory than a process theory.

2. Within such a structural theory, the objective would be to predict the agent of decision making above and beyond any consideration of effective decision making for specific caregiving tasks. In other words, in family caregiving one wants to know who will make the decisions and whether the type of decision making will be autonomous or paternalistic. This focus results from the dependency of the elderly member of the dyad.

3. One must understand the antecedents that determine the agent of decision making and the consequences for effective decision making, as well as any ethical concerns with what "ought to be."

DYADIC DECISION-MAKING MODEL

To provide an overview of dyadic decision making, a general model or schematic diagram of the basic categories and their relationship is presented in Figure 4.1.

The general hypothesis is that the context of decision making facilitates or restricts the decision-making process, and both context and process directly influence decisional outcomes. The above may involve either task decision making or relational decision making (in which the decision is concerned with the relationship between the individuals rather than an external task).

This general approach to dyadic decision making (albeit with various modifications) has been followed by different researchers (e.g., Jaccard et al., 1989; Poole & Billingsley, 1989; Scanzoni, 1989). In such a general schematic representation as found in Figure 4.1, context, process, and outcome

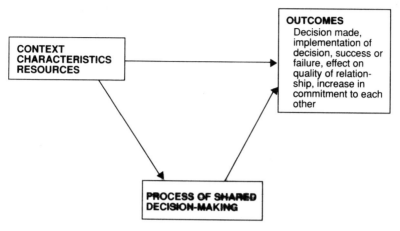

Figure 4.1. General model of dyadic decision making

are generic categories representing various specific variables used in different theories. An elaboration on each of the above generic categories would provide a relevant background for my own theory of dyadic family caregiving decision making.

OUTCOME

The objective of any dyadic decision-making model or theory is to explain and predict the decisional outcome. There are multiple outcomes of any decision, however, and which outcome is viewed as central depends upon the researcher's focus or objective (as well as that of the participants in the decision). One may consider many outcomes or only the one that interests the researcher or focus on one and consider others as side effects. In any event, the concern here is to make the reader aware of some of the different outcomes that may be relevant.

The first outcome, and perhaps the most important, is the actual decision made, or the final selection of an alternative or choice. For some theorists, this is the main concern. For others, outcome would also include the implementation of the decision, or the actual behavior or course of action followed to attain the goal of the decision. A further step is to determine the success or failure of implementing the decision—did it attain the goal of the decision? Was it actually beneficial or harmful to one or both members of the dyad? Was it worth the effort in terms of cost/benefit analysis; in other words, did it lead to maximum benefit and minimum cost? Finally, what was the effect upon the quality of the relationship between the dyad members? For example, did it improve the closeness of the dyad members, or did it lead to alienation between them? Was there greater or less commitment to each other? Which outcome is paramount, which outcomes are considered as side effects, and whether multiple outcomes are considered with equal status will depend upon the researcher's theory.

PROCESS

Process is concerned with the patterns of interaction that emerge as dyad members interact to make a decision. How partners interact may be unpredictable in advance, but certain decision-making styles do seem to exist.

Sillars and Kalblesch (1989) identified implicit and explicit decision-making styles. Although these styles were based upon research dealing with communication and marital conflict, they may be extended to the process of decision making in general.

In explicit decision making (Sillars & Kalblesch, 1989), partners make direct, conscious, verbal agreements. They are prospective in their approach; they engage in discussion with the clear goal of making a decision. They are proactive in that they plan ahead in an organized manner, taking a rationalistic approach to their decision making. This approach is reflected further in their management of the process of discussion. They have an agreed-upon set of procedures, such as a time and place for discussion, participation rules, and so on. This process would be analogous to families holding regular meetings according to some sort of rules. There is direct engagement regarding conflict. Conflict issues are directly verbalized.

Members of the dyad may confront the issue by analysis, threats, insults, hostile jokes, criticisms, and so on.

According to Sillars and Kalblesch (1989), when a decision needs to be made, those using an explicit decision-making style take a mastery approach; that is, they want to attack the problem head-on. The problem is a challenge to be solved and requires explicit communication between the partners. Their syntax is more differentiated and fully elaborated. They use long sentences with greater structural complexity, (e.g., subordinate clauses, uncommon adjectives, adverbs), resulting in a more explicit, elaborated and effortful form of communication.

According to Sillars and Kalblesch (1989), an implicit decision-making style is just the opposite of the explicit style. Rather than explicit agreements, the partners have silent arrangements; that is, decisions are made, reached, or evolved without verbal agreement in an unconscious or partially conscious manner. Silent arrangements occur because it may never occur to the partners to decide things in any other way. Such agreements tend to be retrospective; the partners do not self-consciously view themselves as making decisions except after the fact. Decisions for them simply may be part of a larger ongoing activity, such as going shopping or having meals. Rarely is decision making a separate, self-conscious event. Sillars and Kalblesch also make the point that decision making is incremental rather than proactive. With limited explicit communication or direct attention to the decision process, no master plan or rational procedure exists for carrying it out. The partners tend to muddle through the decision making one step at a time. Even when criteria have been laid down in advance, dyad members may ignore them and use more emotional criteria as they make a decision. For example, two individuals may have listed in advance all the criteria for buying a house but then make the decision more spontaneously when a house is seen that fits some fantasized way of living. Then too, spontaneous decision making may bring unexpected rewards that break old routines and bring the partners even closer together. Decision making may be more personally satisfying when less carefully structured.

When implicit decision making occurs, it is guided more by implicit unverbalized rules than by explicit verbal discussions. Conflicts may be partially acknowledged, joked about, avoided, or even denied. The partners may be vague in their comments, change the topic, walk away from each other, obscure the issue, and so on.

Their language tends to be more pragmatic than that used in explicit decision making. Dyad members may use brief utterances, short sentences, or only a few words. They take verbal shortcuts in expressing themselves. They operate within a common context; for example, they know when silence means approval or rejection.

Sillars and Kalblesch (1989) discussed various factors that account for the differences between explicit and implicit decision-making styles. Implicit decision making appears to be more characteristic of pairs who have shared experiences or role expectations (norms, cultural standards, traditional family background) and greater intimacy and stability in their relationship. In addition, it seems related to decisional overload. The latter occurs when resources are limited and demands are great, that is, many decisions are required. Given decisional overload within the context of similarity, intimacy, and stability, implicit decision making is expedient. As many of the daily decisions are embedded in ongoing life, they simply are made implicitly as part of carrying out other activities.

Explicit decision making appears to be more characteristic of pairs who are nontraditional, individualistic, and independent minded. Such pairs seem to need to make decision making more of a conscious, separate event with much greater verbal communication and agreement than pairs who use implicit decision making.

Another viewpoint on decision-making style is that of Raush, Barry, Hertel, and Swain (1974), who identified three components of style: cognitive, affiliative, and coercive. Persons higher on the cognitive and affiliative components and lower on the coercive component exhibit positive communication in decision making. They tend to be more oriented toward problem solving, friendlier, and less domineering than those using other styles. Those pairs lower on the cognitive and affiliative components and higher on the coercive component exhibit negative styles in decision making. These contrasting styles can facilitate or inhibit the decision-making process.

A further example of decision-making style is from the work of Pruitt (1981). These authors suggested a continuum along which are found four kinds of bargaining behaviors: problem solving, compensatory, compromise, and competitive. Other process variables could be identified (e.g., the power relationship), but the important point is that the sequence of interactions between the pair may involve many dimensions influencing the decision-making process and the final selection of an alternative.

CONTEXT, CHARACTERISTICS, AND RESOURCES

Context, characteristics, and resources refer to what the partners bring to the decision-making process. These variables may facilitate or retard decision making, either influencing outcome directly or influencing it indirectly through their actions on process.

Context refers to the situational constraints within which the pair interacts, such as the proximity of residence. It also may refer to the external characteristics of the partners, such as age, sex, and marital status.

Characteristics as used here refers to such internal features as personality and the emotional, physical, and mental attributes of the partners.

Resources refers to the means that the individual has available to deal with the task, such as money, time, and expertise relative to the task.

Such variables may enhance or inhibit the process of decision making. Thus an individual who is highly individualistic may prefer a decisional outcome that fits personal needs above and beyond any need to maintain the relationship with a partner (Scanzoni, 1989).

THEORY OF DYADIC FAMILY CAREGIVING
DECISION MAKING

The schematic diagram presented in Figure 4.1 identified three broad categories of decision making. This general view was used to derive the more specific decision-making model presented in Figure 4.2.

The present theory is a structural theory in that outcome is related only to contextual and personal-social variables. This does not deny the importance of process but represents a focus imposed by limited research money and time. Some justification exists, however, for an emphasis on contextual and personal-social variables since these variables may account for a large portion of the variance in the dependent variable. As previously stated, there is a long history of the relationships between the family members in aging families. If the dyadic family relationships are reasonably positive, then implicit decision-making styles should predominate. But the long history of the relationship also should lead to predictable patterns of interaction following from contextual and personal-social variables. Therefore the direct effects of these variables may be just as predictive of decision-making outcomes as a combination of their direct effects and their indirect effects operating through the process of decision making.

The specific theory diagrammed in Figure 4.2 represents the three generic categories of Figure 4.1 discussed earlier.

OUTCOME OR DEPENDENT VARIABLES

As previously stated, multiple outcomes of decision making can be identified. The dyadic family caregiving decision-making theory is concerned, however, with an aspect of the relationship between the partners. Most theories of dyadic decision making are concerned with identifying context and/or process variables that lead to more effective decision making, given a particular type of task. (One may be concerned with the number, breadth, or complexity of the task and whether

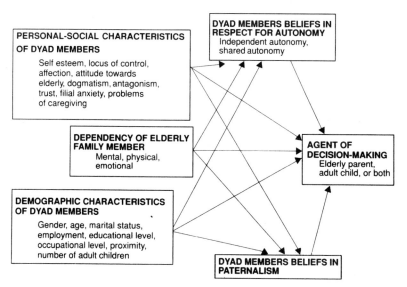

Figure 4.2. Model of dyadic family caregiving decision making

the task is a major or minor one in a person's life.) Dyadic decision making not only concerns making decisions regarding a task but also the relationship between the partners themselves. In the theory of dyadic family caregiving decision making, this relationship becomes the central focus. I am concerned with trying to predict who will be the decisionmaker in regard to caregiving tasks rather than predicting effective decision making for such tasks. (Obviously, the agent of decision making may in turn influence effective decision making.) I am not only trying to predict which member of the pair will be the decisionmaker, but the associated decision-making style as well. Thus if the outcome is a paternalistic decision, then a family caregiver will have made the final decision in some form after interacting with the care receiver. On the other hand, if the outcome is a decision respecting the autonomy of the elder, then the interaction between the pair will have led to the care receiver's exercise of autonomous decision making in some form. Either type of dyadic decisionmaker will have some influence on effective decision making regarding caregiving tasks and some feedback on the quality of the relationship itself. Both of these interesting issues go beyond present concerns.

ANTECEDENT VARIABLES

In applying the theoretical approach diagrammed in Figure 4.2, one is concerned with identifying variables that are predictors of the agent of decision making. This identification involves selecting specific variables from the general categories of contextual and personal-social variables and justifying their selection, as well as hypothesizing their relationship to the agent of decision making.

Dependency

If an elderly family member was not dependent to a degree that help was required for that person to survive, adapt to the community, or adjust to everyday living needs, there would be no need for a caregiver or for decisions on the type and amount of care to be provided. The existence and degree of dependency is the driving force and most fundamental variable in caregiving theories. The very existence of a caregiver-care receiver dyad is predicated upon the dependency needs of an elder and the fulfillment of those dependency needs by a caregiver (Cicirelli, 1983a; Kahana & Young, 1990).

In theory, the degree of dependency of the elderly parent (i.e., the type and amount of help needed during caregiving) is related to paternalistic caregiving (Collopy, 1986). Certainly this is true in many areas of medical care and social services (Beauchamp & Childress, 1983; Marshall, 1981; Moody, 1987). Thus one would expect indicators of dependency to be important predictors of a belief in paternalism.

One may hypothesize a curvilinear relationship between dependency and the agent of decision making. In such a relationship, as dependency increases, the caregiver's allowance or promotion of the exercise of the elder's autonomy continues until the elder reaches a point of decline or deterioration such that some degree of paternalistic decision making becomes necessary to care for the elderly person's needs and autonomy begins to decline. This threshold will vary, depending upon the type of physical, mental, or emotional dependency (or some combination thereof) involved.

Demographic Variables

The demographic variables represent the external context within which the family caregiving dyad exists. Such variables as age, marital status, education, and employment not only influence who the family caregiver will be but the way in which caregiving decisions are made.

Personal-Social Variables

In dyadic decision making, personal-social variables not only can influence the decision-making process but can themselves be altered as a result of the process or outcome.

In the present form of the dyadic family decision-making model, however, only the effects of the personal-social variables upon the determination of the agent of decision making are considered and not effects in the opposite direction. This is a matter of expediency rather than a denial of reciprocal effects; they will be considered at some later time.

Under the rubric of personal-social variables, individual personality characteristics, beliefs, and attitudes are included, as well as variables describing the interpersonal relationships between the members of the dyad.

Given a family caregiving dyad dealing with caregiving tasks, it is hypothesized that the locus of control beliefs of caregiver and care receiver are related to their beliefs in respect for autonomy and paternalism, and thus indirectly related to the agent of decision making. For example, an elderly parent with a strong internal locus of control belief is hypothesized to hold also a strong belief in autonomy.

Self-esteem also should be related to belief in respect for autonomy and indirectly to the exercise of autonomous decision making. Individuals with a high internal locus of control and high self-esteem usually want to control their own destiny.

In addition, trust in the other member of the family caregiving dyad is hypothesized to be related to respect in belief for autonomy and autonomous decision making. A dyadic relationship in which mutual trust is involved should include allowing others to make their own decisions, as well as trusting others to make decisions in that person's behalf.

In attempting to identify variables that might be related to belief in paternalism and paternalistic decision making, the concept of paternalism was examined more closely. When one intervenes in another person's decision making, one feels that he or she knows what is best for the other person by virtue of superior knowledge, abilities, or maturity (or some combination thereof) and thus can bring about a better outcome than an autonomous decision by the person being cared for (Gert & Culver, 1979). The intervener is motivated by concern for the welfare of the care receiver, which is judged as having priority over that person's freedom of choice.

Although reasons exist why an adult child might feel more competent than a parent who is very dependent or confused mentally, one must consider also the general stereotype in our society that older people as a group are less competent than younger people. Many studies (e.g., Bennett & Eckman, 1973; Kite & Johnson, 1988) have reported negative attitudes toward elders held by older people themselves, as well as by the young. If such attitudes are held, then an adult child caregiver would in general be regarded as more competent than an elderly parent and thus would feel justified in intervening paternalistically.

In addition to a negative attitude toward the elderly, a dogmatic personality is hypothesized to lead to a stronger belief in paternalism. Dogmatism involves having a strong set of beliefs based upon appeal to authority (rather than upon evaluation of empirical evidence) and a mind closed to others' ideas and beliefs (Ehrlich, 1978; Rokeach, 1960). Caregivers with a mind closed to an elderly person's point of view and with the belief that their own ideas are correct would be more likely to believe that paternalistic decisions should be made.

If paternalism also involves caring for the welfare of elderly people (even at the expense of their freedom of choice), it implies a sustained motivation and commitment of the caregiver to provide help to the care receiver. Adult attachment theory (Bowlby, 1979, 1980; Cicirelli, 1983a, in press) holds that a child's early attachment to the parent continues throughout life. Protection of the attached figure is an aspect of attachment that develops somewhat later in time than the early childhood bond itself; it has the aim of protecting and preserving the continued existence of the attached figure. An adult child with a strong attachment to the parent (e.g., a daughter's bond to the mother) is hypothesized to have a stronger belief in paternalism than an adult child with a weak attachment bond. In situations in which the parent's continued existence might be threatened, a child's paternalistic decision gives the parent's welfare priority over any concern for the parent's freedom of choice.

Beliefs

Various mediators may come into play to modify the relationship between other antecedent variables and outcome. Beliefs can be important mediators of this sort, as for example in the health belief model (Fincham & Wertheimer, 1985; Sigel, 1985; Woodward & Wallston, 1987). *Beliefs* are subjective judgments that objects (or ideas) exist and have certain attributes (Fishbein & Ajzen, 1975). Beliefs are held with varying degrees of certainty but tend to be durable and contribute to the guidance or influence of behavior.

Sigel's work (1985) provides support for the expected influence of beliefs on behavior. He found that when beliefs are "action-oriented" they are strong predictors of behavior. For example, in studies of parents teaching children, parents' beliefs that children learn best by directly instructing them as to what they should do (an action-oriented belief) was related to their actual behavior in teaching their children. That is, Sigel found that the parental belief predicted the parents' behavior in helping their children learn.

The beliefs in respect for autonomy and paternalism are action-oriented, since they express a belief in what an adult child should do in a caregiving decision situation. Reasoning by analogy from Sigel's (1985) findings, one would expect beliefs about autonomy and paternalism to predict decision-making behavior.

The present study has focused upon two ethical beliefs held by family members regarding caregiving decision making: belief in respect for autonomy and belief in paternalism. It is hypothesized that strong beliefs in autonomy and paternalism predispose the dyad toward either the exercise of autonomous or paternalistic decision making. The beliefs of each member of the dyad may be important predictors. If decision making is dyadic, however, then one also should be concerned with the degree of agreement between the beliefs of the elder and the family caregiver about the appropriate agent of decision making in old age. Thus one would be interested in relating the degree of agreement or disagreement of belief in respect for autonomy to autonomous decision making, and the degree of agreement and disagreement of belief in paternalism to paternalistic decision making.

Certain types of caregiver-care receiver dyads may exist, characterized by particular combinations of the beliefs held by each member regarding respect for paternalism and the autonomy of the elder. (For example, one type might consist of a caregiver with a strong belief in paternalism and a weak belief in respect for autonomy and a care receiver with a weak belief in paternalism and a strong belief in respect for autonomy.)

Assessment of Beliefs in Paternalism and Respect for Autonomy

Studying autonomy and paternalism in the course of family caregiving behaviors is important if one is to determine just what the influences on the older person's autonomy are in the context of family decision making and family life.

Thus one needs to assess both autonomy-related and paternalistic caregiving by family members. To study autonomy-related or paternalistic caregiving practices directly may not always be possible, or it may be too time-consuming. Consequently it would seem important to identify antecedent factors that could be assessed conveniently to predict autonomy-related caregiving practices. Beliefs regarding autonomy and paternalism have been hypothesized to be such antecedent factors (see Chapter 4). In addition to the convenience of measuring beliefs in contrast to measuring caregiving behaviors, measurement of beliefs would be applicable not only to actual but to potential family caregivers and care receivers, thus making prediction of later caregiving behaviors possible.

A first step in studying family members' autonomy-related beliefs was the development of suitable instruments to measure such beliefs. Accordingly a major research effort was directed toward the development of measures to assess an individual's beliefs about paternalism and respect for autonomy in relation to an aging family member. Although it was recognized that other family members are important caregivers, it was decided to develop measures specific to adult children and their elderly parents. (For example, relationships between spouses are very complex, and it remains to be determined how paternalism and respect for autonomy among spouse caregivers are modified by the division of responsibilities within the marital dyad. Instruments were developed, however, so that, with some minor rewording of items, they could be applied also to the measurement of other family members' beliefs.)

An additional objective was to construct two separate instruments—one to measure autonomy-respecting beliefs and another to measure paternalism beliefs—rather than to measure the two as part of a single dimension on the same instrument. If only strong forms of autonomy and paternalism are considered, they would appear to be at opposite poles of the same underlying dimension. This polar relationship is not immediately apparent, however, if more moderate conceptions of these terms are considered. Therefore it was decided to construct two separate instruments with the question of the possible dependence of the two beliefs to be settled empirically.

A further consideration was the desire to construct measuring instruments that could be used with either adult child caregivers or their elderly parents and that would be specific to beliefs about paternalism and respect for autonomy as applied to caregiving situations involving an elderly parent and an adult child. It was felt that such instruments would be more useful if they could be employed to assess beliefs of both the parent and the adult child. One could then determine how parent and child differ in their beliefs and how the beliefs of each influence actual caregiving practices.

INSTRUMENT CONSTRUCTION

Plan for Representation of Relevant Content Areas

In constructing the respect-for-autonomy instrument, items were written to represent each of five subtypes of autonomy (direct, consultive, joint, delegated, and surrogate) appearing to some extent in the writings of various ethicists (Collopy, 1986; Dworkin, 1988; Gillon, 1985; Young, 1986). Since the subtypes as delineated in the literature formed only nominal categories, the further distinction was added that these subtypes involve a degree of participation by others in the decision-making process, thereby converting the nominal to an ordinal scale (see Chapter 2). To review, these categories are as follows:

1. Direct autonomy is the case in which the elderly person makes decisions alone.
2. Consultive autonomy is the case in which the elderly person makes decisions after consulting with another individual (e.g., an adult child).
3. Joint autonomy is the case in which the elderly person and another individual make decisions together.
4. Delegated autonomy is the case in which the elderly person freely delegates decision making to another individual, but such decisions are made in accordance with the elderly person's values and life plan. (A further subtype of delegated autonomy is possible when the parent freely consents to have the child make the decisions according to the child's wishes.)
5. Surrogate autonomy is the case in which another individual voluntarily assumes decision-making power if and when the elderly person is no longer competent to make decisions, or when the elderly person designates the other person to make such decisions in the event of loss of decision-making competence at some time in the future. In either case, decisions should be made in accordance with the values and life plan of the elderly individual.

In addition to the five subtypes of autonomy, three general types of family caregiving decision situations were represented (health decisions, financial decisions, and everyday living decisions). Finally, items were written depicting care receivers with high and low levels of competence. A given item, for example, might describe a situation in which a financial decision must be made, joint autonomy, and an elderly parent at a high level of competence.

A similar plan was used for the paternalism instrument (see Chapter 2), with items representing six types of paternalism (direct, indirect, benevolent, moderate, weak, and default) that have been derived from a consideration of the writings of such ethicists as Collopy (1986), Dworkin (1988), Gillon (1985), and Young (1986). To review, the paternalism categories are as follows:

1. Direct or strong paternalism is the case in which the person in authority intervenes in another person's decision making without that person's request, consent, and/or awareness, for that person's welfare.
2. Indirect paternalism is the case in which the person in authority uses deception or subtle manipulation to intervene.
3. Benevolent paternalism is the case in which the person in authority participates in the decision, explaining its necessity.
4. Moderate paternalism is the case in which the person in authority intervenes only to prevent harm.
5. Weak paternalism is the case in which the person in authority intervenes only when there is mental deterioration.
6. Paternalism by default is the case in which an otherwise capable dependent person is indifferent to making reasoned decisions, so the person in authority must make necessary decisions.

In addition, items represented the three types of family caregiving decision situations (health decisions, financial decisions, and everyday living situations) and care receivers with high and low levels of competence.

Construction of Item Pools and Pre-Tryouts

The first step in instrument construction consisted in writing pools of 80 items dealing with belief in respect for autonomy and 80 items dealing with paternalism. Items of the Likert type were constructed to apply to situations involving adult children and elderly parents. Item statements included a brief description of the decision situation (e.g., a health decision) and level of competence (stated or implied) of the elderly parent, followed by an assertion that the adult child caregiver should exercise a given type of respect for autonomy or paternalism in making the decision. For example, an item depicting a health decision representing strong paternalism reads as follows: "No matter how much an elderly parent objects, the adult child should do whatever he/she thinks is best for the parent's health in the long run." In responding to an item, the interviewee is asked to indicate the extent of agreement with the statement on a 5-point scale ranging from "strongly agree" (5 points) to "strongly disagree" (1 point).

After an initial review and editing of the entire pool of items to make sure they met the specifications for item construction, the 40 respect-for-autonomy items judged by the research staff to be best were selected for the pre-tryout form of the autonomy instrument; the 40 paternalism items judged to be best were selected for the pre-tryout form of the paternalism instrument.

A pre-tryout administration of the initial versions of the two instruments was carried out with 20 interviewees: 10 adult children and 10 elderly parents. In each case, subjects' responses to the items were probed to determine whether item content was misunderstood or ambiguous, whether the vocabulary and usage was understood easily, and whether the subjects' responses indicated that the items achieved the objective of measuring belief in respect for autonomy or belief in paternalism. In addition, it was possible to identify any items that were unsuitable for the assessment of both elderly parents and adult children.

Tryouts of Instruments

Based upon the information gained from the pre-tryout, the tryout versions of the Respect for Autonomy Scale and the Paternalism Scale were constructed. Each consisted of 30 items, developed from the pre-tryout versions of the instruments by selecting the best items, modifying others, eliminating poor items, and adding an item or two where needed.

A field tryout of the resulting instruments was carried out, with the two instruments administered to 31 adult children and 39 elderly parents. Using data from the tryout, item analyses were carried out for the two measures for each group of subjects. These analyses included internal consistency reliabilities, item-total score correlations, and item discriminations for the total subscore and for subscores corresponding to the subtypes of autonomy and paternalism. Internal consistency reliabilities (Cronbach's alpha) were adequate for each of the instruments for both the adult child and elderly parent groups. In addition, item-total correlations were satisfactory for almost all items, as were item discriminations. On the basis of this information, a few items on each instrument were modified slightly to yield final forms of the instruments. Copies of the two scales are found in Appendix A.

Field Testing of Instruments

The two instruments in their final form were field-tested using two separate samples. The first was a sample of 147 adult children, each of whom had at least one living elderly parent. Although most of these adult children were providing some care to their parents, the provision of care was not considered to be a qualification for the selection of the sample, since the scales measured beliefs rather than actual caregiving behavior.

There were 38 adult sons and 109 adult daughters, ranging in age from 27 to 78, with a mean age of 52.2 years (*SD* = 11.5 years). The second sample consisted of 81 elderly parents, each of whom had at least one living adult child. There were 17 elderly fathers and 64 elderly mothers, ranging in age from 60-97, with a mean age of 79.9 years (*SD* = 8.5 years). All resided in a medium-sized midwestern city and its suburban area, with a population of approximately 100,000. In the field test, the instruments were administered individually in the individual's home as part of an interview-questionnaire.

ADMINISTRATION AND SCORING OF THE INSTRUMENTS

The population for which the Respect for Autonomy Scale and the Paternalism Scale were designed includes both adult children (family caregivers) and elderly parents (care receivers). Although it is possible to administer the scales as paper-and-pencil instruments, it is recommended that they be administered individually by a trained interviewer. Items are read individually to the person whose beliefs are being assessed; then the person is asked to indicate verbally the degree of agreement or disagreement with each statement. Individual administration offers the advantage of allowing the interviewer to detect and remedy any difficulties in comprehension of a particular item. In addition, a researcher or family counselor using the instruments can often gain additional information about the subject's beliefs from spontaneous remarks made in the course of responding to the items. The instruments may be administered to small groups, provided that no group members have hearing or vision problems that would hamper comprehension. Each scale takes approximately 20 minutes to administer.

Each item is scored on a 5-point scale, ranging from 5 points for a "strongly agree" response to 1 point for a "strongly disagree" response. To obtain a particular score based upon the scale, the appropriate item scores are summed. In each case, a higher score indicates a greater belief in respect for autonomy or in paternalism.

Subscores for each of the five subtypes of respect for autonomy can be obtained as follows:

Direct autonomy. Sum of scores for items 1, 6, 11, 16, 21, 26.
Consultive autonomy. Sum of scores for items 4, 9, 14, 19, 24, 29.
Joint autonomy. Sum of scores for items 2, 7, 12, 17, 22, 27.
Delegated autonomy. Sum of scores for items 5, 10, 15, 20, 25, 30.
Surrogate autonomy. Sum of scores for items 3, 8, 13, 18, 23, 28.

The possible score range for each of the above subscales is from 6 to 30 points. In addition to the subscores, factor scores (to be discussed later in this chapter) can be obtained as follows:

Independent autonomy. Sum of scores for items 1, 4, 6, 9, 11, 14, 16, 19, 21, 24, 26, 29.
Or, Direct autonomy + Consultive autonomy.
Shared autonomy. Sum of scores for items 2, 3, 5, 7, 8, 10, 12, 13, 15, 17, 18, 20, 22, 23, 25, 27, 28, 30.
Or, Joint Autonomy + Delegated Autonomy + Surrogate Autonomy.

The possible score range for the Independent Autonomy score is from 12 to 60 points; the possible score range for the Shared Autonomy score is from 18 to 90 points.

Like the Respect for Autonomy Scale, each item on the Paternalism Scale is scored on a 5-point range. To obtain a particular score based upon the scale, the appropriate item scores are summed; in each case, a high score indicates greater paternalism of the given type. Subscores for the six types of paternalism can be obtained as follows:

Strong paternalism. Sum of scores for items 1, 9, 14, 19, 26.
Indirect paternalism. Sum of scores for items 4, 12, 17, 21, 23.
Benevolent paternalism. Sum of scores for items 2, 7, 15, 25, 30.
Moderate paternalism. Sum of scores for items 5, 10, 18, 22, 29.
Weak paternalism. Sum of scores for items 3, 8, 13, 20, 24.
Default paternalism. Sum of scores for items 6, 11, 16, 27, 28.

The possible score range for each of the above subscales is from 5 to 25 points.

The Total Paternalism score can be obtained as follows:

Total Paternalism. Sum of scores for items 1 through 30.

Or, Strong Paternalism + Indirect Paternalism + Benevolent Paternalism + Moderate Paternalism + Weak Paternalism + Default Paternalism.

The possible score range for the Total Paternalism score is from 30 to 150 points.

INTERNAL CONSISTENCY RELIABILITY OF THE SUBSCALES

The internal consistency reliabilities (Cronbach's alpha coefficient) for each of the subscales of the Respect for Autonomy Scale and the Paternalism Scale are presented in Table 5.1 for the adult child group and the elderly parent group.

Subscale reliabilities for the five types of autonomy assessed by the Respect for Autonomy Scale ranged from .50 to .73 for the adult child group and from .43 to .54 for the elderly parent group. Similarly, subscale reliabilities for the six types of paternalism assessed by the Paternalism Scale ranged from .67 to .79 for the adult child group and from .48 to .76 for the elderly parent group.

For the adult child group, all of the subscore reliabilities for the two scales except the Joint Autonomy subscore equal or exceed the level of .50 recommended by Nunnally (1967) as sufficient for research work, while the reliabilities of a number of the subscores exceed the level of .70 recommended for comparisons involving groups.

For the elderly parent group, all of the subscore reliabilities for the two scales exceeded the magnitude of .50 recommended for research work, except the Joint Autonomy subscore on the Respect for Autonomy Scale and the Moderate

Table 5.1 Internal Consistency Reliabilities (Cronbach's Alpha) of
Subscores on the Respect for Autonomy Scale
and the Paternalism Scale

Measure	Number items	Reliability	
		Adult child	Elderly parent
Direct autonomy	6	.73	.52
Consultive autonomy	6	.59	.54
Joint autonomy	6	.58	.43
Surrogate autonomy	6	.50	.51
Delegated autonomy	6	.66	.51
Strong paternalism	5	.76	.76
Benevolent paternalism	5	.82	.76
Weak paternalism	5	.72	.66
Indirect paternalism	5	.67	.70
Moderate paternalism	5	.77	.48
Default paternalism	5	.84	.64

Paternalism subscore on the Paternalism Scale, while three of
the Paternalism subscores were of a magnitude sufficient for
comparisons involving groups.

CONTENT DOMAINS

To determine whether beliefs in respect for autonomy and
paternalism depended upon the particular content domain
involved, separate subscores were constructed for health, finances, and everyday living. Internal consistency reliabilities
of the three content domains of the Respect for Autonomy Scale
ranged from .52 to .60 for the adult children and from .49 to .58
for the elderly parents. Reliabilities of the three content domains of the Paternalism Scale ranged from .82 to .85 for adult
children and from .75 to .78 for elderly parents.

A repeated measures analysis of variance, followed by ad
hoc t-tests, was carried out to determine whether any difference existed among the three domain subscore means in belief
in respect for autonomy of the elder. The mean for respect for
autonomy in everyday living was significantly greater than

the means for either health or finances; no difference existed between the latter two means. The difference among the three means, however, was too small to have any practical relevance. Findings were similar for both the adult child and the elderly parent groups. When a similar analysis was carried out for the domain subscores of the Paternalism Scale, no significant differences existed between the means. Overall, then, it can be said that the beliefs regarding respect for autonomy and paternalism appear to be relatively constant over the three content domains.

FACTOR STRUCTURE OF THE INSTRUMENTS

A principal components factor analysis with varimax rotation was carried out for the 30 items of the Respect for Autonomy Scale, using the sample of 147 adult children. Two factors were identified with eigenvalues greater than one. Items loading on the first factor were largely from the subscales for Joint Autonomy, Delegated Autonomy, and Surrogate Autonomy, while items loading on the second factor were largely from the Direct Autonomy and Consultive Autonomy subscales.

A similar principal components factor analysis of the 30 Paternalism Scale items indicated that only a single factor was present.

A second factor analysis was carried out to investigate the question of whether autonomy and paternalism were separate dimensions or were merely polar extremes of the same dimension. Since the sample size was not large enough to deal with the 60 items of both the Respect for Autonomy and the Paternalism scales in a single analysis, the 11 subscores were used in an analysis instead. The results of this analysis are presented in Table 5.2. There were three factors with eigenvalues greater than one, accounting for 73% of the variance in the subscores. The first factor, termed Paternalism, was composed of the six paternalism subscores. The second factor, termed Shared Autonomy, was composed of Joint Autonomy, Delegated Autonomy, and Surrogate Autonomy. The third

Table 5.2 Loadings of Respect for Autonomy and Paternalism
Subscale Scores on Three Belief Factors for
Adult Children ($N = 147$)

| | Factor Loading | | |
Subscale	I	II	III
Direct autonomy	−.15	−.06	.90
Consultive autonomy	−.18	.19	.85
Joint autonomy	.24	.69	−.09
Delegated autonomy	.10	.88	.01
Surrogate autonomy	.13	.83	.22
Strong paternalism	.90	.12	−.11
Benevolent paternalism	.86	.25	−.04
Weak paternalism	.75	.15	−.20
Indirect paternalism	.74	.03	−.01
Moderate paternalism	.82	.14	−.19
Default paternalism	.75	.24	−.19

factor, termed Independent Autonomy, was composed of Direct Autonomy and Consultive Autonomy. The Shared Autonomy factor is made up of those subscales composed of items in which the adult child participates with the parent in making the final decision. The Independent Autonomy factor is made up of those subscales composed of items in which the elderly parent alone makes the final decision (although the parent may consult the adult child for information or advice).

Internal consistencies of the three factors are presented in Table 5.3. For the adult child group, reliabilities were .74 for Independent Autonomy, .78 for Shared Autonomy, and .93 for Paternalism; for the elderly parent group, reliabilities were .70 for Independent Autonomy, .74 for Shared Autonomy, and .90 for Paternalism. All reliabilities are considered to be satisfactory for making comparisons between groups, while the reliability of the Total Paternalism score is at a level sufficient for the interpretation of individual scores, as well as for comparisons involving groups. Because these reliabilities are better than those for the original subscales (Table 5.1), and because the factors represent meaningful conceptions of autonomy, the factor scores were used for the analyses discussed in the present volume and are recommended for any use by others.

Table 5.3 Internal Consistency Reliabilities of Factor Scores

		Reliability	
Measure	Number items	Adult child	Elderly parent
Independent autonomy	12	.74	.70
Shared autonomy	18	.78	.74
Total paternalism	30	.93	.90

STABILITY

To determine the stability of the measures, randomly selected subgroups of adult children and elderly parents ($n = 60$) were retested after a 20-week interval. For the adult child group, the test-retest correlations were .63 for Independent Autonomy, .52 for Shared Autonomy, and .88 for Total Paternalism. For the elderly parent group, the test-retest correlations were .60 for Independent Autonomy, .39 for Shared Autonomy, and .49 for Total Paternalism. All test-retest correlations were statistically significant, indicating considerable stability over a 4½-month interval. Scores for Shared Autonomy, however, were less stable than the other measures, and scores for elderly parents were less stable than those of the younger generation. As yet, I am unable to explain why this is the case.

INDEPENDENCE OF FACTORS

The factor analysis indicated that three distinct factors existed, and, therefore, that belief in respect for autonomy and belief in paternalism should not be regarded as opposite poles of the same dimension. Intercorrelations between the three scores, however, were computed to determine their relative independence. These intercorrelations are presented in Table 5.4, with correlations for the adult child group above the diagonal and correlations for the elderly group below the diagonal.

Among the adult children, Independent Autonomy and Shared Autonomy had a correlation of only .07, while among the elderly the correlation was .25. Thus, the two autonomy

Table 5.4 Intercorrelations of Independent Autonomy,
Shared Autonomy, and Paternalism

Measure	Independent Autonomy	Shared Autonomy	Total Paternalism
Independent autonomy	—	.07	−.31
Shared autonomy	.25	—	.40
Total paternalism	−.02	.52	—

NOTE: Correlations for 147 adult children are located above the diagonal, while correlations for 81 elderly parents are located below the diagonal.

belief scores may be considered to be essentially independent of each other. Independent Autonomy and Paternalism were correlated −.31 for adult children and −.02 for the elderly, providing little indication that these variables are extremes of a single bipolar dimension. Finally, Shared Autonomy and Paternalism were correlated .40 for adult children and .52 for the elderly. The weak to moderate correlations observed between these two measures suggest some degree of overlap, but not enough to consider them as making up a single dimension. If any conclusion can be drawn from these intercorrelations, it is that belief in shared autonomy has more in common with belief in paternalism than it has with belief in independent autonomy. Once the belief is held that an adult child should participate in an elderly parent's decision making, it seems only a small conceptual step to a belief that adult children should take over a parent's decision making entirely.

VALIDITY

Face and Content Validity

An instrument may be said to have face validity when it appears to be measuring what it is intended to measure. Since the content of the Respect for Autonomy Scale and the

Paternalism Scale is straightforward in nature, the measures may be said to have face validity.

The scales also may be said to have content validity, since the items represent carefully defined types of autonomy and paternalism, as well as three major domains of caregiving decision situations (everyday living, health, and finances).

Criterion Validity

Establishing criterion validity presented difficulties because this is a relatively new area of inquiry and established measures were not available. Some degree of criterion validity was established, however, by comparing scores on Independent Autonomy, Shared Autonomy, and Paternalism to scores on two other instruments developed especially for the project: the Ethical Belief situation Test (see Appendix C) and the Caregiving Practices Inventory. (An additional instrument developed for the project, the Autonomy/Paternalism Diagnostic Measures, also is included in Appendix C although it was not used for work reported in this volume. A forced choice instrument, it assesses the respondent's preferred or most frequent mode of responding to caregiving decision situations. It is felt that this instrument and the Ethical Belief Situation Test might be of use to counselors and similar practitioners working with family caregivers of the elderly in stimulating a discussion of the issues involved in respect for autonomy and paternalism and in probing the views of clients.)

The first instrument was the Ethical Belief Situation Test. It presented 12 situations involving caregiving decision dilemmas (4 concerned with everyday living, 4 with health, and 4 with finances) in which an elderly parent and an adult child have opposing views on the proper decision in a particular situation. The dilemma is whether a paternalistic decision should be made by the child or the parent's autonomy should be respected. Six of the dilemmas were adapted from those presented by Collopy (1986), and the remainder were written by me. An example of these dilemmas follows:

> Philip M., a widowed 83-year-old man, lives alone in the small house that he and his wife bought 60 years earlier. Mr. M has always taken great pride in his home and still keeps it in good repair.
>
> However, the neighborhood has gone downhill, and there has been a good deal of crime lately. Mr. M's house was broken into once when he was out, although only a few small items were taken. Recently, he was mugged on the way to the store and his wallet taken. When a neighbor was beaten to death right across the street, Mr. M's son said, "That's enough, Dad! You must move out of this neighborhood right away. I don't want to see you dead too, or in the hospital."
>
> Mr. M said, "I want to stay right here. I love this house. All my memories of the happy years with your mother are here. I know the neighborhood is not as good as it used to be, but I still have friends nearby. I don't keep much money around, and I don't go out at night. Anyway, at my age I don't have too much longer to live, and I want to be where I am happy." The son said, "I think you're too old to see the danger you're in. I'll move you out by force if I have to."
>
> Who has the right to decide what should be done, son or father? _____
>
> Why do you feel the (son, father) has the right to make the decision in this case? _____

The respondent is asked to indicate whether the parent's view or the child's view is the correct one in the given situation and to explain the reasoning behind this response. Both the respondent's judgment and the reasons for that judgment are considered to determine whether the responses to an item indicate a belief in respect for the parent's autonomy or a belief in paternalism. The Situational Autonomy score is the number of dilemmas in which the respondent supports the elderly parent's decision. Internal consistency reliability of the measure was .61 for adult children and .60 for elderly parents.

One would expect the Independent Autonomy score to be positively correlated with the Situational Autonomy score, and one would expect the Paternalism score to be negatively correlated with the Situational Autonomy score. Using the field test sample of 147 adult children of elderly parents, Independent Autonomy was correlated .40 ($p < .01$) with the Situational Autonomy score; similarly, Paternalism was correlated $-.57$ ($p < .01$) with Situational Autonomy. (Although no specific prediction was made regarding Shared Autonomy, it was correlated $-.22$ ($p < .01$) with Situational Autonomy; this was not surprising in view of the positive correlation between Shared Autonomy and Paternalism.) Using the field test sample of 81 elderly parents, Independent Autonomy was correlated .20 ($p < .10$) with Situational Autonomy, while Paternalism was correlated $-.39$ ($p < .01$) with Situational Autonomy. (The correlation between Shared Autonomy and Situational Autonomy was not significant.) Thus evidence exists for the validity of the Independent Autonomy and Paternalism scores, although this evidence is weaker for the elderly parent group than for the adult child group.

The second measure used to establish criterion validity was the Caregiving Practices Inventory. In responding to this inventory, the interviewee reports who makes decisions relative to a set of 40 common caregiving areas. One would expect Paternalism to be related to the number of areas in which decisions are made by the adult child and Independent Autonomy to be related to the number of areas in which decisions are made by the elderly parent.

Using the field test sample of adult children, Paternalism was correlated .29 with the number of decisions made by the adult child and $-.22$ with the number of decisions made by the elderly parent. Independent Autonomy was correlated .32 with the number of decisions made by the parent and $-.22$ with the number of decisions made by the adult child. Using the field test sample of elderly parents, Independent Autonomy was correlated .22 with the number of decisions made by the parent and $-.20$ with the number of decisions made by the adult child. Paternalism was correlated .23 with the number of decisions made by the adult child and −.35 with the number of decisions made by the elderly parent. Also, Shared Autonomy was correlated .28 with the number of decisions made jointly by parent and child.

Although these correlations are small in magnitude, they are statistically significant and in the expected direction, thus providing some support for the validity of the instrument. They support the hypothesized connection between beliefs regarding autonomy and paternalism and actual paternalism and respect for autonomy in the family caregiving situation, as reported by both adult children and elderly. Two possible reasons exist why the correlations were not higher. First, among the adult children and the elderly parents in the field test samples, the extent of actual caregiving was low. The resulting restriction of range in the number of decisions made by the adult child may be responsible for the low correlations. Second, the measure of caregiving decisions was a simple checklist type of procedure. It is expected that the relationships would be stronger if a more refined measure of caregiving decision making were available.

Construct Validity

Considering the definitions of *belief in respect for autonomy* and *belief in paternalism,* one may hypothesize that the measures obtained from the scales would be related to certain other psychological concepts, thus providing a test of the construct validity of the measures.

First, it was hypothesized that adult children with more authoritarian personalities would be more likely to exert authority over those perceived as weaker or less knowledgeable than themselves, using coercion or deception if necessary (Byrne & Kelley, 1981), and thus would have greater Paternalism scores. By the same reasoning, they should have lower scores on Independent Autonomy. The Balanced F-Scale (Cherry & Byrne, 1977), on which a low score indicates greater authoritarianism, was used as the measure of that concept.

For the adult child field sample, scores on the F-Scale were correlated −.43 with Paternalism and .24 with Independent Autonomy; both correlations were in the predicted direction. Using the elderly parent field sample, scores on the F-Scale were correlated −.22 with Paternalism; again, this is in the predicted direction.

It was also predicted that the greater the adult child's concern for the well-being of the parent, the greater the belief in paternalism. The measure of the adult child's concern was one of the two subscales of the Filial Anxiety Scale (Cicirelli, 1988). The anxiety of the child about the parent's well-being was correlated .24 with Paternalism and .28 with Shared Autonomy. In both cases, greater child concern for the parent was related to greater participation in decisions affecting the parent's life.

Finally, to determine whether social desirability had a significant influence upon responses to the Respect for Autonomy and Paternalism scales, correlations were computed between scores on the autonomy and paternalism measures and the Marlow-Crowne Social Desirability Scale (Crowne & Marlow, 1960). For the adult child group, social desirability was correlated −.01 with Independent Autonomy, −.01 with Shared Autonomy, and .16 with Paternalism. For the elderly parent group, social desirability was correlated .12 with Independent Autonomy, −.02 with Shared Autonomy, and .17 with Paternalism. Thus social desirability has at best a weak influence upon the responses of adult children and elderly parents to the Respect for Autonomy Scale and the Paternalism Scale.

NORMS

The gathering of norm data based upon representative samples was beyond the scope of the research project leading to the present volume. Some normative data based upon groups to whom the measures have been administered in the course of the project are presented in Appendix B. Interested readers and potential users of the instruments may use the means and standard deviations reported in the tables as a basis of comparison for their own work.

CONCLUDING COMMENTS

The process of instrument development described in this chapter led to two scales to assess the beliefs of adult children and elderly parents about autonomy and paternalism: the Respect for Autonomy Scale and the Paternalism Scale. Three factors identified through analysis of these scales (Independent Autonomy, Shared Autonomy, and Total Paternalism) were found to have satisfactory reliability. In addition, some evidence for their validity was obtained.

It should be noted, however, that establishing the reliability and validity of an instrument is an open-ended and ongoing process that continues as the instrument is used with new populations and to test new hypotheses. Obviously the measures of autonomy and paternalism are in an early stage of development. Nevertheless, a need exists for gerontological research into questions regarding respect for autonomy of the elderly and paternalism in family caregiving, and the measures provide a tool to use in such explorations. The work described in this volume was carried out in this spirit and should be interpreted as one stage in a continuing investigatory process.

PART THREE

Study of Autonomy and Paternalism Beliefs

Intergenerational Congruence of Beliefs

If elderly parents and their adult children agreed completely about *who* should make decisions affecting the parents' care and *what* those decisions should be, then questions of respecting the parents' autonomy would be irrelevant. In the real world, however, parents and their children do not always see eye-to-eye, and it becomes important to know just how well parents and adult children do agree on matters pertinent to the parents' care. Since some evidence exists (Schlesinger, Tobin, & Kulys, 1980) that care receivers have enhanced well-being when they perceive that their caregivers will act in accord with their wishes should they be unable to decide for themselves, lack of respect for the care receiver's autonomy can have serious consequences for the dependent elderly person. Although little research has been done on respect for the parents' autonomy in family caregiving situations, the existing studies in related areas provide some clues to the congruence between adult children and their elderly parents.

87

Health Status and Needs for Help

Studies of congruence between parents' and adult children's reports of the parents' health indicate the degree of parent-child agreement in this area. Rakowski and Hickey (Dengiz, Rakowski, & Hickey, 1982; Rakowski & Hickey, 1979, 1983) examined the congruence of elderly patients at a geriatric clinic and their family resource persons, measuring health status and other health-related variables. Even when elderly patients had the opportunity to discuss their condition with family members, congruence did not improve. Adult children, however, constituted only about 31% of Rakowski and Hickey's sample, making their findings of limited applicability to the question of parent-child congruence in itself.

Cicirelli (1981) investigated the difference between adult children's and elderly parents' perceptions of the parents' needs for caregiving assistance, although congruence was not specifically examined. Important differences were noted, however, in the relative importance that the two generations attached to various caregiving services, as well as in reports by parents and children of the actual amounts of services provided.

Cicirelli (1983b) also investigated congruence of reports on health status variables given by elderly parents and their adult children. Parent and child each were asked to report on the number and severity of the parent's chronic ailments, number and persistence of the parent's symptoms, parent's mobility, and parent's self-sufficiency in maintaining everyday activities. Congruence was indicated by the correlations between the elderly parents' and adult children's views of the parents' health. These correlations ranged from .33 to .79, with the highest correlations found for the two measures of the parents' functional adequacy (mobility and self-sufficiency in everyday activities) and the lowest correlations found for the two measures of the parents' health symptoms. It is interesting that congruence was greater regarding the parents' functional adequacy, which is more immediately and objectively observable, than for health symptoms, which are often unobservable (e.g., pain) and experienced subjectively.

In the work of Horowitz (Horowitz & Reinhardt, 1988; Horowitz et al., in press) comparing elders' and family caregivers' perceptions of whether the caregivers' help was appropriate to the need, the elders were found to be more likely than the caregivers to report receiving too little help in certain areas.

A recent study (Zweibel & Lydens, 1990) examined the congruence between responses of an older person and the family caregiver (68% were adult children) in regard to 18 aspects of the caregiving relationship. For seven items dealing with perceptions of the care receiver's ability to complete instrumental activities of daily living, from 24% to 40% of the dyads disagreed in their perceptions. Lack of congruence regarding perceptions of the level of assistance provided by the caregiver ranged from 4% to 44% over the seven items, with the greatest disagreement regarding extent of assistance with travel and shopping and the least with bathing and laundry. The lack of congruence was greatest for the four items dealing with subjective perceptions of the caregiving relationship, ranging from 47% disagreement regarding the availability of additional caregivers to 70% disagreement regarding the overall dependence of the care receiver.

The direction of the disagreement was significant only for two items. Caregivers regarded care receivers as more dependent than the care receivers perceived themselves to be, and caregivers regarded themselves as more impatient with the care receiver than care receivers perceived them to be. In other words, although disagreement was relatively high for many items, most of the children had one view, while most of the parents had the opposite view.

Overall the studies related to congruence in regard to the parents' health status and dependency needs indicated only a moderate degree of congruence between the perceptions of adult children and elderly parents. Also, congruence was greater in regard to objective, easily observable variables than when more subjective variables were considered.

Health Care Decisions

An aspect of parent-child congruence that is more closely relevant to issues of autonomy and paternalism concerns decisions about health care. The few existing studies of predictions of elderly persons' preferences by family members and other decisionmakers have been concerned with major medical decisions.

One such study (Uhlmann, Pearlman, & Cain, 1988) dealt with spouses' predictions of elderly patients' preferences for cardiopulmonary resuscitation under various severe health status scenarios. The subjects of the study were elderly, non-terminal chronic disease patients under the current care of a physician and their spouses. The spouses' correct predictions of the patients' resuscitation preferences ranged from 42% to 94%. (In every case, a higher percentage of spouses predicted that the patients would prefer resuscitation than did the patients themselves.) Those spouses who felt sure they were accurate in predicting their mates' preferences, however, did no better than those who were unsure. Thus family members who claim to know the elderly patients' wishes regarding treatment may or may not be correct. It is clear that the family needs to understand better the elderly patients' wishes regarding care before acting as surrogate decisionmakers. This need makes discussion of these matters essential. But, one reason why such discussions may not occur is that spouses tend to feel that they already understand their mates' wishes when in fact they may not understand them at all.

Another recent study (Tomlinson, Howe, Notman, & Rossmiller, 1990) aimed to determine how accurately family members could make substituted judgments for the elderly person in a simulated decision situation. The family members studied included spouses, brothers, sisters, daughters, sons, and others. Subject-kin pairs were assigned randomly to one of two different groups. In one group the family member was asked to make judgments of the elderly's treatment preferences for various medical scenarios in the way he or she thought the elderly person would make them. In the second group the family member was asked to make judgments about treatment according to what he or she thought was best for the elderly person. In both groups, the elderly person was asked for his or her own judgment. Greater disagreement existed between elders and their relatives in the second group than in the first group. This result demonstrated that when family members are asked to make judgments in the way they believe the older people would, they are in greater agreement with the judgments made by the older people themselves than when asked to make judgments according to what they think is best. The extent of agreement did not appear to depend upon the type of family member making the judgment (adult child, sibling, spouse, etc.), age differences, frequency of contact, or the relatives' ratings of their ability to make an accurate substituted judgment for the older family members.

Warren et al. (1986) carried out a study in which real rather than simulated decisions had to be made. They investigated the question of whether family members (the majority of whom were adult children) acting as proxies or surrogates for incompetent elderly nursing home patients actually would make decisions in the way they believed the older person would decide. The family members were asked to decide whether their elderly relative should participate in a minimal-risk research study to be carried out in the nursing home. The family members were divided into two groups according to whether they believed that their relative in the nursing home would give consent to participate in the research study.

In the group that believed the patient would refuse consent, 31% actually gave consent in opposition to their perceptions of the patient's wishes. In the group that believed the patient would consent, approximately 20% of the family members refused to give consent for the patient to participate in the research study. These findings suggest that family members acting as proxies or surrogates for an elderly person may not respect the autonomy of the elder, even when they believe they know what the elder's wishes are.

Thus it would appear important to understand the reasons why family members decide as they do in an elder's behalf.

Their ethical beliefs regarding respect for autonomy and paternalism could have considerable relevance. Indeed, when Warren et al. (1986) asked the 20% of family members who refused to give consent for their reasons, the most frequent reason was concern for the patient's welfare (suggesting paternalism), followed by reluctance to decide for the patient (perhaps suggesting respect for the patient's autonomy).

Zweibel and Cassel (1989) also studied the congruence on medical decisions between elderly patients receiving outpatient care at a large metropolitan hospital and their adult children (or nieces and nephews). Children and parents were asked to respond to five case vignettes in which decisions about life-extending care were required and the patient was incapable of responding. Patients and their adult children disagreed on the decision up to half of the time, with opposite choices occurring from 24% of the time for a decision about tube feeding to 50% of the time for a decision about chemotherapy. For four of the five decision scenarios (ventilation, chemotherapy, amputation, and tube feeding), the direction of discrepant responses was such that the adult child would choose to provide care that the elderly patient did not want, while for the fifth decision scenario (cardiopulmonary resuscitation) the adult child would choose *not* to provide care that the elderly patient did want. In a second part of the study, the adult children were asked what treatments they would want for themselves in each of the five decision scenarios. What they decided for themselves was highly concordant (ranging from 93% to 95%) with what they would decide for their elderly family member.

These findings suggest that the discrepancy between the decisions of elderly patients and family members on the decision scenarios existed because family members were using their own views in deciding what was best for the elderly patient rather than attempting to take the elderly patient's point of view. Looking at the findings from another perspective, it may be that for cases in which family members agreed with the patient regarding decisions, the agreement may have been the result of the coincidence of views reflecting underlying common values rather than the result of any active consideration of the elderly patient's wishes.

Caregiving Decisions

Only a few studies have been concerned with the extent of agreement between parent and child over caregiving decisions. Pratt et al. (1989) looked at decision making by elderly mothers and their caregiving daughters in regard to six areas of decisions: routine daily care, daily financial decisions, major financial decisions, routine health care, major health care, and housing. Both mother and daughter responded to questions about the degree of the mother's involvement in the decisions, the degree of the daughter's involvement, the degree of confidence in the mother's decision-making abilities, who had the "final say" in making decisions, and satisfaction with the decision-making process. Study findings revealed no difference between mothers' and daughters' perceptions of the degree of the mothers' involvement in decisions or their perceptions of satisfaction. There was less congruence, however, regarding the extent of the daughters' involvement in decision making, who had the "final say" in decisions, and confidence in the mothers' decision-making abilities. In comparison with the mothers, more daughters felt they had a greater involvement, were more likely to have the "final say" in the decisions, and felt less confidence in the mothers' ability to make decisions.

In a study of caregiving decision making involving a small number of respondents (Horowitz & Reinhardt, 1988; Horowitz et al., in press), conflicts surrounding caregiving decisions were explored. In reports of 66 caregiving decisions, conflicts between the elder and the family caregiver occurred in about a third of the cases. Caregivers were more likely to report that the elders would "give in," while elders were more likely to report that they had the last word on the decision. Despite the substantial percentage of decisions for which a difference of opinion occurred, the authors concluded that no

significant conflict existed around decision making. This conclusion, however, appeared to be based more upon the fact that
the conflicts were settled amicably than upon the fact that
differences of opinion did occur.

Attitudes and Beliefs About
Respect for Autonomy and Paternalism

Another part of Horowitz's work (Horowitz & Reinhardt,
1988; Horowitz et al., in press) dealt with the subjects' responses to a series of vignettes depicting family caregiving
situations in which autonomy issues were involved. Little
congruence was shown between caregivers' and elders' responses. For example, regarding a vignette depicting an elderly
father who refused needed help with food and medications,
74% of the elderly respondents felt that the father should be
persuaded or forced to accept children's help (paternalism),
while adult children felt that alternative autonomy-respecting
solutions should be tried. Similarly, in regard to a vignette
depicting an elderly mother with careless and forgetful smoking habits, all of the elderly respondents felt that the daughter
should not permit the mother to continue smoking (paternalism), while two thirds of the caregivers felt that the mother
had a right to continue to smoke (perhaps supervised in
some way). Thus the caregivers appeared to view the autonomy of the elderly more favorably than did the elders themselves. The authors observed that the elderly people they
studied were concerned primarily with the welfare of the
older people in the vignettes and viewed autonomy as having
secondary importance.

In a later phase of the present project, I determined the
congruence between elderly parents' and their adult children's
beliefs in respect for autonomy and paternalism. The sample,
described in detail in Chapter 8, consisted of 62 parent-child
pairs (46 mother-daughter pairs, 10 mother-son pairs, 3 father-
daughter pairs, and 3 father-son pairs). Correlations between the parent and child scores were computed for the three

measures: Independent Autonomy, Shared Autonomy, and Paternalism. These are presented in Table 6.1.

The correlations presented in the first column of Table 6.1 are for the entire group of 62 parent-child pairs. The correlations are extremely low in magnitude; the largest value of .22 for Shared Autonomy fails to reach statistical significance. Thus little congruence exists between the beliefs of parent and child.

Because it is possible that differing relationships for the four sex combinations of parent-child pairs could have affected adversely the overall congruence of the total group, the correlations also were carried out for the mother-daughter group alone (the sample sizes for the other three sex combinations were too small to permit analysis). These correlations are found in the second column of Table 6.1. Although the correlations are a little greater in magnitude than found for the total group, they still indicate a low level of agreement between the beliefs of mother and daughter regarding respect for autonomy and paternalism.

Since parent-child congruence on the belief measures was so low, the next question is whether they agree on who is actually making caregiving decisions. Using the Caregiving Practices Inventory, an inventory assessing who makes decisions in 40 common caregiving areas (see Chapter 5), scores were obtained for the number of decisions made by the adult child, number of decisions made by the elderly parent, and number of shared decisions. The correlations between the elderly parent's scores on the inventory and the adult child's scores also are presented in Table 6.1. The correlations between the two reports are strong for all three decision measures, indicating a high degree of congruence on the number of decisions made by the elderly parent, and somewhat less congruence on the number of decisions made by the adult child and the number of decisions made jointly by parent and child. As was found for the belief measures, the congruences were slightly greater when only the mother-daughter pairs were considered than when the total sample containing all four sex combinations was used. Yet the differences between the two samples were small.

Table 6.1 Correlations Between Elderly Parents and Adult Children
          on Measures of Belief in Respect for Autonomy and
              Paternalism and on Caregiving Decisions for
          62 Parent-Child Pairs and 46 Mother-Daughter Pairs

Measure	Total Group	Mother-Daughter Group
Independent autonomy	.09	.22
Shared autonomy	.22	.27
Paternalism	.09	.14
Number parent decisions	.87	.91
Number child decisions	.71	.72
Number shared decisions	.61	.65

It is apparent that elderly parents and adult children agree
rather well on their objective reports of who actually makes decisions in relation to caregiving, whereas there is little agreement in their beliefs about who should be making such
decisions. This finding suggests a possibility for conflict and
dissatisfaction surrounding caregiving decision making, as has
been observed (Horowitz & Reinhardt, 1988; Horowitz, et al.,
in press).

Adult Children's Knowledge of Parents' Wishes for Care

The studies reviewed thus far in this chapter indicate that
reports of elderly parents and their adult children have a high
level of congruence in relation to objective, easily observable
measures of health status, needs for care, or caregiving decisions, but a much lower level of congruence when more subjective variables are involved. In the case of beliefs about
respect for autonomy and paternalism, very little agreement
exists between parent and child.

Another topic that has implications for questions of autonomy and paternalism is adult children's knowledge of parents'
wishes relating to care. Parents' wishes regarding their own
care may be spelled out carefully to their adult child, or parents
may assume that the child should know without being told.

A child who knows clearly what the parents' wishes are in a given caregiving situation is better fitted to respect the parents' autonomy than one who has only a vague idea of what the parents' views are.

How well, then, do adult children feel that they know their parents' wishes for care? How well do elderly parents feel that their adult children know and understand these wishes? To probe these questions, we asked the adult children in our sample of 62 parent-child pairs to respond to the following questions:

1. To what extent would you know what your parent's wishes (for everyday care/for health care/about financial matters) would be if something serious were to happen and he/she could not decide this for himself/herself?
2. Have you and your parent ever discussed the parent's wishes (for everyday care/for health care/about financial matters)?
3. To what extent do you agree with your parent's wishes (for everyday care/for health care/about financial matters)?
4. Is there another person who would know your parent's wishes about (everyday care/health care/financial matters) better than you? If so, who?

Elderly parents were asked a set of similar questions about how well the adult child would know their views, whether they had ever discussed their wishes with the child, whether they agreed with their child's views, and whether anyone else would know their views better than the child. As indicated in the parentheses in the questions themselves, the questions were repeated for each domain of caregiving decisions: everyday living, health, and financial.

Parents and adult children were asked to respond to the first question on a 6-point scale, ranging from "would not know well at all" to "would know extremely well." Responses to the second question were on a 5-point scale, ranging from "have never discussed it" to "parent has made wishes known in great detail." Responses to the third question were on a 5-point scale, ranging from "strongly agree" to "strongly disagree." Responses to the fourth question were open-ended.

Because responses for the three types of decisions (everyday living, health, financial) differed only slightly, the mean of the three responses was used for analysis purposes. Findings are presented for the entire sample of 62 elderly parent-adult child pairs; differences between this group and the smaller group of mother-daughter pairs were negligible.

The correlation between the elderly parents' and adult children's mean scores for responses to the first question about the extent of the child's knowledge of the parent's wishes was .42, representing only a moderate congruence. Looking at the congruence in another way, only 30% of parents and children, averaged over the three domains, agreed exactly on responses to the first question. The responses of some 71% differed by no more than one category on the response scale. The responses of 29%, however, differed by two or more categories. Table 6.2 presents the percentages of elderly parents and adult children choosing various response alternatives to the first question.

Some 48% of the elderly parents and 57% of the adult children felt that the child would know the parent's wishes "very well" or "extremely well," while 47% of the elderly parents and 36% of the adult children felt that the child would know the parent's wishes "somewhat" or "pretty well." Only 5% of the parents and 7% of the adult children felt that the child would know the parent's wishes "not well at all" or "not too well." These data indicate that the great majority of respondents felt the adult children knew the elderly parents' wishes reasonably well.

Despite their responses indicating the adult child's rather good knowledge of the parent's wishes, the responses to the second question raise doubts about the source of that knowledge (see Table 6.3). Some 42% of the elderly parents and 20% of the adult children reported that the parent and child had never discussed the parent's wishes or that they had tried to discuss it but the other person would not talk about it. Another 25% of the parents and 28% of the adult children indicated that they had discussed some things but not all. Finally, 33% of the elderly parents and 52% of the adult children

Table 6.2 Percentages of Elderly Parents and Adult Children
Choosing Various Response Alternatives to the
Question of How Well the Child Knows the
Parent's Wishes for 62 Parent-Child Pairs

Response Alternative	Children	Parents
1. Not well at all	3	2
2. Not too well	4	3
3. Somewhat	13	12
4. Pretty well	23	35
5. Very well	41	28
6. Extremely well	16	20

Table 6.3 Percentages of Elderly Parents and Adult Children
Choosing Various Response Alternatives to the
Question of Whether They Had Discussed the
Parents' Wishes for 62 Parent-Child Pairs

Response Alternative	Children	Parents
1. Never discussed	10	18
2. Tried, but other person wouldn't	10	24
3. Some things, but not all	28	25
4. Most things	36	26
5. In great detail	16	7

responded that they had discussed most things or that the
parent's wishes had been made known in great detail.

The correlation between the elderly parents' and the adult
children's mean scores for responses to the second question
was .64. Thus greater congruence of responses existed regarding the extent of discussion of the parent's wishes than for the
more subjective first question of how well the adult child knew
the parent's wishes. On the average, responses for 70% of the
pairs did not differ by more than one response category, while
30% differed by two or more response categories. This finding
is consistent with the differences in the overall responses of
parents and children observed in Table 6.3.

Table 6.4 Percentages of Elderly Parents and Adult Children
Naming Various Members of Parent's Social
Network as Person Best Knowing Parent's
Wishes for 62 Parent-Child Pairs

	Health		Everyday Living		Finances	
Relationship	C	P	C	P	C	P
Caregiving child	82	75	78	80	64	70
Parent's spouse	5	7	5	5	5	7
Parent's sister	3	6	5	3	4	3
Parent's brother	0	2	2	0	8	5
Child's sister	7	7	7	4	7	2
Child's brother	0	3	0	6	9	13
In-law	1	0	1	2	0	0
Other relative	0	0	0	0	0	0
Nonrelative	2	0	2	0	3	0

NOTE: C = caregiving child; P = elderly parent.

When asked if another person would know the parent's
wishes better than the adult child who was in the caregiver
role, substantial congruence existed in the responses given
by elderly parents and adult children. The point-biserial correlations (caregiving child versus someone else) between parents and children for the three decision domains ranged from
.48 to .54. Differences existed, however, among the three domains in the degree to which someone other than the caregiver was named. Table 6.4 presents the percentages of various
members of the elderly person's social network regarded as
most knowledgeable.

For decisions about the elderly parents' health, 18% of the
adult children and 25% of the elderly parents listed someone
else. For decisions about everyday living, 22% of the adult
children and 20% of the elderly parents listed someone other
than the caregiving child. The percentage was considerably
larger for decisions about financial matters; 36% of adult children and 30% of elderly parents considered the caregiving
child less knowledgeable about the parents' wishes than someone else. A sibling of the caregiving child tended to be most
frequently named, with a sibling of the elderly parent the next

most frequently listed. In regard to financial matters, a brother typically was named.

In regard to the third question concerning the degree of perceived agreement between parent and child on the parent's wishes, some 89% of the responses of parents and children differed by no more than one response category. Only 11% of the parent-child pairs differed by two or more response categories. This apparent high level of congruence is somewhat spurious, since most individuals used only three of the five response categories. Looking at overall responses to the third question, 80% of the elderly parents and 75% of adult children indicated that they agreed or strongly agreed with the other. Another 20% of elderly parents and 22% of adult children responded that they neither agreed nor disagreed. Only 3% of adult children and no elderly parents perceived a disagreement in views.

Some important points should be made about the above findings. First, congruence between parents' and children's responses about the extent of discussion of the parents' wishes is not high, since substantially higher percentages of adult children than parents reported that discussions had taken place. Second, an inconsistency seems to exist between responses about discussion of the parents' wishes and responses about the degree to which the children know the parents' wishes. Although 42% of the elderly parents claimed not to have discussed their wishes with their children, only 5% felt that the children would not know their wishes too well. And although 68% of adult children said they would know their parents' wishes very well or extremely well, only 52% of adult children reported that they had discussed most things with their parents or their parents had made their wishes known in great detail. Third, the majority of families perceived considerable agreement between parents and children regarding the parents' wishes, despite the fact that little or no discussion had taken place.

Two interpretations seem possible. Many families may operate on the basis of "tacit understandings" (High & Turner, 1987) about the parents' wishes rather than on the basis of open discussions between parent and child. Or, even though both parent and child maintain that the child knows the parent's wishes, this could be a "tacit misunderstanding." No data indicated what the elderly person's wishes were or the adult child's version of these wishes. Both parent and child may have assumed that they would agree on what those wishes were, but in reality little congruence may exist between the two.

More important, it seems that parent and child may depend more upon nonverbal than verbal communication, and though little disagreement was reported, the percentage of parents and adult children who neither agreed nor disagreed may represent either an attempt to mask suspected disagreement or a recognition that not enough was known about the other's views to agree or disagree. For most pairs in the sample, the adult child who occupied the caregiver role was considered by parent and child to be the one who best knew the parent's wishes. Since even this adult child may not know what the parent would wish, the need for better communication of the parent's wishes to his or her adult children is clear.

Implications of Congruence
for the Elderly Parent's Autonomy
in Caregiving Decision Making

Whether elderly parents and their adult children have highly congruent beliefs, values, and knowledge of each other's wishes regarding caregiving decisions is of little importance when an elderly parent is able to make independent decisions. When the older person must delegate certain decisions to the adult child (delegated autonomy), or when the child must make a decision due to the parent's incapacity (surrogate autonomy), then the question of congruence assumes greater importance.

The role of the family in surrogate decision making for the elderly has been studied in some detail by High (High, 1987, 1988, 1989a, 1989b, 1990a, 1990b; High & Turner, 1987). When he asked elderly people about their preferences and concerns in the event that they were too ill to make their own health care decisions, some 90% chose a close family member to act as surrogate decisionmaker. Half the sample wanted the surrogate decisionmaker to exercise substituted judgment (i.e., choose as the older person would have wanted); the remaining half of the sample, however, wanted the surrogate to decide according to what he or she thinks is in the best interest of the older person. In the latter group, congruence was not even a matter of concern to the elderly.

Considering first those elderly who prefer the use of substituted judgment by the surrogate decisionmaker, existing findings raise some doubts that accurate substituted judgments are made by close family members. The studies reviewed in this chapter (Cicirelli, 1981, 1983b; Dengiz et al., 1982; Horowitz & Reinhardt, 1988; Horowitz et al., in press; Rakowski & Hickey, 1979, 1983; Zweibel & Lydens, 1990) found, at best, moderate congruence between the elderly and family members regarding perceptions of the older person's health and care needs. Congruence was high only for the most obvious objective indicators of health status and care needs. In studies of how accurately family members could make substituted judgments for older people regarding major health care decisions (Tomlinson et al., 1990; Uhlmann et al., 1988; Warren et al., 1986; Zweibel & Cassel, 1989) family members acting as decisionmakers were not only unable to predict elder's preferences correctly in an alarmingly high proportion of cases, but did not tend to decide in the way that the elderly person would even when the member felt that he or she knew what the older person's wishes were.

Studies of decision making in the family caregiving situation (Horowitz & Reinhardt, 1988; Horowitz et al., in press; Pratt et al., 1989) did not investigate the accuracy of surrogate judgments as such, but nevertheless revealed considerable lack of agreement between elders and caregivers about who was most involved in the decision making and who had the final voice in caregiving decisions, or about the decision itself and the degree of confidence in the elders' decision-making ability. My own work suggested little congruence in the beliefs of adult children and their elderly parents about respect for the autonomy of the elder and paternalism. In contrast to the evidence regarding lack of congruence, most of the parent-child pairs I studied felt that the adult children knew the parents' wishes regarding caregiving decisions reasonably well and that there was a high degree of agreement between them. One can only conclude that such perceptions of agreement may well be illusory. Those elderly who prefer that family members exercise substituted judgment in their behalf would be well advised to spell out their wishes carefully in advance.

Parent-child congruence would seem to have no implications for the autonomy of the elderly who prefer that surrogate decision makers use their own judgments as to the best interests of the elderly (High, 1989b). Choice of a person to act as surrogate, however, tends to be based upon feelings of trust and confidence that the elder and the surrogate share basic values and beliefs and would be likely to decide things in much the same way (High & Turner, 1987; Jecker, 1990). Jecker has argued that intimate family members have access to rich and detailed knowledge about an elderly parent's wishes and values (including knowledge of an intuitive and nonverbal nature); the same would seem to be true of the parent's knowledge of the adult child's views. From such a perspective, an elderly person's preference to have the child decide things in the best interest of the parent could mean merely shifting the responsibility of decision to one who would not be expected to stray far from parental wishes and values. In my own depth interviewing of elderly mothers regarding their affirmation of belief in paternalism, they seemed to have great trust that adult children who decided paternalistically would make decisions that the parents would see as quite reasonable. It never seemed to occur to them that adult children might make unreasonable decisions. Since the existing studies reviewed in this chapter point to the existence of considerable differences between the views of elderly parents and adult children, parents' unquestioning confidence in their children's possible decisions for them seems unrealistic. One may ask whether a parent's trust in children is a sufficient reason to allow them to make decisions for the parent, or whether there should be more concern about the accuracy of children's conceptions of the parent's wishes and their willingness to attempt to make decisions in accordance with such wishes.

The literature (Cassel & Zweibel, 1987; High, 1988; High & Turner, 1987) reveals that only a small percentage of older medical patients (ranging from 4% to 17% in various studies) have given any specific advance instructions of their wishes regarding treatments to their families or their doctors. In this work regarding caregiving decisions (see Table 6.3), similar low percentages of parents and children reported detailed discussions of the parents' wishes, although percentages were greater regarding more casual discussion of certain topics. On the other hand, 42% of elderly parents and 20% of adult children reported that no discussions of these topics had taken place. The clear implication of the findings on parent-child congruence seems to be that if an adult child might at some point make decisions for an elderly parent, explicit discussions between parent and child should be held so that wishes, values, and views of the parent can be unambiguously expressed and understood by the child. In addition, the adult child should indicate an intent to make decisions in accordance with the parent's wishes, provided the parent desire the child to do so.

SEVEN

Intergenerational Differences in Beliefs

Intergenerational congruence between measures obtained for elderly parents and their adult children is a measure of the degree to which members of a parent-child pair agree on a given measure; that is, the degree to which one can predict a given child's score by knowing the parent's score (or vice versa). On the other hand, an intergenerational difference indicates whether elderly parents as a group differ in their mean score on the measure from adult children as a group; that is, whether parents in general have higher or lower scores than children in general, regardless of whether parents tend to agree with their own children. A high degree of parent-child congruence on a characteristic implies that the characteristic may be transmitted either genetically or by socialization from parent to child (e.g., tall parents tend to have tall children, while short parents tend to have short children; or, parents have taught their children the beliefs that they have concerning money). A large intergenerational difference on a characteristic implies that some genetic or social cultural cohort factor influences the generation as a whole (e.g., adult children tend to be taller than their parents, in general).

When the degree of congruence between elderly parents and adult children regarding beliefs in respect for autonomy and paternalism was examined in Chapter 6, findings indicated little congruence for the three belief measures studied. The next logical step is to determine whether any intergenerational differences between parents' and children's scores on these measures exist and then to consider the meaning of these findings.

It is often assumed that congruence exists—that family members hold similar beliefs, attitudes, values, and knowledge as a result of their long and intimate interaction within the family scene, with such characteristics transmitted from parent to child through socialization (Elias, 1982). The extent of transmission of such characteristics across generations, however, is open to question in modern society as cohort effects or social forces in the larger environment may override any family socialization. Rapid technological and social change has led to a society characterized by greater individualism, age stratification, and greater intergenerational conflict (Dreitzel, 1984), as well as increased emancipation of women from family responsibilities (Hagemann-White, 1984; Treas, 1977).

Such changes have extended to norms and expectations regarding care of the dependent elderly (Bengtson, Cutler, Mangen, & Marshall, 1985; Mangen & Westbrook, 1988; Shanas, 1980; Treas, 1977), with elderly parents expressing stronger adherence to the norms of familism than adult children (Bengtson et al., 1985; Mangen & Westbrook, 1988). Scant literature exists, however, about who should take responsibility for decisions affecting the dependent elderly. The traditional concept of role reversal (Blenkner, 1965) implies that the adult child should take over the role of "parental" authority with respect to an aging parent. It would seem that this role would include making decisions for the parent. With regard to authority over household matters, Held (1984) noted that the elderly, particularly women, tend to lose their authority with increasing age. If this is true, then it is important to learn whether differences exist between the views of elderly parents and their adult children about who should make decisions for aging parents.

Differences in Beliefs

In the sample of 62 pairs of adult children and elderly parents first discussed in the previous chapter and described more fully in Chapter 8, matched pair *t*-tests were used to test the significance of any differences between parents and their children on the three belief measures studied: Independent Autonomy, Shared Autonomy, and Paternalism. These tests are summarized in Table 7.1. Tests for differences between the 46 pairs of mothers and daughters included in the larger sample also are summarized in Table 7.1.

The findings for the sample of mother-daughter pairs are closely similar to those for the larger group of parent-child pairs. In the analysis of data for parent-child pairs, adult children ($M = 37.37$, $SD = 5.62$) scored higher than their parents ($M = 36.87$, $SD = 5.30$) on the Independent Autonomy measure, but the differences were not statistically significant, $t(61) = -0.53$, $p > .05$. Based upon the Horowitz's finding (Horowitz & Reinhardt, 1988; Horowitz et al., in press) that family caregivers seemed to view the autonomy of the elderly more favorably than did the elderly themselves, one might have expected this difference in beliefs of parents and children to be significant.

Elderly parents ($M = 69.87$, $SD = 5.50$) scored slightly higher than their children ($M = 69.55$, $SD = 7.41$) on the Shared Autonomy measure, but these differences were not statistically significant either, $t(61) = 0.31$, $p > .05$. Thus parents and children held quite similar beliefs about shared autonomy in the family caregiving situation.

In the analyses for Paternalism, the elderly parents ($M = 103.68$, $SD = 12.96$) scored significantly higher than their adult children ($M = 89.87$, $SD = 16.84$), $t(61) = 5.35$, $p < .01$. The difference in scores between the two generations was nearly a standard deviation in magnitude. This finding is in agreement with the comment (Horowitz & Reinhardt, 1988; Horowitz et al., in press) that elderly care receivers were more concerned with issues about the health and safety of the older people in the vignettes presented to them than they

Table 7.1 Summary of *t*-tests for Differences on Measures of Belief
in Respect for Autonomy and Paternalism for 62
Parent-Child Pairs and 46 Mother-Daughter Pairs

Quantity	Independent Autonomy	Shared Autonomy	Paternalism
Elderly parents			
Mean	36.87	69.87	103.68
SD	5.30	5.50	12.96
Adult children			
Mean	37.37	69.55	89.87
SD	5.62	7.41	16.84
t	−0.53	0.31	5.35**
Elderly mothers			
Mean	36.46	69.63	103.61
SD	4.86	5.66	13.62
Adult daughters			
Mean	37.63	68.85	88.41
SD	5.05	7.54	16.45
t	−1.29	0.65	5.18**

**p < .01

were with any considerations of autonomy. That is, the elderly respondents seemed to feel that paternalism was to be preferred if it ensured that the welfare of the older people in the vignettes would be protected. At any rate, when the vignettes used by Horowitz are examined, interviewees' responses to the vignettes appear to be interpreted within a forced-choice framework (paternalistic regard for health and safety vs. autonomy). In my present research, beliefs about autonomy and paternalism were measured separately. The above findings make it clear that adult children's beliefs in the autonomy of the elderly are only slightly greater than those of their parents, while elderly parents' beliefs in paternalism are much stronger than those of their adult children.

One also may examine the above findings from another perspective. Since the Independent Autonomy, Shared Autonomy, and Paternalism measures are based upon different numbers of items, it is difficult to make direct comparisons between the measures. By calculating a mean score per item for each of the three measures, more direct comparisons can be made. As might be expected, mothers' and daughters' item means differed little for Independent Autonomy (mothers' mean = 3.04; daughters' mean = 3.14) and Shared Autonomy (mothers' mean = 3.87; daughters' mean = 3.82), and mothers' item means for Paternalism ($M = 3.45$) were significantly greater than daughters' item means ($M = 2.94$). The order of magnitude for the item means on the three measures, however, was different for the mothers and daughters. For the mothers, Shared Autonomy was the highest, followed by Paternalism and then by Independent Autonomy. For the daughters, Shared Autonomy was also the highest, but it was followed by Independent Autonomy and then by Paternalism. These findings seem to imply that daughters believe most strongly in sharing decision making with their mothers, or in simply respecting the mothers' independent decisions, and less strongly in making paternalistic decisions for their mothers. For their part, elderly mothers seem to believe most strongly in sharing decision making with their daughters, or in submitting to daughters' paternalistic decisions for them, and less strongly in making their own decisions independently. Such inferences must, of course, be viewed with great caution at the present stage of knowledge about beliefs and decision making.

Global Beliefs

In addition, open-end questions were used to probe the global beliefs of mothers and daughters about caregiving decision making. Daughters were asked: Do you think that you should make decisions for your mother in regard to your mother's everyday activities? Why do you feel that way? A corresponding question was addressed to the mothers: Do you think that your daughter should make decisions for you in regard to your everyday activities? Why do you feel that way? Similar questions were asked regarding decisions about health matters and financial matters.

Regarding decisions about everyday activities, only 7% of the daughters but 18% of the mothers felt that the daughters should make decisions for the mothers regarding everyday activities. Reasons for their views also differed. Among the daughters, 5% felt that the parents were incapable of deciding, while 2% felt that the parents were apathetic about needed decisions. Among the mothers, 11% felt that their daughters knew best, 3% felt that their daughters knew what they wanted and so should make the decision, 2% felt that their daughters had their best interest at heart, and 2% felt that their daughters should make the decisions since they were the ones who had to provide the care. Of the 93% of the daughters who felt that they should not make decisions about everyday activities for their mothers, 88% felt that their mothers were quite capable of making their own decisions, 3% felt that their mothers were quite happy while making their own decisions, and 2% felt that their mothers got upset if the daughters tried to make decisions for them. Of the 82% of the mothers who felt that their daughters should not make decisions for them, 78% felt perfectly capable of making their own decisions, while 4% felt that they should discuss things with their daughters but have the final decision.

Regarding decisions about health matters, 27% of the daughters and 27% of the mothers felt that the daughters should make the decisions. Although no difference existed between the two percentages, mothers' and daughters' reasons for their decisions did differ. Among the daughters, 9% felt that the mothers' decisions would lead to a poor outcome, 5% felt that the mothers were unaware of their own health problems, 6% felt that the mothers were apathetic about health care decisions, 2% felt that the mothers did not see the daughters' concerns as important, 3% felt that the mothers needed the daughters' help in making decisions, and 2% felt that daughters should make decisions for the mothers if asked to do so. Among the mothers, 15% felt that the daughters knew more than they did, 5% felt that they needed help in making health care decisions, 3% felt that their own decisions led to a poor outcome, 2% felt that the daughters should make the decisions because they "mean well," and 2% felt that the daughters should decide because they were the ones giving the care. Of the 73% of the daughters who felt that they should not make health care decisions for their mothers, 64% felt that the mothers were capable of making their own decisions in these matters, 5% felt that the mothers should discuss the decisions with the daughters but make their own decisions, and 4% felt that they should not make the decisions but a health professional should. Of the 73% of the mothers who felt that their daughters should not make health care decisions for them, 53% felt that they were capable of making their own decisions, and 20% felt that they should discuss the decisions with their daughters but make their own decisions.

Regarding decisions about financial matters, 20% of the daughters and 16% of the mothers felt that the daughters should make such decisions for their mothers. Again, reasons for these beliefs varied. Among the daughters, 9% felt that their mothers were not capable of making decisions about money, 4% felt that their mothers just didn't want to be bothered about such things, 3% felt that they knew more than their mothers about financial matters, 2% felt that their mothers were too vulnerable to harm if poor decisions were made, and 2% felt that they should make the decisions if their mothers asked. Among the mothers, 9% felt that their daughters knew more about financial matters than they did, 5% didn't want to be bothered about such things, and 2% felt that their daughters should decide because they had the mothers' best interests at heart. Of the 80% of the daughters who felt that they should not make decisions about financial matters for their mothers, 73% felt that their mothers were capable of making their own decisions, 3% felt that they had no right to decide since it was their mothers' money, 2% felt that they should not decide because other relatives knew more about it, and 2% felt that their mothers should discuss the decisions with them but make the decisions themselves. Of the 84% of the mothers who felt that their daughters should not make decisions about financial matters for them, 58% felt that they were capable of making their own decisions, 17% felt that they should discuss the matter with their daughters but decide for themselves, 6% felt that they should decide since it was their own money, and 3% felt that a professional should make the decision rather than the daughters.

Over all three decision domains (everyday living, health, and financial matters), the majority of mothers and daughters interviewed believed that the mothers should make their own decisions in these areas. This is not surprising, since all the mothers who were interviewed had sufficient cognitive abilities to comprehend and respond to a wide variety of questions even though they had needs for physical care. The highest percentages of respondents who felt that the mothers should make their own decisions were found for matters of everyday living, followed by financial matters, and in turn by health matters. Among those who believed that daughters should make decisions for the mothers, daughters' reasons for this belief centered around the mothers' incapability to make adequate decisions or their lack of awareness and interest in the matter. On the other hand, mothers' reasons for believing that their daughters should make the decisions centered around their belief that their daughters knew more about it than they did and that the daughters had their best interests at heart. A substantial percentage of the mothers felt that they should discuss decisions with their daughters before making the final decisions for themselves.

Because the first three of the global-belief questions asked for the respondent's views about the mother-daughter dyad of which she was a part, a fourth and more general question was asked: Under what circumstances do you think that an adult child should make decisions for an aging parent? Mental incompetence of the parent was the major reason given by both daughters (76%) and mothers (84%). The parent's request for the child to decide was mentioned by 16% of the daughters and 4% of the mothers. Some 6% of the daughters and 5% of the mothers felt that children should decide when the outcomes of parents' decisions would be harmful to the parents themselves or to someone else. In addition, 2% of the daughters felt that adult children should make decisions for their parents when the parents were apathetic or uncomfortable about making decisions; 7% of the mothers felt that adult children should take over decision making when parents were physically ill or disabled.

If any conclusion can be drawn from the responses to the open-end questions, it is that the mothers seem to have a stronger belief than their daughters that adult children should take over decision making for their parents when the parents are no longer capable or willing to do so. Although the majority feel that the mothers at present are capable of making their own decisions, the remainder feel that their daughters should become involved in the decision making for a variety of reasons.

Explanations of Findings

One can speculate as to why parents' belief in paternalism may be greater than that of their children. One possibility is that the elderly group's greater scores may be due to simple response acquiescence tendencies or to social desirability.

Response acquiescence tendencies may be dismissed quickly as a possible explanation. Since the Paternalism Scale and the Respect for Autonomy Scale have the same structure, one would expect parent-child score differences due to response acquiescence tendencies to be found for Independent Autonomy and Shared Autonomy, as well as for the Paternalism measure. No such differences were found, however.

With respect to social desirability as a possible explanation for elderly parents' greater belief in paternalism, it is possible that adult children could regard making paternalistic decisions for their parents as socially undesirable. On the other hand, it could be seen as socially undesirable for adult children *not* to intervene paternalistically if their parents' health and safety were at stake. Similarly, elderly parents might consider it socially desirable for older people to submit to their adult children's decisions for them. Some evidence bearing on this question exists. During the process of instrument development, correlations were computed between the Independent Autonomy, Shared Autonomy, and Paternalism scores and scores on the Marlow-Crowne Social Desirability Scale for the field sample (Crowne & Marlowe, 1960). For the field test group of adult children ($N = 147$), social desirability was correlated $-.01$ with Independent Autonomy, $-.01$ with Shared Autonomy, and .16 with Paternalism. For the elderly parent group ($N = 81$) social desirability was correlated .12 with Independent Autonomy, $-.02$ with Shared Autonomy, and .17 with Paternalism. Thus social desirability responding would appear to be minimal; in any event, it would appear that scores of parents and children both would be affected in the same direction.

Elderly parents' greater belief in paternalism may be related to the cultural context in another way. One may hypothesize a cohort effect based upon the traditional autocratic ideology of families in America (Nye & Berardo, 1973). Such families were socialized to follow the philosophy that the father (or the parent) knew best (paternalism in child rearing) in regard to any matters affecting family members; parents' views about what was right tended to be held rigidly. At the same time, a general view was held that aging was accompanied by a decline in mental competence (Cole, 1985, 1987). In such an event, family authority was assumed by adult children. According to Nye and Berardo (1973), traditional families of this sort are more typical of an older generation and lower socioeconomic status. The fact that most elderly parents were reared in traditional families might provide some explanation of parents' greater belief in paternalism.

The more recent emphasis on personal freedom in American society (Treas, 1977), especially the freedom of women, may be another explanation for adult children's lesser belief in paternalism as compared with their parents. Such cultural forces as more democratic educational systems, the greater emancipation of women, women's increased participation in the work force, increased geographic mobility, and the greater openness of society in general have contributed to the weakening of the traditional family. In addition, these forces would affect the generation of adult children more than the elderly.

Still another possibility is that adult children might hold slightly ambivalent views about paternalism. One of the project staff members (L. Tarr, personal communication, September 5, 1990) observed that adult children's relatively lower paternalistic beliefs might be somewhat illusory. In probing why certain interviewees responded to items on the Paternalism Scale as they did, she found that some interviewees apparently felt that adult children should intervene paternalistically in their parents' decision making but preferred more euphemistic statements about such intervention than those of the scale items. In other words, if they believed that adult children should be paternalistic, they didn't care to have it labeled as such.

Elderly parents' greater belief in paternalism than their adult children could be related also to changes in their desire for personal control with advancing age. It has been theorized (Rothbaum, Weisz, & Snyder, 1982; Schulz, 1986) that secondary control (aligning with powerful others who act in one's best interests) increases after age 60 and that primary control (directly shaping events to achieve one's goals) decreases as the ability to maintain such control erodes with age. Schulz contended that the person who yields control to appropriate and beneficent others ultimately may achieve better control over events than the person who does not give up primary control. To the extent that belief in paternalism is related to beliefs about locus of control, this contention might provide a satisfactory explanation of elderly parents' greater belief in paternalism. Reid's (1984) notion of participatory control also would seem to be relevant in this connection. In such a view the individual would form a partnership with a powerful other (one with greater knowledge and authority in the situation), participating in cooperative decision making together with that person. Reid's position would seem, however, to be more compatible with belief in shared autonomy with the adult child than with paternalism. It does not appear to account for parents' greater belief in paternalism. (The reader should recall that the factor score for Shared Autonomy includes Delegated Autonomy, the case in which a parent expressly requests that a child make certain decisions. This term is different conceptually from paternalism, in which the child makes decisions without any request or agreement from the parent.)

Influence of Dyadic Differences in Paternalism on Beliefs

If the family is a system, then one might expect the beliefs of one family member to have an influence upon the beliefs of another. Although little overall congruence existed between the beliefs of elderly parents and their adult children about autonomy and paternalism, the difference in their beliefs in paternalism raised the question of whether the beliefs of one might have some effect upon the beliefs of another.

To examine this question, the beliefs of 46 mother-daughter dyads were examined in relation to their differences in beliefs about paternalism. Through the use of the median of the daughters' Paternalism scores and the median of the mothers' Paternalism scores as cutting points, a two-way classification of the mother-daughter pairs was carried out to form four approximately equal subgroups. (It should be noted that the two medians were not the same, since mothers had higher paternalism scores than their daughters. Thus the cutting point for the mothers was at a Paternalism score of 104, while the cutting point for the daughters was at a Paternalism score of 90.) Ten pairs were contained in the Both High subgroup (both the mother and her daughter scored above their respective group medians on Paternalism), 12 pairs in the Daughter High subgroup (the daughter scored above the daughters' group median on Paternalism, while her mother scored below the mothers' group median), 13 pairs in the Mother High subgroup (the mother scored above the median on Paternalism, while her daughter scored below the median), and 11 pairs in the Low Low group (both the mother and the daughter scored below their respective group medians on Paternalism). Simple analysis of variance was used to compare the four subgroups on the beliefs held by mother and daughter.

The daughters' belief in Independent Autonomy showed a significant difference between the four subgroup scores, F (3, 42) = 4.17, $p < .05$. Daughters' Independent Autonomy scores were higher for the Mother High ($M = 40.08$, $SD = 4.54$) and Both Low ($M = 39.73$, $SD = 3.93$) subgroups than for the Both High ($M = 35.30$, $SD = 5.58$) and Daughter High ($M = 35.00$, $SD = 4.31$) subgroups. (Daughters held low Paternalism beliefs in the Mother High and Both Low subgroups, while mothers' Paternalism beliefs varied from high to low. The implication is that mothers' Paternalism beliefs are not related to daughters' Independent Autonomy scores. A similar argument may be given for Both High and Daughter High subgroups, in which daughters held high Paternalism beliefs while mothers' beliefs varied from high to low.) Thus the daughters' beliefs about Independent Autonomy were related only to their own beliefs about Paternalism and were independent of any beliefs that their mothers held about Paternalism.

When the mothers' belief in Independent Autonomy was examined similarly, the difference between the four subgroups was not significant, F (3, 42) = 0.78, $p > .05$. This finding indicated that the mothers' belief in Independent Autonomy was independent of their daughters' belief in Paternalism, as well as their own. The pattern of the subgroup means, however, suggested that mothers' belief in Independent Autonomy was lower when both mother and daughter held high beliefs in Paternalism ($M = 34.40$, $SD = 3.57$) than for the other three groups. The means of the other three groups were: Daughter High ($M = 37.00$, $SD = 5.27$), Mother High ($M = 36.77$, $SD = 6.22$) and Both Low ($M = 37.36$, $SD = 3.50$). These tendencies suggest that when at least one member of the mother-daughter dyad has relatively low beliefs in Paternalism, the mother's belief in Independent Autonomy appears to be enhanced. It is of particular interest that the adult daughter's belief in Independent Autonomy appears to be related only to her own belief about Paternalism and not to her mother's, while the mothers' belief seems to depend upon the combination of beliefs held by the dyad.

In regard to the daughters' belief in Shared Autonomy, no significant difference was found between the four subgroup means, $F(3, 42) = 0.13$, $p > .05$. Only small differences were found between the means for the Both High group ($M = 69.60$, $SD = 3.57$), the Daughter High group ($M = 68.08$, $SD = 7.14$), the Mother High group ($M = 68.31$, $SD = 10.30$), and the Both Low group ($M = 69.64$, $SD = 6.76$). These findings indicated that daughters' belief in Shared Autonomy did not depend upon the dyadic combinations of mothers' and daughters' beliefs in Paternalism.

Mothers' belief in Shared Autonomy for the four subgroups, however, was significantly different, $F(3, 42) = 5.03$, $p < .05$. Belief in Shared Autonomy was higher for the Both High subgroup ($M = 71.30$, $SD = 4.83$) and the Mother High subgroup ($M = 72.69$, $SD = 6.65$) than for the Daughter High subgroup ($M = 65.25$, $SD = 4.49$) or the Both Low subgroup ($M = 69.27$, $SD = 3.13$). It can be observed in addition that the mothers' means for the two subgroups in which the daughters had low Paternalism belief (the Mother High and the Low Low subgroups) were greater than for their counterparts in which the daughters had greater belief in Paternalism (the High High and the Daughter High subgroups, respectively.) Here, mothers' belief in Shared Autonomy appeared to depend largely upon the strength of their own Paternalism belief and to a much smaller degree on the Paternalism belief held by their daughters.

This presentation of dyadic subgroup comparisons, although limited by small subgroup sizes, has yielded several interesting findings. In regard to daughters' beliefs, the dyadic analysis indicates that daughters' beliefs in Independent Autonomy and Shared autonomy were independent of any influence of their mothers' Paternalism belief. In the case of the elderly mothers, mothers' Independent Autonomy scores were enhanced when either mother or daughter held a relatively weak Paternalism belief, and their belief in Shared Autonomy was influenced by the daughters' Paternalism belief. Overall, it would seem that the mothers' beliefs about autonomy were more susceptible to influence by the daughters than vice versa. This apparent reversal of the traditional direction of influence from parent to child is not too surprising in view of the mothers' more vulnerable position of dependency.

Some Conclusions

Based upon the small amount of evidence presented here, one can conclude that a substantial intergenerational difference exists in mothers' and daughters' Paternalism beliefs, with mothers holding a stronger belief in Paternalism than their daughters. This was the case despite the mothers' greater susceptibility to influence by the daughters' views than vice versa. This difference in views was found to be the case for the responses to the global-belief questions, as well as for the belief measures, as daughters seemed to take a more cautious approach to intervention in parents' decisions than did mothers. This finding supports the work of Hansson et al. (1990). Pratt et al. (1987) also have noted daughters' reservations about making decisions for parents. At present, the most tenable explanation for these differences in beliefs seems to be the more traditional family backgrounds of mothers in the older generation, as compared with their daughters, and the recent social trends toward greater personal independence of women.

The observed differences in paternalism beliefs are compatible with High's (1989b) findings that half of his elderly sample preferred to have family members acting as surrogates make decisions paternalistically in their behalf, rather than have the surrogates make decisions consistent with the elders' own views. This tendency may be related to the hypothesized rise in secondary control in old age (Rothbaum et al., 1982; Schulz, 1986), in which an elder with declining physical and or mental abilities transfers control to someone better able to achieve control over events. The present findings suggest that this situation may be more likely with regard to financial and health decisions than for decisions about everyday living, although Hansson et al. (1990) found the opposite order. As discussed earlier in this volume, locus of control beliefs and beliefs regarding paternalism and autonomy are different, although there may be some overlap in the concepts. Nevertheless, this area warrants further investigation in view of the observed intergenerational differences in paternalism beliefs. The theories of Schulz and Rothbaum et al. imply that intergenerational differences in paternalism beliefs between the elderly and their adult children may be the result of developmental or maturational changes in old age, rather than due to broader changes in the social structure of the family. Obviously, these sources of change need not be mutually exclusive (Bengtson et al., 1985); each may contribute to the intergenerational differences in belief revealed by the data presented here.

The implication of these intergenerational differences in belief for caregiving decision making seems to be that adult children may be somewhat less ready to make paternalistic decisions in their parents' behalf than parents are ready to submit to such decisions.

EIGHT

Contextual Correlates of Beliefs

The importance of contextual variables has been well recognized by developmental psychologists. Both the demographic characteristics of the individuals concerned and the characteristics of their physical and social environment can be important factors in explaining individual differences in variables of interest.

Despite this importance, few of the studies relevant to caregiving decision making have considered the possible effect of such contextual factors as demographic variables, family structure, and dependency indicators. Pratt et al. (1989) found that a measure of elderly mothers' dependency was correlated significantly with their daughters' involvement and influence on decision making. On the other hand, Warren et al. (1986) investigated the relationship of a variety of demographic variables and dependency indicators on proxy decision making by family members but found they had no relationship to decisions. Although other studies reported demographic characteristics of the samples used, they did not attempt to relate these characteristics to decision making.

This chapter focuses on the influence of various contextual variables on beliefs held by adult daughters and their elderly mothers regarding autonomy and paternalism in family caregiving.

Because this is a new area of inquiry with little previous literature to guide the selection of variables for study, many variables were examined. Although only a limited number of significant relationships between contextual variables and beliefs were found, they are presented here in considerable detail to gain a fuller understanding of the possible influence of context and to assist others who may wish to study beliefs about caregiving decision making.

SAMPLE SELECTION

The first phase of the research project referred to in this volume involved various samples of adult children and elderly parents used in the development of measures of autonomy and paternalism beliefs and in their validation. In the second phase of this research project, a sample of 62 adult children and their elderly parents was selected, with at least one member of each pair residing in a central Indiana city with a population of approximately 100,000 and the other within 50 miles. To be eligible for the study, the parent needed to be at least 60 years of age and of sufficient cognitive ability and physical health to be interviewed (in the judgment of the interviewer and/or family members). The adult child needed to be providing some degree of regular care required by the parent for everyday activities. Both parent and child needed to give formal consent before the pair could be included in the sample.

Subjects were volunteers obtained through the local Area Council on Aging in response to a newsletter advertisement in the local paper, seeking adult children and their elderly parents for which the child was providing "some degree of care" to the parent. This conception of a caregiver follows that of Horowitz and Dobrof (1982), who defined a *caregiver* as someone providing some degree of care in response to the older person's needs, rather than any set group of tasks or amount of time spent. My desire to interview both parent and child precluded the sampling of caregivers with heavy caregiving loads, as most parents of such caregivers are too frail and/or cognitively impaired to be interviewed. Nonetheless, the sample was considered to be adequate for my purpose.

The local Area Council on Aging conveyed to me the names of volunteers who responded to the advertisement; these people then were telephoned to determine their eligibility for the study and their willingness to participate. The final sample obtained consisted of 62 adult children and their elderly parents, representing 78% of the 79 pairs initially contacted. (All were white and of predominantly northern European background.) This sample consisted of 46 mother-daughter pairs, 3 mother-son pairs, 10 father-daughter pairs, and 3 father-son pairs. Since the other subgroups were not large enough to assess gender differences adequately, only the 46 mother-daughter pairs were used in the work described in this and the following chapters. This group represented 84% of the 55 mother-daughter pairs initially contacted.

MEASURES OF CONTEXTUAL VARIABLES

Three groups of contextual variables were measured in the study reported here: demographic characteristics, family structure variables, and indicators of the elderly parent's dependency. Variables in each group will be discussed in turn.

Demographic Characteristics

The characteristics of mother and daughter that were measured included age, marital status, educational level, occupational level, employment status, geographic proximity, and mother's living arrangement.

Chronological age was measured in years from the date of birth, as reported by the respondent.

Current marital status was recorded as one of five response alternatives: married and living with the spouse, widowed, divorced, married but separated from the spouse, and never married.

Educational level was recorded as the number of years of schooling completed. This information was coded into the 7-point scale of educational level devised by Hollingshead (1957). The categories of educational level were: 1. 0-6 years, 2. 7-9 years, 3. some high school, 4. high school graduate, 5. some college or vocational training, 6. college graduate, and 7. postgraduate work or advanced degree.

To determine occupational level, the respondent was asked for the occupational title of the position she currently held, if working, or the title of her most recent position if she was not currently working or was retired. The 7-point Hollingshead scale (1957) was used to code the occupational titles: 1. unskilled manual labor; 2. semi-skilled manual labor; 3. skilled manual labor; 4. clerical, sales, or technical positions; 5. administrative personnel, semiprofessionals, or small business owners; 6. business managers, lesser professionals, and owners of medium-sized businesses; and 7. higher executives, major professionals, or owners of large businesses. In coding, each occupation reported by the respondent was matched with one of the seven categories of occupational titles provided by Hollingshead. Although the Hollingshead scale is somewhat dated, it was used because the occupational titles listed for the seven categories provided good matches for the positions held by the older women studied. Also, it was felt that socioeconomic status levels implied by the categories were valid reflections of the way women in the age groups studied regarded the occupations they currently or previously held. To ensure reliability, two different coders worked independently to code the occupational titles listed by the respondents; they agreed exactly on 96% of the occupations reported and disagreed by no more than one level on the remaining 4%. The few cases in which there was disagreement between the coders were resolved through discussion.

Employment status was measured by asking the interviewee whether she was currently working, and probing to get a full response. Responses were coded into the following categories, as used in earlier studies (Cicirelli, 1981); working full time (35 hours/week or more); working part time (1-34 hours per week); not working because of temporary illness, layoff, or strike; unemployed, laid off, looking for work; retired; and keeping house. Preliminary inspection of the data indicated that no study participants were in the "not working . . ." and "unemployed . . ." categories; also, little difference was found between those participants working full time and those working part time in terms of number of hours worked. Therefore the categories were collapsed to form a dichotomous classification: working and not working.

Geographic proximity of the dyad, or the distance between the residences of the mother and the daughter, was ascertained by asking where each lived and determining the distance between them. In the event that they lived in the same city but not in the same household, the interviewee was asked whether they usually walked between the two residences. If one member of the dyad lived out of town, the distance was determined by referring to the Rand McNally Road Atlas (1987). Distances were coded into the 8-category scale of proximity used in my earlier work (Cicirelli, 1981): 1. more than 1000 miles, 2. 500-1000 miles, 3. 100-500 miles, 4. 50-100 miles, 5. within 50 miles but not in the same city, 6. in the same city, 7. in walking distance (a few blocks), and 8. parent and child live together. The first four categories of the proximity scale were irrelevant to the caregiving dyads represented in the study, since a criterion for selection of the sample was that the mother and daughter live within 50 miles of one another.

Finally, the elderly mother's living arrangements were categorized as follows: 1. mother living in her own home or apartment in the community, 2. mother living in the home of an adult child or other family member, 3. mother living in a retirement village or apartment, and 4. other living arrangement.

Family Structure Variables

Only a limited attempt was made to assess the family structure of mother and daughter. The daughters were asked to indicate the numbers of brothers and sisters they had, as well as the numbers still alive, while mothers were asked for similar information about their sons and daughters. This knowledge thus pertains to both generations of the family.

Dependency Variables

The degree of the elderly mother's dependency was assessed in several ways. First, a respondent was asked to make global ratings of the elderly mother's health status. Separate ratings were made for physical health, emotional health, and intellectual functioning (e.g., degree of forgetfulness, mental confusion, poor decision making). Ratings were made on a 6-point scale as follows: 1. very poor, 2. poor, 3. not so good, 4. good, 5. very good, and 6. excellent.

Another indicator was a rating of the frequency of the mother's current needs for help in carrying out ordinary activities. A 5-point scale was used, ranging from "rarely" to "all of the time."

Still another indicator of the mother's dependency was a checklist of whether the mother needed help in each of 15 different areas. Some 13 of these areas were identified in earlier work (Cicirelli, 1981), and two additional ones were added. They were: home health care, personal care, homemaking, transportation, maintenance, housing, income, mediation, checks on mother's well-being, protection, social support, emotional support, spiritual support, recreation support, and dealing with socially unacceptable behaviors. All 15 areas were included in daughters' interviews, but only the first 14 were presented to the mothers. The total number of areas in which help was needed was used as an overall indicator of dependency.

Another dependency variable was the respondent's estimate of the number of hours per week currently spent by the adult daughter in helping her elderly mother. Each respondent also was asked to indicate the number of hours of help per week she might provide in the future when the mother's needs for help increased, as well as an estimate of how soon such increased help might be needed. The imminence of increased care needs may be viewed as yet another indicator of the mother's dependency.

These multiple indicators provide information about different aspects of the mother's dependency. Although each has its limitations, taken together they present an integrated picture of the mother's health, functioning, and needs for care. Further, since information about the contextual variables was obtained separately from the elderly mothers and adult daughters, any differences in the perspectives of the two can be detected.

DESCRIPTION OF THE CONTEXTUAL SITUATION

Before proceeding to determine the relationship of the contextual variables to beliefs regarding autonomy and paternalism, a summary of the characteristics of the mother-daughter dyads studied will be given. Although this information is given in some detail, it is provided to give the reader a better understanding of the mother-daughter dyads whose views about paternalism and autonomy are the subject matter of this volume.

Demographic Characteristics

Table 8.1 presents summary information about the demographic variables. The first column of the table contains the information as reported by the adult daughters, while the

Table 8.1 Demographic Characteristics of Mother-Daughter Dyads Reported by Mothers and Their Daughters

Variable	Data Source	
	Daughters	*Mothers*
Daughters' mean age	49.67	50.00
Standard deviation	8.64	8.32
Daughters' marital status		
Married	60%	60%
Widowed	7%	7%
Divorced	30%	30%
Never married	3%	3%
Daughters' educational level		
7-9 years	2%	2%
Some high school	5%	5%
High school graduate	15%	23%
Some college or vocational training	46%	37%
College graduate	15%	20%
Postgraduate work or advanced degree	17%	13%
Daughters' employment status		
Working	76%	78%
Not working	24%	22%
Daughters' occupational level		
Unskilled manual labor (includes housewife)	13%	4%
Semi-skilled manual labor	4%	11%
Skilled manual labor	7%	2%
Clerical, sales, and technical positions	37%	41%
Administrative, semi-professional, small business	15%	13%
Managers, lesser professional, medium business	22%	26%
Higher executives, major professional, large business	2%	2%
Mothers' mean age	77.61	77.76
Standard deviation	7.07	7.09
Mothers' marital status		
Married	15%	15%
Widowed	85%	85%
Mothers' educational level		
0-6 years	2%	2%
7-9 years	11%	9%
Some high school	20%	24%
High school graduate	30%	26%
Some college or vocational training	22%	26%
College graduate	15%	13%
Mothers' employment status		
Working	2%	2%
Not working	98%	98%

(continued)

Table 8.1 Continued

	Data Source	
Variable	Daughters	Mothers
Mothers' occupational level		
Unskilled manual labor (includes housewife)	30%	28%
Semi-skilled manual labor	22%	20%
Skilled manual labor	4%	4%
Clerical, sales, and technical positions	17%	22%
Administrative, semi-professional, small business	9%	11%
Managers, lesser professional, medium business	17%	15%
Mother-daughter proximity		
Coresidence	13%	13%
Within walking distance	15%	15%
In same city	55%	55%
Within 50 miles	17%	17%
Mothers' living arrangement		
In own home or apartment	72%	72%
With child or other family member	15%	15%
In a retirement village or apartment	13%	13%

second column contains the same information as reported by the elderly mothers. As can be noted in Table 8.1, the two reports agree exactly for some variables and are slightly different for others. In the main, congruence regarding these demographic characteristics is quite good, with correlations between the two reports ranging from 1.00 to .77. On the basis of t-tests, mothers' and daughters' reports were not significantly different.

The daughters ranged in age from 27-66 years, with a mean age of 49.67 years, while the mothers ranged in age from 61-95 years, with a mean age of 77.61 years. Although a few daughters were older than the youngest of the mothers, the role of the daughter in providing help to the mother was the important qualification for inclusion in the study and not age. Some 85% of the mothers were widowed, while 40% of the daughters were widowed, divorced, or never married. All of the mother-daughter pairs lived within 50 miles of each other, and 83% lived in the same city. Only 13% of the pairs shared the same residence. Most of the mothers, 72%, lived at least somewhat independently in their own home or apartment, while another 13% lived in a retirement village or apartment and 15% lived with a family member.

As can be seen in Table 8.1, the educational level of the daughters surpasses that of the mothers, with 78% of the daughters having some education beyond high school in comparison to only 37% of the mothers. Only 2% of the mothers were still employed (and that mother only on a part-time basis), while 76% of their adult daughters were employed at least on a part-time basis outside the home. The modal occupations for the daughters were on the clerical, sales clerk, or technician levels, while the modal occupations for the mothers were as housewives or unskilled manual labor positions. Thus the adult daughters as a group illustrate clearly modern social trends for women to be better educated than their mothers and to be a part of the work force.

Family Structure

Table 8.2 presents the percentages of elderly mothers with various numbers of adult children. (The reader should note that the number of the adult daughters' sisters is equal to one less than the number of the mothers' daughters reported in the table. For example, if 40% of the mothers have two living daughters, this implies that 40% of the adult daughters have one living sister.) Although 22% of the mothers in the sample had no sons born to them, all the mothers had at least one daughter. This follows from the fact that the sample consisted only of mother-daughter pairs.

The mothers had an average of 2.15 living daughters and 1.44 living sons. By implication, the daughters had an average of 1.15 living sisters and 1.44 living brothers; thus they were slightly more likely to have a brother than a sister to share the caregiving load. Only 13% had no living brothers or sisters.

Table 8.2 Family Structure Characteristics: Percentages of Elderly
Mothers with Various Numbers of Adult Children

| | Number of Children | | | | | | | | |
Variable	0	1	2	3	4	5	6	7	8
Daughters born	0	26	41	17	11	4	0	0	0
Daughters living	0	30	40	19	7	4	0	0	0
Sons born	22	30	22	17	0	7	0	0	2
Sons living	30	27	21	15	5	2	0	0	0

Mothers' Dependency

Table 8.3 presents information reported independently
by mothers and daughters about the degree of the mothers'
dependency, as indicated by the various measures used. The
first column of the table presents the daughters' reports about
the mothers' dependency, while the second column of the table
presents the mothers' reports.

First are the ratings of the mothers' health. When daughters
rated their mothers' physical health, 8% saw it as excellent, 9%
very good, 48% good, 24% not so good, 9% poor, and 2% very
poor. Mothers' self-ratings of physical health were 11% excellent, 9% very good, 56% good, 15% not so good, and 9% poor.
In regard to emotional health, daughters' ratings were 15%
excellent, 26% very good, 28% good, 22% not so good, and 9%
poor, while mothers' self-ratings were 9% excellent, 26% very
good, 54% good, 7% not so good, 2% poor, and 2% very poor.
Finally, when intellectual functioning was rated similarly, 17%
of the daughters perceived their mothers' intellectual functioning as excellent, 28% as very good, 28% as good, 22% as not so
good, and 5% as poor. Mothers' self-ratings of intellectual functioning were 6% excellent, 31% very good, 52% good, 9% not
so good, and 2% very poor. Overall the mothers perceived
themselves to be in slightly better physical, emotional, and
intellectual health than their daughters perceived them to be.
This result was expected, as older persons' self-perceptions of
health have been found to be more positive than those of health
professionals and family members (Dengiz et al., 1982; Linn,

Table 8.3 Indicators of Mothers' Dependency Reported by
Mothers and Their Daughters

	Data Source	
Variable	Daughters	Mothers
Mothers' physical health		
Excellent	8%	11%
Very good	9%	9%
Good	48%	56%
Not so good	24%	15%
Poor	9%	9%
Very poor	2%	0%
Mothers' emotional health		
Excellent	15%	9%
Very good	26%	26%
Good	28%	54%
Not so good	22%	7%
Poor	9%	2%
Very poor	0%	2%
Mothers' intellectual functioning		
Excellent	17%	6%
Very good	28%	31%
Good	28%	52%
Not so good	22%	9%
Poor	5%	0%
Very poor	0%	2%
Frequency of mothers' care needs		
All of the time	7%	2%
Most of the time	11%	11%
Often	22%	18%
Occasionally	36%	45%
Almost never	24%	24%
Number of kinds of help needed		
Mean	6.96	6.50
Standard deviation	3.06	2.99
Hours of care weekly		
Mean	6.61	6.41
Standard deviation	7.67	8.46
Estimated time to increased care needs		
Within 6 months	16%	11%
6 months to a year away	6%	0%
1-2 years away	20%	21%
2-5 years away	34%	29%
More than 5 years away	22%	32%
Never	2%	7%
Future hours of care weekly		
Mean	27.00	15.22
Standard deviation	29.52	21.07

Linn, & Knopka, 1978; Maddox & Douglas, 1973; Rakowski & Hickey, 1983). The *t*-tests for the difference between mothers' and daughters' ratings were not significant.

With regard to the frequency of mothers' care needs, 40% of the daughters and 31% of the mothers reported that the mothers needed help often or more frequently, while another 36% of the daughters and 45% of the mothers reported that the mothers needed occasional help. Overall, 76% of the mothers and 76% of the daughters felt that the mothers needed some help in carrying out their ordinary activities of living.

On the average, daughters saw their mothers as needing help with 7.0 of the 15 basic categories of help measured on the checklist, while mothers felt that they needed help with 6.5 categories. The most frequently checked categories, in descending order, were: social support, emotional support, transportation, checks on daily health or security, home maintenance, homemaking, and mediation for services. Least frequently checked were: dealing with socially unacceptable behaviors, income, housing, home health care, personal care, and protection.

In terms of actual help provided by the adult daughters, daughters reported helping their mothers for a mean of 6.6 hours each week, while mothers reported receiving 6.4 hours of help each week. The distribution was somewhat skewed, however, with only 36% of the daughters and 35% of the mothers indicating that 7 or more hours of help were provided each week; only 9% of both groups reported 20 or more hours of help weekly.

The remaining two indicators of the mothers' dependency concerned expectations about how soon increased needs for help would occur and how much help the daughter would be likely to provide in such an eventuality. Here, 22% of the daughters but only 11% of the mothers expected increased care needs within the next year, while 39% of the mothers but only 24% of the daughters expected that any increase in the mothers' care needs would be more than five years away, if ever. Thus the daughters seemed to have less positive expectations than their mothers regarding the time course of the mothers' dependency needs. If and when such a contingency occurred, the daughters expected to provide a mean of 27.0 hours of care weekly, while their mothers' expected them to provide only 15.2 hours.

Agreement of the information about dependency provided by mothers and daughters was less than that for the demographic variables. Correlations between mothers' and daughters' reports for the various dependency indicators were as follows: physical health, .56; emotional health, .29; intellectual functioning, .26; frequency of mothers' care needs, .72; number of kinds of help needed, .69; hours of care weekly, .44; expectation of increased future care needs, .27; and expected future hours of care weekly, .31. Consensus between mother and daughters was greatest for such easily observable quantities as the frequency of the mothers' care needs and hours of care weekly and least for variables involving more subjective judgments, such as emotional health, intellectual functioning, and future expectations.

When *t*-tests were used to compare mothers' and daughters' reports, the difference was significant only for the expected future hours of care weekly.

Reflecting upon the evidence presented here regarding the mothers' dependency, it is evident that although most of the mothers had some needs for help at the present time, these needs were moderate. Thus while only a portion of the adult daughters in the sample bore heavy caregiving responsibilities, all daughters gave at least some help that seemed important for their mothers' continued existence in the community.

RELATION OF CONTEXTUAL VARIABLES TO BELIEFS ABOUT AUTONOMY AND PATERNALISM

To determine the relationship of contextual variables to mothers' and daughters' beliefs about autonomy and paternalism, correlations were computed between the contextual variables and Independent Autonomy, Shared Autonomy, and Paternalism. Two independent correlational analyses were carried out: one for adult daughters, using data obtained from the daughters; and one for elderly mothers, using data obtained from the mothers. As noted earlier in this chapter, the congruence between mothers' and daughters' reports about the mothers' dependency is relatively low for some of the measures of dependency. It is assumed, however, that the perceptions of each individual about the variables in question influence that individual's beliefs rather than any objective reality.

In addition to employment status that had been recoded already as a dichotomous variable, two other variables were recoded for purposes of the correlational analysis. Marital status was recoded into two categories: married and not married (widowed, divorced, never married). In the case of mothers, the not-married group consisted entirely of widows, while in the case of daughters, the not-married group consisted primarily of those who were divorced. The mothers' living arrangement was recoded into two categories: those living independently in their own home or apartment and those with other living arrangements (living with a child or other family member, or living in a retirement village or apartment). With regard to the family structure variables, a score representing the proportion of adult sons in the family (number of sons/ number of adult children) was computed, since recent literature has suggested that family gender composition might be important (Brody, 1990; Coward & Dwyer, 1990). In addition, a subscore was computed for the number of kinds of help needed by the mother that included only instrumental forms of help and not various types of social and intangible support.

Findings for Adult Daughters

Table 8.4 presents the correlations of the contextual variables with the measures of adult daughters' beliefs: Independent Autonomy, Shared Autonomy, and Paternalism.

Look first at the correlations with Independent Autonomy. The only demographic variable that was significantly related

Table 8.4 Correlations of Contextual Variables with Adult
Daughters' Independent Autonomy,
Shared Autonomy, and Paternalism Scores

Variable	Independent Autonomy	Shared Autonomy	Paternalism
DEMOGRAPHIC VARIABLES			
Daughter's age	−.23	.24	.25
Daughter's marital status	−.15	−.23	.36*
Daughter's education	.14	.03	−.40*
Daughter's employment	−.17	.31*	.15
Daughter's occupation	.14	−.07	−.34*
Mother's age	−.24	.21	.32*
Mother's marital status	−.12	.31*	.11
Mother's education	.09	.03	−.26
Mother's employment	−.07	−.06	.15
Mother's occupation	.10	−.02	−.16
Proximity	−.21	−.01	.21
Mother's living arrangement	−.39*	−.22	.27
FAMILY STRUCTURE VARIABLES			
Number of adult children	−.14	.07	.32*
Number of adult sons	−.13	.03	.32*
Number of adult daughters	−.07	.08	.15
Number of living children	−.09	.02	.25
Number of living sons	−.17	−.05	.30*
Number of living daughters	.04	.10	.07
Proportion of sons	−.14	−.08	.22
DEPENDENCY VARIABLES			
Mother's physical health	.07	−.23	−.01
Mother's emotional health	.01	.01	.02
M's intellectual functioning	.28	−.17	−.16
Frequency of M's care needs	−.16	.27	.05
Number of kinds of help needed	−.27	.24	.13
Instrumental help	−.27	.30*	.16
Hours of care weekly	−.12	.18	.21
Time to increased care needs	.11	−.24	−.08
Future hours of care weekly	.11	.18	−.04

*$p < .05$.

was the mother's living arrangement ($r = −.39$), when independent living arrangements were coded "1" and other arrangements coded "2." Thus daughters with mothers who lived independently in their own homes or apartments

held stronger beliefs regarding respect for the parent's autonomy than daughters whose mothers had other kinds of living
arrangements (living with adult children, retirement apartments, etc.). One does not know, however, whether the
mothers' living arrangements influenced the daughters' beliefs or vice versa. No significant correlations were found
between beliefs and either the family structure variables or the
dependency variables.

With regard to the daughters' belief in Shared Autonomy,
significant correlations were found with two of the demographic variables, daughter's employment ($r = .31$) and
mother's marital status ($r = .31$). Daughters who were not
employed believed more strongly that an elderly parent's decision making should be shared with an adult child than
daughters who were employed outside the home. Daughters
whose mothers were widowed believed more strongly in
Shared Autonomy than daughters whose mothers still had a
living spouse. None of the family structure variables were
related to Shared Autonomy. Of the dependency indicators,
only the number of kinds of instrumental help needed was
significantly related ($r = .30$). Here, daughters whose mothers
had a greater number of instrumental help needs believed more
strongly in Shared Autonomy than daughters whose mothers
had fewer instrumental help needs.

Examining next the correlations with belief in Paternalism,
several of the demographic variables were significantly related: daughter's marital status ($r = .36$), daughter's educational level ($r = -.40$), daughter's occupational level ($r = -.34$),
and mother's age ($r = .32$). Daughters who were in the not-married group, who were of lower educational and occupational
levels, and whose mothers were older had stronger beliefs in
Paternalism than daughters who were married, who were of
higher educational and occupational levels, and whose mothers were younger. Indicators of the mother's dependency were
not significantly related to the daughters' belief in Paternalism.

Findings for Elderly Mothers

Table 8.5 presents the correlations of the contextual variables with the measures of elderly mothers' beliefs: Independent Autonomy, Shared Autonomy, and Paternalism.

It can be seen from an inspection of Table 8.5 that none of the contextual variables were related to mothers' belief in Independent Autonomy. In regard to Shared Autonomy, only the mother's living arrangement ($r = -.35$) and the proportion of adult sons in the family ($r = -.34$) were significantly correlated. Mothers who lived in their own homes or apartments had a stronger belief in Shared Autonomy than those who had other living arrangements. Also mothers who had a smaller proportion of adult sons among their children held a stronger belief in Shared Autonomy than mothers who had a higher proportion of adult sons. No significant relationship was found between dependency variables and Shared Autonomy.

In regard to Paternalism, only the daughter's marital status was significantly related to mothers' belief in Paternalism ($r = .37$). Here, mothers whose daughters were in the not-married group had a stronger belief in Paternalism than mothers whose daughters were married.

IMPLICATIONS OF FINDINGS

A limited number of relationships between the contextual variables and the daughters' beliefs were discovered in the correlational analysis. Three suggestive trends do seem to emerge. In regard to autonomy, it seems that critical life events may influence the degree of belief in Independent Autonomy and Shared Autonomy. When a mother becomes more dependent upon others in her living arrangements, the daughter tends to have less belief in Independent Autonomy; when a mother has become widowed and has a greater need for instrumental help, there is greater respect for Shared Autonomy; and

Table 8.5 Correlations of Contextual Variables with Elderly
Mothers' Independent Autonomy,
Shared Autonomy, and Paternalism Scores

Variable	Independent Autonomy	Shared Autonomy	Paternalism
DEMOGRAPHIC VARIABLES			
Daughter's age	−.05	−.01	.09
Daughter's marital status	−.21	−.06	.37*
Daughter's education	−.20	.01	−.10
Daughter's employment	.08	.05	.02
Daughter's occupation	−.24	.05	−.01
Mother's age	−.05	−.11	.11
Mother's marital status	.18	−.02	.20
Mother's education	−.01	.27	−.09
Mother's employment	−.23	−.09	.21
Mother's occupation	.13	.25	.11
Proximity	.12	.17	.16
Mother's living arrangement	−.08	−.35*	−.13
FAMILY STRUCTURE VARIABLES			
Number of adult children	−.23	−.04	−.05
Number of adult sons	−.22	−.20	−.03
Number of adult daughters	−.11	.22	−.06
Number of living children	−.21	.01	−.08
Number of living sons	−.16	−.20	−.04
Number of living daughters	−.15	.23	−.08
Proportion of sons	−.20	−.34*	−.04
DEPENDENCY VARIABLES			
Mother's physical health	.20	.06	.05
Mother's emotional health	.17	.02	.04
M's intellectual functioning	.02	−.04	−.14
Frequency of M's care needs	−.22	−.16	−.08
Number of kinds of help needed	−.15	−.03	.13
Instrumental help	−.21	.02	.16
Hours of care weekly	−.05	−.02	.20
Time to increased care needs	.24	−.12	−.27
Future hours of care weekly	−.15	−.16	.18

*$p < .05$.

when the daughter herself is not employed outside the home,
there is a greater belief in respect for Shared Autonomy.

To account for the association of these diverse life events
with an apparent shift from Independent Autonomy to Shared
Autonomy, one might hypothesize that when events occurring

in the life of either mother or daughter impose environmental restrictions, less belief exists that an elderly parent should make decisions independently and a greater belief exists that independence should be maintained through the mechanism of Shared Autonomy.

Perhaps the findings of greatest conceptual importance involve the relationships to daughters' belief in Paternalism. Daughters' Paternalism beliefs were related to their educational and occupational levels, their marital status, their mothers' age, and the number of adult sons in the families, but not to indicators of the mothers' dependency. This finding suggests the importance of general cultural factors in accounting for Paternalism beliefs, rather than the demands of the specific caregiving situation. Male-dominated families of lower socioeconomic levels tend to follow a more traditional autocratic ideology in which the father knew best (Nye & Berardo, 1973). It is not surprising that adult daughters reared in such families would have a greater belief in Paternalism.

It is possible that the lack of relationships between the belief measures and the indicators of dependency might be because the mothers studied were not sufficiently frail or dependent to reveal such a relationship. To examine this possibility, we subdivided the sample into two equal groups based upon the number of hours of help weekly provided by the daughters, and repeated the correlations for each group. Even in the subgroup providing the most help, the correlations were still not significant. In order to resolve this question, larger samples involving parents who are more dependent than those studied here are needed.

With regard to the family dyadic belief model presented in Chapter 4 (see Figure 4.2), the findings here indicate that the contextual variables play a serious part only in relation to Paternalism beliefs. It is possible, however, that they may have a direct relationship to actual caregiving decision making. Before examining such a possibility in Chapter 10, the relationship of personal-social variables to beliefs will be considered in Chapter 9.

NINE

Personal-Social Correlates of Beliefs

In addition to the effect of contextual variables upon beliefs in respect for autonomy and paternalism, it was hypothesized in Chapter 4 that personal-social variables also would bear a relationship to beliefs and caregiving decision making. Among the variables investigated as possible antecedents of beliefs in the present project were a set of personality characteristics and a set of variables describing the interpersonal relationship between the members of the dyad.

PERSONALITY CHARACTERISTICS

In attempting to hypothesize personality characteristics that might be related to beliefs, the concepts of independent autonomy, shared autonomy, and paternalism were reexamined carefully. The strategy used was to identify and analyze the attributes of these concepts to infer personality characteristics that might be related.

Locus of Control

First, a belief in independent autonomy is a belief that elderly people have the right to make decisions affecting their own lives without interference from others, regardless of the consequences. Although I argued earlier (see Chapter 2) that important distinctions exist between autonomy and personal control, both concepts have in common the notion of making and executing decisions that affect one's life. The concept of an internal locus of control (Rotter, 1966) refers to individuals' expectations of control over external reinforcers; that is, they expect that what happens to them will be the result of their own behavior. An external locus of control refers to individuals' expectations that what happens to them will be the result of such external forces as fate, chance, or powerful others. Those with an internal locus of control deliberate carefully when making decisions (Wheeler & Davis, 1979), while those with an external locus of control have been found to depend more upon the advice of others (Pines, 1973). (Whether the degree of internal and external locus of control are constant or vary with domains, e.g., health or finances, is not an issue here.)

Thus how an older person feels about decision making should depend at least in part upon whether he or she desires or expects to have control over events through such decisions (Coulton, Dunkle, Haug, Chow, & Vielhaber, 1989; Reid, Haas, & Hawkings, 1977; Ziegler & Reid, 1979). In this sense, an elderly person's belief in independent autonomy should be positively related to measures of expected control over events. Similarly, expectations that external forces are in control over events should be related to belief in paternalism (in essence, relinquishing control to others) and to shared autonomy (making an alliance with a "powerful other" to control events). The notions of participatory control (Reid, 1984) and secondary control (Rothbaum et al., 1982; Schulz, 1986) suggest that older people may prefer alliances with others in order to achieve better control over events. Also, one might expect that an adult child caregiver with a high expectation of control over events would have a stronger belief in paternalism than one with a belief that external forces controlled events.

Self-Esteem

Following from the above reasoning for locus of control, one would expect that an elder's belief in independent autonomy would be related to a more positive sense of self-esteem, since self-esteem has been found to be related to measures of an internal locus of desired control (Reid et al., 1977; Wolk, 1976).

Attitudes Toward the Elderly

With regard to paternalism, a belief in paternalism is basically a belief in the existence of an ethical prescription that one should intervene in another person's decision making and/or the implementation of such decisions for that person's welfare but without that person's consent (Gert & Culver, 1979; Halper, 1980). Such a belief involves four main attributes: (a) one assumes that one knows what is best for another person better than that person does; that is, one is more competent than the other person (in terms of knowledge, ability, maturity, and so on) and thus by implication the other person is viewed as inferior; (b) intervening will do more good and/or less harm than if the other person makes the decision; (c) one is motivated to care for the welfare of the other person, to want to help for the good of that person; and (d) the welfare of the other person has priority over that person's freedom, with freedom a means to ultimate welfare and happiness rather than an end in itself. The first two attributes of paternalism appear to involve feelings of superiority on the part of the helper, while the second two attributes appear to involve altruistic concern for the well-being of the other person.

If paternalism involves the notion that the helper is more competent than the elderly family member, then it implies a negative attitude toward older people. It is not surprising that an adult child might feel more competent than an elderly parent who is very dependent or mentally impaired. Above and beyond this, however, in American society a general cultural stereotype exists that older people as a group are less competent than younger people (Cole, 1985, 1987; Hummert, 1990; Lachman & McArthur, 1986; Levin, 1988). Many studies (e.g., Bennett & Eckman, 1973; Kite & Johnson, 1988) have reported negative attitudes toward elders held by older people, as well as young. If an adult child holds negative attitudes toward the elderly, then that child would be expected to have a stronger belief in paternalism and to intervene paternalistically. Similarly, if an elderly parent holds negative attitudes toward old people in general, then that parent might be expected to have a stronger belief in paternalism in relation to dependent elderly. On the other hand, those adult children and elderly parents who hold positive attitudes toward old people in general might be expected to have a stronger belief in respect for autonomy.

Dogmatism

In addition, a dogmatic personality is hypothesized to lead to a stronger belief in paternalism. Dogmatism involves having a strong set of beliefs based upon appeal to authority (rather than upon evaluation of empirical evidence) and a mind closed to others' ideas and beliefs (Ehrlich, 1978; Rokeach, 1960). A caregiver whose mind is closed to an elderly parent's point of view and who believes that his or her own ideas are correct would be more likely to believe that paternalistic decisions should be made. Some support for this hypothesis has been provided by Phillips and Rempusheski (1985). In the process of validating their instrument to assess beliefs about proper caregiving behavior, dogmatism was significantly correlated with caregiving beliefs. Although many of the items described paternalistic actions by the family caregiver, unfortunately the authors did not conceptualize their scale in this way and no relevant subscales were developed.

CHARACTERISTICS OF THE
INTERPERSONAL RELATIONSHIP

Family caregiving involves a close interpersonal relationship of long standing between elderly parent and adult child. Since the quality of the parent-child relationship has been demonstrated to influence adult children's helping behavior (e.g., Montada & Bierhoff, in press; Montada, Schmitt, & Dalbert, in press), one also might expect that the quality of their relationship would be related to the beliefs of parent and child regarding paternalism and autonomy. The characteristics of the interpersonal relationship considered here are indicators of a specific relationship between a given mother-daughter pair and are to be interpreted on that level. (The attitude toward old people, in contrast, is considered to be a pervasive disposition toward old people in general. It is possible that one could have a negative attitude about the competence of old people in general but regard the competence of one's own mother very positively.)

Feelings of Attachment

If paternalism involves caring for the welfare of another person, even at the expense of that person's freedom of choice, then it implies a concern for that person's welfare, as well as a sustained motivation and commitment to provide help. As discussed in Chapter 4, adult attachment theory (Bowlby, 1979, 1980; Cicirelli, 1983a, in press) holds that a child's early bond to the parent continues throughout life. Protection of the attached figure is another aspect of attachment that develops somewhat later in time; it has the aim of protecting and preserving the continued existence of the attachment figure. An adult child with a strong attachment bond to the parent is hypothesized to have a stronger belief in paternalism than an adult child with a weak attachment bond. For situations in which the parent's continued existence might be threatened, a child's paternalistic decision gives the parent's welfare priority over any concern for the parent's freedom of choice.

Although it is debatable whether elderly parents have reciprocal feelings of attachment for their children, they do have strong affectional bonds. It is hypothesized that parents who have strong feelings of affection for their adult children will be more likely to believe that the children should make decisions in their behalf or share in such decisions.

Concern for Parent's Well-Being

As a corollary to the reasoning about the relationship between an adult child's feelings of attachment and belief in paternalism, one also might expect that an adult child with greater feelings of concern for an elderly parent's well being (Cicirelli, 1988) also would be more likely to believe in paternalism. For such adult children, one would expect that the parents' welfare would be given priority over the parents' independence.

Trust

According to High (High, 1988; High & Turner, 1987), elderly parents' frequent assumption that their adult children will make satisfactory surrogate decisions in their behalf rests upon a basic sense of trust in their children. *Trust* in an interpersonal relationship has been defined as belief by a person in the integrity of another individual, that is, in the benevolence, honesty, and sincerity of the other individual (Larzelere & Huston, 1980; Stinnett & Walters, 1977). This type of trust is distinguished from a generalized sense of trust in which the person has a belief in the integrity of people in general (Rotter,

1971); the individual may feel trust in another person with whom there is a close relationship but feel little trust in regard to people in general. The belief in the benevolence of the other member of the dyad is the belief that the other person is interested in one's welfare and not just in his or her own welfare. This attribution about the other person is highly relevant to the question of decision making for the elderly. Thus an elderly parent with a high sense of trust in his or her own child would be more likely to believe that an elderly parent should share decisions with a child and also more likely to believe that a child's paternalistic decisions would have a parent's welfare at heart. From the adult child's point of view, an adult child with a high sense of trust in his or her own parent would be more likely to believe that the parent's autonomous decision making would be carried out honestly and with the welfare of the child (and other family members) at heart.

Antagonism

Interpersonal relationships also can involve negative aspects, such as conflict and feelings of antagonism between the members of the dyad (Braiker & Kelley, 1979). It is hypothesized that elderly parents with such feelings would be less likely to believe that adult children should make decisions for their parents. Similarly, adult children with such feelings are hypothesized to be less likely to respect the autonomy of the parents.

MEASURES

The measure of locus of control was the Locus of Desired Control Interview Questionnaire (Reid et al., 1977), designed to measure generalized control expectancies in an older population. The measure consisted of two subscales: a 7-item desired control scale on which subjects indicated how desirable or important each of several generally valued outcomes was for them personally, and a 7-item expected control scale on which subjects indicated how much they felt they could influence or cause each of the outcomes. Responses on each subscale were made on a 4-point scale. (A total score, the sum of the cross-product of the items in each subscale, also could be obtained.) A high score on the Desired Control subscale indicates a greater desire for control, while a high score on the Expected Control subscale indicates a greater expectation of control. Reid et al. reported an internal consistency reliability of .64; the hypothesized correlation of .46 with self-concept provided some evidence for validity.

Self-esteem was measured using the Rosenberg (1965) Self-Esteem Scale. This scale was selected because its content was appropriate for middle-aged, as well as elderly, adults and it has satisfactory reliability and validity. The scale consists of ten 4-point items, with the total score the sum of the item scores. (Rosenberg devised a complex scoring scheme; it has been shown, however, that these scores are equivalent to the simpler item sums.) Internal consistency reliability of the scale was .77. Rosenberg has presented extensive evidence for the validity of the measure.

Attitude toward elders was measured using the Old People Scale (Kogan, 1961). The scale was designed to measure attitudes toward old people in regard to such things as tension in the presence of old people, personal qualities of old people, residential aspects of age, and intergenerational relationships. Two 17-item subscales were used, one consisting of positive statements regarding the elderly and one consisting of negative statements regarding the elderly. Since the two subscales correlated somewhat differently with criterion variables, they appeared to have differences in meaning beyond being simple opposites. A 7-point response scale was used for each item. Kogan reported odd-even Spearman-Brown reliabilities for the two subscales ranging from .73 to .83 for the negative attitude subscale and from .51 to .77 for the positive attitude subscale. Evidence for validity included significant correlations with attitudes toward minorities and physically disabled groups.

Dogmatism was measured using Form E of the 40-item Dogmatism Scale developed by Rokeach (1960). According to Rokeach, *dogmatism* is a relatively closed set of beliefs about reality, organized around a central set of beliefs about absolute authority. The Dogmatism Scale was designed to measure individual differences in the openness-closedness of such belief systems (i.e., how difficult it might be to modify beliefs to accommodate new evidence or changing situations). The items consist of statements of beliefs about various social and personal topics; the total score is the sum of the item scores. Rokeach reported split-half reliabilities ranging from .68 to .93 for various sample groups and presented extensive evidence for validity that included comparisons between known groups, as well as experimental findings.

Affective feelings was used as an indicator of the adult child's feelings of attachment to the parent, as well as an indicator of the parent's feelings for the adult child. The measure of affective feelings developed for Bengtson's Southern California Three Generations Study (Gronvold, 1988) was used as the measure of the affective feeling of parent and child regarding each other. The 5 items dealing with the feelings that the respondent has about a significant other person in a relationship (the short form of the instrument) were used in the research reported here. (An additional 5 items of the scale elicited feelings attributed to the other person; Gronvold indicated, however, that the short form could be used with little loss of information.) Each item had a 6-point response scale ranging from "not at all" to "extremely." The total score was the sum of the item scores, with a high score indicating a more positive affective relationship. Reliabilities for the short form ranged from .89 to .91. In addition to factorial validity, correlations with a global measure of closeness of feeling ranged from .64 to .75.

Feelings of concern for the parent were measured using one of the two subscales of the Filial Anxiety Scale (Cicirelli, 1988). Filial anxiety B, a 6-item subscore, measures the extent of an adult child's anxiety or concern over the welfare of an elderly parent in declining health. Item responses were made on a

5-point scale; the total score was the sum of the item scores. Internal consistency of the measure was .77. Hypothesized correlations with measures of the adult child's feelings of attachment to the parent, parent symptoms, and parent mobility provided evidence for the validity of the scale. (This measure was used for the adult children only.)

Trust in the other member of the dyad was measured using the Dyadic Trust Scale (Larzelere & Huston, 1980). This measure consists of seven items, each measured on a 7-point response scale. The total score is the sum of the item scores, with a high score indicating a high degree of trust in the other dyad member. Internal consistency reliability of the trust measure was .93. Its validity was indicated by the hypothesized correlations with love for the partner, depth of self-disclosure, and relationship status.

Finally, interpersonal antagonism was measured using the 10-item Antagonism Measure of Mancini, Thompson, Blieszner, and Travis (1985). Each item had a 5-point response scale. The total score was the sum of the item scores, with a high score indicating a high degree of antagonism toward the other member of the dyad. The scale had an internal consistency reliability of .80. I have presented evidence for factorial validity.

RELATION OF PERSONAL-SOCIAL MEASURES TO AUTONOMY AND PATERNALISM BELIEFS

As a preliminary step in determining the relationship of the personal-social variables, means and standard deviations of these variables for adult daughters and elderly mothers were examined. They are presented in Table 9.1.

Substantial differences between mothers' and daughters' scores were noted for several of the personal-social variables; when *t*-tests for paired samples were carried out, significant differences were found for self-esteem, dogmatism, desired locus of control, negative attitude toward old people, trust in the other, and antagonism toward the other. Adult daughters,

Table 9.1 Means and Standard Deviations of Personal-Social
Variables for Adult Daughters and Elderly Mothers

Variable	Daughters		Mothers	
	Mean	SD	Mean	SD
Self-esteem	30.70	3.90	28.52	3.37
Dogmatism	124.84	21.55	149.62	20.31
Locus of control				
Desired	22.91	3.25	21.38	4.11
Expected	20.84	2.75	20.29	3.41
Attitude toward old people				
Positive attitude	86.56	8.23	86.11	8.87
Negative attitude	45.87	8.80	60.78	12.97
Filial anxiety				
Concern for parent	19.85	3.75	—	—
Affection for the other	25.80	3.37	25.96	2.64
Trust in the other	44.69	7.78	48.27	5.03
Antagonism toward the other	22.04	3.94	19.22	3.48

on the average, had a more positive self-esteem than their
elderly mothers and also desired a greater degree of control
over events in their lives. Mothers, however, were more dogmatic than their daughters and also had a more negative
attitude toward old people. With regard to their interpersonal relationship, elderly mothers felt a greater sense of trust
in their daughters than vice versa, while daughters felt more
antagonism toward their mothers than their mothers did toward them.

Correlations for Daughters

Table 9.2 presents the correlations of adult daughters' scores
on the measures of the personal-social variables with their
scores on the three belief measures: Independent Autonomy,
Shared Autonomy, and Paternalism.

Only a few of the correlations were large enough to be statistically significant. None of the correlations of the personal-
social variables with Independent Autonomy were significant.

Table 9.2 Correlations of Personal-Social Variables with Adult
Daughters' Independent Autonomy, Shared
Autonomy, and Paternalism Scores

Variable	Independent Autonomy	Shared Autonomy	Paternalism
Self-esteem	−.07	−.01	−.25
Dogmatism	.17	−.03	.33*
Locus of control			
Desired	.07	−.22	−.16
Expected	−.09	−.30*	−.17
Attitude toward old people			
Positive attitude	.15	−.10	−.03
Negative attitude	−.19	.09	.55*
Filial anxiety			
Concern for parent	.05	.20	.06
Affection for mother	−.22	−.23	.26
Trust in mother	.09	−.02	−.03
Antagonism toward mother	−.02	.01	.03

*$p < .05$.

In the case of Shared Autonomy, only the correlation with
expected locus of control was significant ($r = -.30$). Here,
daughters who expected a greater degree of control over events
had weaker beliefs in Shared Autonomy than daughters who
expected a smaller degree of control over events. Finally, both
dogmatism ($r = .33$) and negative attitude toward old people
($r = .55$) were significantly correlated with Paternalism scores.
That is, adult daughters who were more dogmatic and who had
a more negative attitude toward old people had stronger Paternalism beliefs than daughter who were less dogmatic and who
had less negative attitudes toward the elderly. Thus many of
the hypotheses about the relationships between the personal-
social variables and beliefs about caregiving decision making
were not borne out. (It should be noted that some of the correlations, such as that between affection for the mother and Paternalism, were in the predicted direction but were not large
enough to be statistically significant. In other cases, such as the
correlations for trust and antagonism, all the correlations were
of negligible magnitude.)

Table 9.3 Correlations of Personal-Social Variables with Elderly
Mothers' Independent Autonomy, Shared Autonomy,
and Paternalism Scores

Variable	Independent Autonomy	Shared Autonomy	Paternalism
Self-esteem	−.13	.09	.09
Dogmatism	.29	.30*	.36*
Locus of control			
Desired	.18	−.01	.01
Expected	.10	.16	−.06
Attitude toward old people			
Positive attitude	.34*	.18	.19
Negative attitude	.18	.27	.33*
Affection for daughter	−.24	−.16	.18
Trust in daughter	−.00	−.04	−.09
Antagonism toward daughter	.10	.15	.01

*$p < .05$.

Correlations for Mothers

Similar correlations between the personal-social variables
and the belief measures were carried out for the group of
elderly mothers. They are presented in Table 9.3.

As was the case for the adult daughters, only a few correlations large enough to be statistically significant were found. In
regard to Independent autonomy, only positive attitude toward old people ($r = .34$) was significantly related; mothers
with more positive attitudes toward old people in general have
a stronger belief in Independent Autonomy than mothers with
less positive attitudes. Shared Autonomy was significantly related to dogmatism ($r = .30$), with more dogmatic mothers
having a stronger belief in Shared Autonomy than less dogmatic mothers. (This correlation may be a reflection of the
substantial relationship between Shared Autonomy and Paternalism found for the elderly mothers.) Finally, as was found
for the adult daughters, both dogmatism ($r = .36$) and negative
attitude toward old people ($r = .33$) were significantly correlated with Paternalism. Mothers who were more dogmatic and
who had more negative attitudes toward the elderly in general

had stronger beliefs in Paternalism than mothers who were less dogmatic and who had weaker beliefs in Paternalism. (Again, some of the correlations, such as between desired locus of control and Independent Autonomy, were in the predicted direction but were not large enough to be significant, while others, such as those for trust and antagonism, were negligible.)

Some Tentative Conclusions

Variables describing the interpersonal relationship between mother and daughter did not seem to be related to beliefs about Autonomy and Paternalism, although daughters' affection for the mother (an indicator of attachment) was in the predicted direction and approached significance. The relations of the personality variables with Paternalism were more interesting, with dogmatism and negative attitude toward old people significantly correlated among both mothers and daughters.

Any interpretation of these findings will be deferred until Chapter 10, where relationships in the proposed model of dyadic family caregiving decision making will be explored.

TEN

Relation of Autonomy and Paternalism Beliefs to Caregiving Decision Making

The objective of this chapter is to provide the reader with an understanding of factors predicting the daughter's paternalistic decision making, the mother's autonomous decision making, or shared decision making by mother and daughter from the characteristics of either the mother or the daughter within a dyadic caregiving situation.

The analysis carried out to attain this objective makes use of the hypothesized relationships between variables formulated in the dyadic family caregiving decision-making model in Chapter 4 and diagrammed in Figure 4.2.

(The reader is reminded that the simplified schematic model depicts only a single direction of influence between categories of variables, although the possibility of reciprocal effects is recognized; more complex models were felt to be premature at this early stage of inquiry.)

An analysis based upon the model can be carried out using data obtained from either the daughter or the mother (or both). As discussed in Chapter 4, when dyad members make a decision, each individual brings to the situation a set of characteristics, beliefs, attitudes, needs, and resources that may influence the decision outcome (Brinberg & Jaccard, 1989; Jaccard et al., 1989). The study of dyadic decision making can be carried out based upon data from one individual or the other, or it can be based upon measures of the dyadic process (Brinberg & Jaccard, 1989; Ransom, Fisher, Phillips, Kokes, & Weiss, 1990). The process may become habitual in a dyad with a close relationship of long standing, and structural factors or characteristics of the individuals in the dyad may become more important in predicting decision making. In addition, this study is focusing on dyadic outcomes (whether decisions are made autonomously by the mother, paternalistically by the daughter, or shared by both). For these reasons the decision-making process itself was not measured. Therefore a structural model seemed appropriate—a model that predicts outcome from characteristics of the dyad members.

Although scores constructed from measures of both individuals in a dyad sometimes have been used, Ransom et al. (1990) point out that statistical difficulties arise in constructing so-called "dyadic measures" such as averages or difference scores based upon measures from each individual, and it seems preferable in most cases not to attempt to aggregate the data in this way. An alternative is to construct a model based upon variables measured for two individuals. Thompson (1990) has noted that while such structural models may be constructed including data from both members of the dyad, these too are difficult to specify and to estimate.

Therefore considering the limited number of dyads studied, data analysis was carried out first using data obtained from the daughter and then using data obtained from the mother. Because each brings a different perspective to the caregiving decision situation, it is recognized that these two parallel analyses may yield different results.

The model guided the analysis. The two main areas of interest were: (a) determining the direct effects of beliefs, mothers' dependency, and background characteristics upon the outcome (the agent of decision making); and (b) determining the indirect effects of background characteristics upon outcome as a result of their effects on beliefs. (Perhaps the ideal analysis to accomplish these objectives would be to base the analysis on longitudinal data and to estimate effects in the structural model using a method such as LISREL. Because the number of mother-daughter pairs studied was not large enough to permit use of analytical methods that could test the model in its entirety, a more limited analytic strategy was used. Regression analysis was employed to estimate direct effects, with hierarchical regression used as a basis for inferring the indirect effects of background variables upon the agent of decision making.)

Thus far the measurement of beliefs and the agent of decision making has been discussed in Chapter 5. In Chapters 8 and 9, the measurement of contextual and personal-social variables was described. In addition, the relationship of each of the contextual and personal-social variables to beliefs about autonomy and paternalism was examined in these chapters, considering the univariate correlations of these antecedent variables first with daughters' beliefs and then with mothers' beliefs.

(Although many contextual and personal-social variables were measured in the course of the project, only a limited number of variables could be included in a regression analysis. In order to maintain the recommended subjects-to-variables ratio of 10:1, the number of predictors that could be entered into the regression equation at any one time was limited to five. Therefore only one or two variables of each type could be selected to represent these categories. In selecting variables for analysis, several criteria were used: the strength of the relationship found in the simple correlations, the adequacy of measurement, the degree to which the variable represented a particular category of variables found in the model, and theoretical relevance.)

PREDICTING THE AGENT OF DECISION MAKING FROM THE DAUGHTERS' PERSPECTIVE

First of all, the relationships among the variables in the model were examined from the daughters' perspective. That is, data gathered from the daughter were used in the analyses. Data about the mothers' as well as the daughters' own characteristics, the relationships with the mothers, autonomy and paternalism beliefs, and the agent of decision making were provided by the daughters.

The first question considered was: What are the direct effects of daughters' autonomy and paternalism beliefs on the agent of decision making? Then, what is the direct effect of the mothers' dependency on the agent of decision making? And, what are the direct effects of the demographic and personal-social characteristics on the agent of decision making? Finally, what are the indirect effects of dependency and background variables (demographic and personal-social characteristics) on the agent of decision making through their influence on beliefs?

Direct Effects of Daughters' Autonomy and Paternalism Beliefs on the Agent of Decision Making

As discussed in Chapter 5, these three autonomy and paternalism beliefs (Independent Autonomy, Shared Autonomy, and Paternalism) are relatively independent of each other. That is, if someone has a strong belief in independent autonomy, it does not necessarily imply that a weak belief in paternalism will also be held by that individual. Rather, an individual may be assessed as holding a profile of the three beliefs, with each belief exerting an effect in determining the agent of decision making.

A daughter's paternalistic decisions (number of decisions made by the daughter), a mother's autonomous decisions (number of decisions made by the mother), and shared decisions (the number of decisions made jointly by mother and daughter) were the three measures of the agent of caregiving decision making. Their means and standard deviations are presented in Table 10.1, as well as their correlations with the measures of daughters' beliefs. Stronger paternalism beliefs and weaker beliefs in independent autonomy were related to a

Table 10.1 Correlations of Daughters' Beliefs with the Agent of
Caregiving Decisions (Mothers, Daughters, or Both)

	Agent of Caregiving Decisions		
Variable	Daughter	Mother	Shared
Independent autonomy	−.29*	.39*	−.07
Shared autonomy	.12	−.21	.29*
Paternalism	.38*	−.33*	−.13
MEAN	3.78	29.44	4.44
STANDARD DEVIATION	6.75	9.50	5.09

*$p < .05$.

greater number of daughters' paternalistic decisions. In the
converse of the previous relationship, weaker paternalism beliefs and stronger beliefs in independent autonomy were related to a greater number of mothers' autonomous decisions.
Finally, a stronger belief in shared autonomy was related to a
greater number of shared decisions.

In separate multiple regression analyses, the three measures
of daughters' beliefs (Independent Autonomy, Shared Autonomy, and Paternalism) were entered as predictors of each of the
three measures of the agent of caregiving decision making.
Table 10.2 presents a summary of these analyses.

Looking first at the analysis for the mothers' autonomous
decisions, the regression was significant, with a resulting R of
.50. Both Independent Autonomy and Shared Autonomy were
significant predictors. The greater a daughter's belief in independent autonomy and the less her belief in shared autonomy,
the greater the number of her mother's autonomous caregiving
decisions. The square of the multiple correlation coefficient, R^2,
was .25, indicating that these two predictors accounted for 25%
of the variance in the mothers' autonomous decisions.

Considering the analysis for the daughters' paternalistic
decisions, the regression was significant, with a resulting R of
.45 and an R^2 of .20. Only Paternalism was a significant predictor; as the strength of the daughter's Paternalism belief increased, the greater the number of the daughter's paternalistic
decisions.

Table 10.2 Summary of Regression Analyses Predicting Agent of Decision from Daughters' Beliefs (*n* = 46)

Variable	B	SE B	Beta	R	R²
MOTHERS' AUTONOMOUS DECISIONS					
Independent autonomy	0.61	0.31	.32*		
Shared autonomy	−0.38	0.17	−.30*		
Paternalism	−0.11	0.10	−.20	.50*	.25
SHARED DECISIONS					
Independent autonomy	−0.24	0.18	−.24		
Shared autonomy	0.20	0.10	.29*		
Paternalism	−0.07	0.06	−.21	.36*	.13
DAUGHTERS' PATERNALISTIC DECISIONS					
Independent autonomy	−0.17	0.23	−.12		
Shared autonomy	0.18	0.13	.20		
Paternalism	0.14	0.07	.34*	.44*	.19

*$p < .05$.

Proceeding to the analysis for shared decisions by mother and daughter, the overall regression was not significant. The beta-coefficient for Shared Autonomy was significant, however, indicating that taken alone it had a significant direct effect upon shared decisions. (In other words, in a simple regression equation with belief in shared autonomy as the only predictor of shared decision making, it would be a significant predictor.) Thus daughters' beliefs in shared autonomy were associated with a greater number of shared decisions.

These results indicate that the pattern of a daughter's profile of beliefs influences who will be the agent of decision making. In summary, when a daughter's belief in independent autonomy is strong and belief in shared autonomy is weak, a greater likelihood of autonomous decisions by the mother exists. When a daughter's belief in paternalism is strong, a greater likelihood of paternalistic decisions by the daughter exists. And, when a daughter's belief in shared autonomy is strong, a greater likelihood of shared decision making exists.

Direct Effects of Mothers' Dependency
Upon the Agent of Decision Making

As one would expect, there would be no need for caregiving or caregiving decision making if the elderly parent were not dependent. In fact, if a parent were seriously dependent, paternalistic decision making probably would be inevitable. In the present study, the mother's dependency was assessed in several ways: global ratings of physical health, mental health, and intellectual functioning; a checklist of types of help needed by the parent; and the number of hours of care provided by the adult child. Inspection of univariate correlations of these variables with the agent of decision making revealed that these variables had negligible relationships with the outcome variables.

This finding was somewhat surprising, since one criterion for participating in the study was that daughters must be providing some degree of care to their mothers. In fact, daughters provided a mean of 6.6 hours of care per week to their mothers, reporting a range of from 1-40 hours of care weekly. At the same time, the need to interview mothers as well as daughters precluded the sampling of mothers with high degrees of dependency. Mothers who required a great deal of care were likely to be too ill, too frail, or too cognitively impaired to be interviewed. The resulting restriction in the range of dependency may have accounted for the low correlations. Some kind of threshold may exist, such that the mother's dependency has no effect upon the agent of decision making until some level of dependency is reached, making it difficult or impossible for the mother to participate further in decision making. With the more limited range of dependency found in the present study, the mother's dependency had no direct effect upon the agent of decision making.

Direct Effects of Background Characteristics
Upon the Agent of Decision Making

Two categories of background characteristics were considered: demographic characteristics and personal-social characteristics. when the correlations of the demographic variables with the agent of decision making were examined, a daughter's educational level and a mother's age appeared to be the most promising as predictors. Similarly, when the relationships of the personal-social variables with the agent of decision making were studied, self-esteem, locus of desired control, antagonism, and trust all had negligible correlations with the outcome variables. Two of the remaining three variables looked promising as predictors (negative attitude toward elders, and dogmatism), and the third (affective feelings toward the mother) had weak correlations with the outcome variables but was of theoretical interest as an indicator of attachment (see Chapter 4). Since a substantial correlation existed between dogmatism and negative attitude toward elders, little was to be gained by including both in a regression analysis. Consequently, two demographic characteristics (daughter's educational level, mother's age) and two personal-social characteristics (negative attitude toward elders, affective feelings toward the mother) were included in a multiple regression equation to determine their direct effects upon the agent of decision making.

When the regression of these four background variables on the mothers' autonomous decisions was examined (see Table D.1, Appendix D), the mother's age and the daughter's negative attitude toward elders were significant predictors, with an R of .52 and an R^2 of .27. The direct effects of the daughter's educational level and affective feelings toward the mother were negligible. The younger the mother and the less negative the daughter's attitude toward elders, the greater the number of the mother's autonomous decisions.

Regarding the number of shared decisions, none of the four background variables were significant predictors (Table D.2, Appendix D); the multiple R was only .13.

The regression of the background variables upon the daughters' paternalistic decisions (Table D.3, Appendix D) was significant, with an R of .48 and an R^2 of .23. The daughter's educational level and negative attitude toward elders were both significant predictors of paternalistic decisions, while the direct effects of daughters' affective feelings toward the mother and the mother's age were negligible.

The question of whether the agent of decision making can be predicted more effectively from autonomy and paternalism beliefs or from the background variables can now be considered. In the case of mothers' autonomous decisions, the beliefs had a multiple correlation of .50 with mothers' decisions, while the background factors had a multiple correlation of .52, only a slight difference. In the case of shared decisions, the beliefs had a multiple correlation of .36 while the background variables had a multiple correlation of .13; since neither of these regressions was significant, both beliefs and background variables do a poor job of predicting shared agents of decision. Finally, the beliefs had a multiple correlation of .45 with daughters' paternalistic decisions, while the background variables had a multiple correlation of .48. Here, the background variables were only slightly better in predicting daughters' autonomous decisions than the belief variables. Thus the beliefs and the background factors appear to have about the same effectiveness in predicting outcomes (either relative to the mothers' autonomous decisions or the daughters' paternalistic decisions).

Indirect Effects of Background Variables

Comparing the relative effects of beliefs and background variables upon the outcome measures is interesting, but it is also important to know whether the effects of the background variables were independent of beliefs. It was hypothesized in

Chapter 4 that the background variables would have indirect effects upon the agent of decision making, acting through the effect of these variables upon beliefs and the subsequent effects of beliefs upon the agent of decision making. If such indirect effects exist, then the overall direct effects of the background variables considered in the previous section would consist of the indirect effects plus any independent direct effects.

One way of detecting the existence of such indirect effects is through hierarchical regression analysis. Measures of belief were entered in the first step of the hierarchical regression, and the selected background variables were entered in the second step of the analysis. The increase in R^2 from the first step of the analysis to the second allows one to determine the extent to which the background characteristics improve prediction above and beyond the effects of belief alone, that is, the extent to which the background variables have independent effects upon outcome in addition to any indirect effects acting through beliefs.

In the case of mothers' autonomous decisions, the hierarchical regression analysis (Table D.4, Appendix D) indicated that the addition of the background variables from step one to step two of the analysis resulted in an increase in R^2 of .09. Since the background variables accounted for an overall R^2 of .27, explaining 27% of the variance in mothers' autonomous decisions, one can infer that the remaining 18% of the variance in mothers' decisions was due to the indirect effects of the background variables through their effects upon beliefs.

A similar analysis carried out for mothers' and daughters' shared decisions (Table D.5, Appendix D) resulted in a change in R^2 of only .02 resulting from the addition of the background variables to the prediction equation. Since the background variables explained only 2% of the variance in shared decisions, one can infer that there were no indirect effects.

With regard to daughters' paternalistic decisions, the hierarchical regression analysis (Table D.6, Appendix D) resulted in a change in R^2 of .11. Since the background variables accounted for an overall R^2 of .23, explaining 23% of the variance in daughters' paternalistic decisions, one can infer that the

remaining 12% of the variance in daughters' paternalistic decisions was due to the indirect effects of the background variables through their effects upon beliefs.

As a check on whether the background variables did indeed
have the inferred effect upon beliefs, additional regressions
were carried out to determine the effect of the background
variables upon belief. With regard to belief in independent
autonomy (Table D.7, Appendix D), the background variables
did indeed have a significant effect, with both negative attitude
toward elders and affective feelings toward the mother significant predictors. When a similar analysis for belief in shared
autonomy was examined, there were no significant effects.
Finally in the case of belief in paternalism (Table D.8, Appendix D), all four of the background variables (negative attitude
toward elders, affective feelings toward the mother, daughter's
education, and mother's age) were significant predictors of
daughters' belief in paternalism.

PREDICTING THE AGENT OF DECISION MAKING
FROM THE MOTHERS' PERSPECTIVE

The analyses discussed thus far in this chapter have used
data collected from the daughters, and the findings reflect the
daughters' perspective on decisions within the mother-daughter dyad. Now the mothers' perspective will be considered in
similar analyses, using data gathered from the mothers. To
maintain comparability between the two sets of analyses, the
same set of contextual and personal-variables was used also
for the analyses of the mothers' data.

Direct Effects of Mothers' Autonomy and
Paternalism Beliefs Upon the Agent of Decision Making

The correlations of the mothers' autonomy and paternalism
beliefs with the three measures of the agent of decision making

(daughter, mother, shared) are presented in Table 10.3, as well as the means and standard deviations of the measures of the agent of decision making. The mothers' belief in paternalism were related to autonomous decision making, with a weaker belief in paternalism associated with more decisions made by the mother. Next, mothers' belief in shared autonomy and belief in paternalism were both significantly correlated with shared decision making. In both cases the stronger the beliefs, the more decisions were shared by mother and daughter. Finally, none of the mothers' beliefs in autonomy and paternalism were significantly related to the daughters' paternalistic decisions.

In separate multiple regression analyses, presented in Table 10.4, the three measures of the mothers' beliefs were entered as predictors of each of the three measures of the agent of caregiving decision making. In the analysis for shared decision making, the regression was significant, with a resulting R^2 of .17. Paradoxically, only the mothers' belief in paternalism was a significant predictor; here, as the strength of the mothers' paternalism belief increased, the greater the number of decisions shared by mother and daughter. In regard to the analyses for the mothers' autonomous decisions and the daughters' paternalistic decisions, there were no significant predictors. It appears that the relationships noted in Table 10.3 were not robust enough to attain significance in the multiple regression.

Effects of Mothers' Dependency Upon the Agent of Decision Making

As in the analyses from the daughters' perspective, the indicators of the mothers' dependency were not related to the agent of decision making as reported by the mothers. As discussed in connection with the analysis for daughters, this result is probably due to the relatively low dependency needs of the mothers in the sample.

Table 10.3 Correlations of Mothers' Beliefs with the Agent of
Caregiving Decisions (Mothers,
Daughters, or Both)

Variable	Agent of Caregiving Decisions		
	Daughter	*Mother*	*Shared*
Independent autonomy	−.21	.17	.15
Shared autonomy	.17	−.12	.30*
Paternalism	.20	−.30*	.33*
MEAN	3.56	26.28	3.74
STANDARD DEVIATION	5.38	8.41	4.74

*$p < .05$.

Direct Effects of Background Characteristics
Upon the Agent of Decision Making

The four background characteristics (negative attitude toward elders, affective feelings toward the daughter, mother's
age, and daughter's educational level) were included in a regression analysis to determine their direct effects upon each of
the three agents of decision making.

In regard to the regression of the background variables on
the mothers' autonomous decisions (see Table D.10 in Appendix D), the multiple R was .45 and R^2 was .20. The mother's age
was the only significant predictor of the mothers' autonomous
decisions. The younger the mother, the greater the number of
the mothers' autonomous decisions.

Regarding the number of shared decisions (Table D.11 in
Appendix D), none of the four background variables were
significant predictors. The multiple R was only .26 and was not
significant.

The regression of the background variables on the daughters' paternalistic decisions was significant, with an R of .52
and an R^2 of .27. Both the educational level of the daughter
and the mother's age were significant predictors of the daughters' paternalistic decisions, while the effects of negative
attitude toward elders and affective feelings toward daughters were negligible. The lower the educational level of the

Table 10.4 Summary of Regression Analyses Predicting Agent of Decision from Mothers' Beliefs (*n* = 46)

Variable	B	SE B	Beta	R	R²
MOTHERS' AUTONOMOUS DECISIONS					
Independent autonomy	0.18	0.27	.11		
Shared autonomy	−0.02	0.25	−.01		
Paternalism	−0.17	0.10	−.27	.32	.10
SHARED DECISIONS					
Independent autonomy	0.20	0.15	.20		
Shared autonomy	0.11	0.14	.13		
Paternalism	0.11	0.05	.32*	.42*	.17
DAUGHTERS' PATERNALISTIC DECISIONS					
Independent autonomy	−0.22	0.17	−.20		
Shared autonomy	0.15	0.16	.16		
Paternalism	0.03	0.07	.09	.29	.08

*$p < .05$.

daughter and the older the mother, the greater the number of paternalistic decisions by the daughter.

The question of whether the agent of decision making can be predicted more effectively from the autonomy and paternalism beliefs than from the background variables can be considered also from the mothers' perspective. In the case of the mothers' autonomous decisions, the mothers' beliefs had a multiple correlation of only .32 with mothers' decisions, while the background variables had a multiple correlation of .45. Regarding shared decisions, the mothers' beliefs had a multiple R of .42 in comparison to an R for the background variables of .26. Finally, in regard to the daughters' paternalistic decisions, the R for beliefs was .29, while the R for the background variables was .52. In summary, background variables seem to be better predictors than mothers' beliefs in regard to the prediction of mothers' autonomous decisions and daughters' paternalistic decisions, while beliefs seem to be better predictors than background variables in the case of shared decisions.

Indirect Effects of Background Variables

In the analyses from the mothers' perspective, the question of whether the background variables have an indirect effect on the agent of decision making through their effect upon beliefs is meaningful only in regard to shared decisions. Mothers' beliefs themselves did not have a significant effect upon mothers' autonomous decisions or upon daughters' paternalistic decisions; thus any indirect effects would be negligible. In the case of shared decisions, although beliefs had a significant effect upon shared decisions, the total effect of the background variables was not significant. Any indirect effects would, therefore, be insignificant as well.

INTERPRETATIONS OF THE
OBSERVED RELATIONSHIPS

The findings presented here furnish evidence that adult daughters' beliefs about autonomy and paternalism are related to the agent of caregiving decision making. A profile of the three beliefs (belief in independent autonomy, belief in shared autonomy, and belief in paternalism) was found to be differentially related to mothers' autonomous decisions, mothers' and daughters' shared decisions, and daughters' paternalistic decisions, although prediction of the shared decisions was poor. That is, daughters' beliefs influence who will be making caregiving decisions: daughters, mothers, or both together. Elderly mothers' beliefs were related individually to the agent of caregiving decisions, but the relationships were weaker than those found for daughters.

Three possible reasons are proposed why daughters' beliefs were stronger predictors of the agent of decision making than mothers' beliefs. One is that the measures of the agent of decision making as reported by mothers may have differed from those reported by daughters. Yet, the correlations between the mothers' and daughters' reports were substantial (.91 for the mothers' autonomous decisions, .66 for shared decisions, and

.75 for daughters' paternalistic decisions), indicating consider-able agreement. Another possible explanation is that the reli-ability of the belief measures was not as high among mothers as it was among daughters (see Chapter 5), thus limiting the magnitude of correlations with other variables. A third reason is that the beliefs of adult daughters, who hold more power in the caregiving situation, may take precedence in dyadic inter-actions between mother and daughter regarding caregiving decisions. Mothers were found to have stronger beliefs in pa-ternalism than their daughters (see Chapter 7); thus the el-derly mothers may have been inclined to accept passively the "rules of the decision-making game" as seen by their caregiv-ing daughters.

The effects of the dependency variables, the personal-social variables, and the demographic variables upon the agent of decision making generally were somewhat less than antici-pated, although a few variables were significant predictors of the agent of decision making. The lack of a relationship be-tween indicators of the mothers' dependency and the agents of decisions was surprising, although it was probably due to low levels of dependency among mothers in the study. A depen-dency threshold is postulated, such that dependency is inde-pendent of the agent of decision making until a level of dependency is reached, making it difficult or impossible for the mother to participate in decision making. After this point, one would expect the level of dependency to be related to the agent of decision making. This threshold hypothesis needs to be tested in a sample with a greater range of dependency among the elderly mothers than the one used here.

Among the four personal-social and demographic variables considered as possible predictors of the agent of decision mak-ing, daughters' negative attitude toward elders stood out in both the prediction of mothers' autonomous decisions and daughters' paternalistic decisions, although the direction of the relationship was different for daughters' decisions from that for mothers. (Dogmatism may bear a similar relationship to the agent of decision making; the reader should remember that it was not included in analyses due to its substantial correlation with negative attitude toward elders.) Daughters' educational level was related to daughters' paternalistic decisions, with daughters at lower educational levels more likely to make paternalistic decisions. The fact that negative attitude toward elders, daughters' educational level, and mothers' age had an indirect effect upon daughters' paternalistic decisions through their effect upon daughters' paternalism beliefs suggests that the general cultural context may be important. Older families and less well-educated families tended to adhere to the traditional autocratic ideology of families in American (Nye & Berardo, 1973), following the philosophy that the parent knows best (paternalism in child rearing) and that aging is accompanied by a decline in competence (negative attitude toward elders). As a consequence, older mothers in the sample would be more likely to rear daughters with stronger paternalistic beliefs and more negative attitudes toward aging; such daughters might be expected also to make more paternalistic caregiving decisions (and their mothers to submit to such decisions).

The limitations of the method of analysis imposed by the small sample size are recognized. It is felt, however, that the conclusions cautiously advanced here may serve as the starting point for future work that can investigate this area more thoroughly.

ELEVEN

The Influence of Siblings
Upon Beliefs and Decision Making

Thus far, the book has considered only the dyad of the elderly parent and the adult child caregiver in relation to beliefs and decision making. This is a valid approach in that the literature (see Chapter 1) has shown consistently that the majority of informal family care is provided by one person, typically an adult daughter (Horowitz & Dobrof, 1982; Johnson & Catalano, 1981; Tennstedt & McKinlay, 1989). The majority of elderly people, however, also report receiving some help from at least one secondary caregiver, most frequently a sibling of the adult child acting as primary caregiver (Horowitz & Dobrof, 1982; Tennstedt, McKinlay, & Sullivan, 1989). These siblings, in addition to helping care for the parent, may also participate in decisions affecting the parent.

It would be of interest to determine the relationship between siblings' participation in caregiving and paternalistic and autonomous decision making. At the present time, no studies bearing on such a relationship exist; in fact, only a few studies deal with sibling caregiving participation itself. Therefore as a first step in exploring this new area, a review of existing sibling studies concerned with shared caregiving is in order. Later in

173

this chapter, the influence of siblings upon beliefs and decision making will be examined to the extent possible.

SIBLINGS AS FAMILY CAREGIVERS

Few studies have examined the contribution of all adult children in the family in a systematic way. Those studies that have been completed, however, indicate that a variety of family caregiving arrangements exist other than that of an adult daughter in the principal caregiver role.

The work of Matthews (Matthews, 1987, 1988; Matthews, Delaney, & Adamek, 1989; Matthews & Rosner, 1988; Matthews & Sprey, 1989) is noteworthy for its careful examination of the contributions of all adult children in the family to the care of an elderly parent. In looking first at the sharing of responsibility by pairs of sisters in a two-child family, Matthews and Rosner (1988) found that pairs of adult sisters tended to share caregiving tasks, with the division of effort becoming more equal when both sisters were employed. In larger families, five types of sibling participation in parent care were identified: routine help, in which regular assistance to the parent was incorporated into the child's ongoing schedule of activities; backup help, in which a sibling not routinely involved in care could be counted on for special emotional support or tangible aid when requested by the siblings giving routine help; circumscribed help, in which the help provided to the parent was limited carefully by amount or type; sporadic help, in which occasional assistance to the parent was provided at the child's own convenience; and dissociation, in which the adult child abdicated from any responsibility to help the parent.

The relative frequencies of these types of help were quite different. In most cases, help from one or more of the adult siblings in these larger families was either circumscribed in nature, sporadic, or nonexistent. According to Matthews (Matthews, 1987; Matthews et al., 1989; Matthews & Rosner, 1988), sisters were more likely to use routine or backup styles of participation, while brothers' help tended to be sporadic or

circumscribed, usually limited to typically male areas of expertise. Brothers spent fewer hours in parent caregiving tasks than
did their sisters and took on fewer caregiving tasks involving
personal care and household chores. Yet, when families consisting only of brothers were examined, the brothers appeared to
be willing to meet their parents' needs for care and to fulfill
their filial obligations.

Recent work by Coward and Dwyer (1990), using data from
a large national survey, sheds further light upon the caregiving
contribution of brothers. Some 683 caregiving sons and daughters were interviewed about the caregiving contributions of
3,742 adult children. The interviewees' sibling networks were
divided into single-gender networks, mixed-gender networks,
and only children to determine the effects of gender composition of the siblingship. Sons from all three types of sibling
networks were less likely than were daughters to participate in
parent care or to become principal caregivers. Participating
sons from networks that had no available sisters, however,
provided essentially as many hours of care as daughters from
networks that had no available brothers. It is not known
whether these sons provided the same types of care as did
daughters, but it is noteworthy that sons did take on caregiving
tasks when they had no sisters to assume the caregiver role.
Only in the mixed-gender network did daughters provide significantly more hours of care than brothers. Since the mixed-
gender networks are far more prevalent than those of other
types, Coward and Dwyer's findings are not at odds with those
of other studies (Matthews et al., 1989; Matthews & Rosner,
1988).

Brody, in studying the contributions of siblings of caregiving daughters of elderly parents (Brody, 1990; Brody, Hoffman,
Kleban, & Schoonover, 1989; Brody, Kleban, Hoffman, &
Schoonover, 1988), found the "daughter as principal caregiver"
model to be supported by her data. Daughters serving as principal caregivers reported that they provided an average of 24
hours of help weekly to their elderly parents (although those
daughters who shared a residence with their parents were
largely responsible for the high average hours of help), while

their sisters living nearby provided 8 hours of help weekly. In contrast, brothers who lived nearby provided only 4 hours of help weekly. Among geographically distant siblings, little help was provided by either sisters or brothers. In Brody's work, only help with ADL and IADL tasks was investigated. Siblings' help in other areas was not measured, although some services of other types can be time-consuming and might have lessened the observed gender differences.

Cicirelli (1981, 1984), in studies of adult children's help to their elderly parents, also investigated the contributions made by the siblings of the adult child who was considered by the elderly parent to be "closest" and the one turned to first for help. Two groups of adult children were studied—those who had intact marriages, and those who had experienced some form of marital disruption (i.e., divorce, widowhood, or remarriage). Adult children with intact marriages reported giving significantly more help to their elderly parents than did their siblings, while those with disrupted marriages gave about the same amount of help as did their siblings. In both cases, gender differences were found in the type of help provided. When asked to indicate which sibling provided the most help with various kinds of services, sisters were named more frequently as helpers with homemaking, personal care, home health care, transportation, and psychological support, while brothers were named more frequently as helpers with maintenance, bureaucratic mediation, and protection. Interviewees were asked also about the amount of help with parent care that they anticipated from their siblings at a future time when parents' needs for care were greater. Little difference was found in the total amount of help expected from brothers and sisters, but the type of help expected again seemed to fall into the traditional male and female role behaviors.

In one portion of the present study, siblings' helping patterns were investigated. On the basis of the respondent's estimations of the percentages of the caregiving load assumed by each sibling, four patterns were identified. These patterns, with the percentage of respondents reporting each type, were as follows: Principal caregiver provides all care while siblings provide none, 5%; principal caregiver provides over half of the caregiving load while siblings share the remainder, 55%; respondent provides more care than siblings but no one provides over half of the caregiving load, 19%; and approximately equal division of caregiving load between respondent and siblings, 21%. When the respondents were asked what kinds of caregiving tasks they and their siblings provided, 37% reported that they and their siblings provided the same types of care, while 61% reported that roles were diversified, with siblings providing types of care complementary to what the respondent provided. (Another 2% of respondents reported that they rotated caregiving with their siblings, with each providing total care for the parent during his or her term of caregiving.)

The findings of the above studies show considerable convergence despite the differences in methodology. Most noteworthy in the present context, the data clearly indicate a great deal more support from siblings than has been generally recognized, particularly for cases in which the daughter has experienced marital disruption or is employed outside the home. Overall, sisters provide more help than brothers; sisters have a greater tendency to share help more equally; and sisters and brothers tend to provide different types of help, structured according to traditional gender norms. That is, sisters provide more help than brothers with routine hands-on personal care tasks, whereas brothers provide more help with traditional male-dominated tasks. The literature indicates that sons provide a more limited range of caregiving tasks (or purchase services) and abdicate caregiving roles sooner than daughters (Brody, 1990; Montgomery & Kamo, 1989), although a recent 7-year study (Stoller, 1990) found no difference in the stability of sons and daughters as caregivers. These conclusions appear to apply to the contributions of all siblings, as well as to the "principal caregiver."

Some controversy has arisen over the contributions of sons and brothers as caregivers. The demographic reality that elderly widows are the predominant group requiring help from adult children may be responsible for the prevalence of daughters as caregivers. Two factors may be involved. First, sons may feel a sex-role taboo preventing them from giving more intimate types of care to their mothers and preventing mothers from asking them to do so (Coward & Dwyer, 1990; Matthews, 1988; Montgomery & Kamo, 1989). Second, researchers' emphasis upon daughters as caregivers and their exclusive concern with a limited group of caregiving tasks has led to a lack of recognition of the contributions of sons (brothers). That is, the tasks used to assess caregiving are the ones that women traditionally have done. Yet these tasks may be required only when the parent is in a stage of advanced frailty; at earlier stages of dependency, other types of assistance are needed. Here brothers and sisters may make more equal contributions. The more intensive types of care may not be required by all parents or may be needed only for a brief period. Further studies are needed to investigate this question. Finally, studies do not exist that examine brothers' and sisters' contributions to the care of elderly fathers as compared with the care of elderly mothers. It may be that sons (brothers) make a greater contribution to the care of elderly fathers than to the care of mothers, depending upon the degree of impairment and the range of caregiving tasks required.

Help from the principal caregiver's siblings may be greater when the parent lives alone than when the parent resides with the principal caregiver (Brody, 1990). When a parent becomes increasingly frail and care needs increase, the likelihood is greater that an adult child and the parent will share a residence so that care needs can be met. In this situation, the major portion of caregiving responsibility falls to that child by virtue of the immediacy of the elder's care needs and the inclusion of other caregiving tasks within the fabric of ongoing household duties (Aldous, 1987; Brody, 1990), regardless of siblings' willingness to help.

When one of the adult children occupies the principal caregiver role, providing a greater amount of the parent's care than do siblings, it is not surprising that some conflict develops between the siblings over the distribution of caregiving responsibilities (Brody, 1990; Matthews & Rosner, 1988; Matthews & Sprey, 1989). The principal caregiver experiences more strain and burden than the siblings acting as secondary caregivers (Brody, 1990), especially when the parent's care needs expand with increasing impairment. Brody reported that 30% of the principal caregivers, 40% of their sisters, and 6% of their brothers reported strain and conflict associated with caregiving. The principal caregivers tried frequently to make the siblings feel guilty or to make them assume a greater caregiving responsibility.

In our present study, 37% of caregiving daughters felt that the division of caregiving responsibilities with their siblings was unfair or very unfair. Some 44% of those daughters who had both brothers and sisters regarded the division of caregiving responsibilities to be unfair or very unfair, compared with 33% of caregiving daughters who had sisters only and 25% of caregiving daughters who had brothers only. Although judgments of unfairness and attempts to make the sibling feel guilty seemed to be directed more toward sisters than toward brothers, a closer examination of the data suggests the principal caregiver's acceptance of an unequal caregiving load depends upon a complex consideration of the sibling's proximity, employment and other competing responsibilities, interest and willingness to help, gender role norms, and the history of family relationships, as well as the principal caregiver's own situation. These more complex considerations help explain why the majority of adult children acting as principal caregivers felt that the distribution of responsibilities among siblings was fair albeit unequal. Brody (1990) referred to this kind of sharing of the caregiving load as "amicable and equitable rather than equal" (p. 118).

In the present study, respondents were asked how well they felt that they understood their siblings' willingness and ability to give help. The responses indicated that 78% of the adult daughters interviewed felt that they understood their siblings' situations regarding caregiving very well; only 22% did not fully understand why their siblings' could not contribute to their parents' care. Since some 79% of the respondents reported an unequal distribution of caregiving responsibility with siblings while only 37% regarded this division as unfair, it is clear that having a good understanding of why a sibling could or could not give care was important in attributions of unfairness. When a caregiving daughter felt that a sibling was in a position to help with a parent's care but did not do so, she regarded this as very unfair.

Sibling Help and Caregiver Burden and Life Satisfaction

According to Brody (1990), daughters who were principal caregivers for aging parents experienced the greatest feelings of stress and burden; their local brothers experienced the least, and their local sisters an intermediate amount. Among geographically distant siblings, sisters felt more stressed and burdened than brothers. When brothers do assume a major caregiving role, however, their feelings of burden may be disproportionately great in view of their objective burden (Montgomery & Kamo, 1989; Spitze & Logan, 1990).

When siblings share the caregiving responsibility, the burden of the principal caregiver is likely to be reduced (Brody, 1990; Zarit, Reever, & Bach-Peterson, 1980). Whether siblings can cooperate in parent caregiving tasks, however, depends upon the history of their relationship. According to Tonti (1988), some families have a history of closeness and care, and caregiving tasks are divided as evenly as possible. In other families, siblings tend to distance themselves emotionally from one another under the stress of caregiving, or old patterns of sibling rivalry are reactivated with active conflict. Matthews and Rosner (1988) found that conflicts among the siblings they studied stemmed from events in their pasts rather than from caregiving responsibilities themselves, although Brody (1990) reported increased conflict as a result of caregiving.

In the present study, 65% of caregiving daughters reported that their feelings toward their siblings had stayed the same as the result of their caregiving experiences, while 23% felt that they had grown closer to their siblings, and 12% said that their relationships with their siblings had deteriorated (particularly when brothers were involved).

Goetting's (1986) review of the developmental tasks of siblingship suggests the hypothesis that the successful cooperation between siblings required to complete the major developmental task of parent caring should be accompanied by heightened life satisfaction. Such a hypothesis has not yet been tested.

COORDINATION OF SIBLING CAREGIVING EFFORTS

The weight of the data reviewed here indicates that, in most cases, siblings of the adult child who is the principal caregiver do indeed provide some degree of help to their dependent elderly parent. Whether these siblings coordinate their helping efforts in some way or act independently in relation to the parent remains to be determined.

The adult children who participated in the present study were asked about how sibling help was managed in their families. First, respondents were asked whether all the adult children worked together in providing help or whether they worked independently. The most frequent response, given by 47% of the principal caregivers, was that all siblings worked together and coordinated their efforts in providing care to the parent. In another 26% of the families, each sibling helped with care as he or she wished, acting independently of the other siblings in the family. Two types of partial coordination of help in larger families were found also in the responses. In 13% of the families, a few of the siblings coordinated their caregiving efforts while the remaining siblings provided no help; and in 7% of the families, a few of the siblings coordinated their caregiving activities while the remaining siblings helped sporadically without any coordination of their efforts with those of the main caregivers. Finally, in 7% of the families, the principal caregiver achieved some measure of coordination by simply asking the siblings to assist in caregiving when it was needed. Overall, some degree of voluntary coordination of caregiving was found in the majority of the families, indicating that these families tended to operate as a system and not as a set of independent parent-child dyads.

A second question was how well the respondent understood the situations of siblings in regard to their willingness and ability to give help to the parent. Some 78% of the adult children felt that they understood their siblings' situations well or very well, while 15% felt that they had only a partial understanding of siblings' situations, and 7% failed to understand why their siblings could not help in caregiving. When asked how well siblings understood the parent's needs, problems, and feelings as compared with the respondent, only 3% of respondents felt that a sibling understood the parent better than they did, while 57% felt that siblings' understanding of the parent was about the same as their own, and 44% felt that siblings' understanding of the parent was less than their own. Thus adult children in the principal caregiver's role seem to be very aware of their siblings' reasons for helping or not helping, as well as the degree of the siblings' understanding of the parents.

The majority of our respondents (57%) felt that they could work together very well with their siblings in providing for parents' care, while 25% felt that they could work together to some degree. Another 4% felt that they could work together with some of their siblings but not with all of them. Finally, 14% of the respondents felt that working together with siblings was either totally impossible or would be difficult and unproductive. It is clear that for the majority of these adult children, poor sibling relationships do not seem to be an impediment to working together for parent caregiving. Since Goetting (1986) considers working together to provide care for parents in their declining years to be a fundamental developmental task of the siblingship in middle age, it is evident that the majority of siblingships represented in this sample were accomplishing this task.

If most sibling groups feel that they can work together to provide care for parents, why is the actual distribution of caregiving responsibility so unequal? One answer may be found in the siblingships themselves. Valid reasons may exist for why certain siblings cannot provide more help than they do, such as heavy competing responsibilities, lack of resources, or geographic distance. In some cases, as Brody (1990) has noted, the principal caregiver volunteers for the role (perhaps for self-serving reasons) and declines any sibling offers of help. And, of course, one adult child's coresidence with the parent produces an unequal caregiving distribution by the very nature of the situation. Another explanation for an unequal distribution of help may be the parent's insistence upon a particular child as caregiver, or the parent's rejection of any proffered help that does not meet traditional gender role expectations. Sometimes the parent does not want the discontinuity of care or the feeling of being an unwanted burden to all the children that might occur when several adult children share caregiving responsibilities. Attempting to understand all the dynamics of a family undertaking caregiving responsibilities is a difficult task indeed.

Sibling Decisions About Caregiving

Little is known thus far about the process by which the adult children in the family decide what should be done for the parent and who should do it. When the study participants were asked about how they developed a plan with their siblings for helping the parents, 43% said that all siblings discussed the parents' needs and devised a plan for providing care. In some cases everyone assembled for a formal meeting, and in others a lot of telephoning was done between the siblings until some sort of consensus was reached. In 18% of the families only one or two of the adult children assumed the entire responsibility, planning and implementing all care. In 34% of the families the adult child who assumed the principal caregiver role simply called upon siblings as required to ask for or assign help with specific caregiving tasks. In 2% of the families no specific plan existed, but whoever happened to be on the scene decided what was to be done in a pragmatic fashion, assuming that the other siblings would concur.

When asked how the siblings decided specifically "who did what" to help the parent, a considerable variation in responses occurred. Only 17% of respondents indicated that all the siblings discussed together who should carry out specific caregiving tasks. In 31% of the families one or two of the siblings would decide things; in another 14% of the families one or two of the siblings would make decisions about specific tasks and then get the approval of the others. In 22% of the families decisions about who should provide certain kinds of care were based pragmatically. That is, the sibling who had particular knowledge or abilities (e.g., business expertise, medical knowledge) was the one to undertake tasks in that area. In another 8% of the families, no decision was made about who should do things. Rather, a loose, informal arrangement existed, with one sibling or another doing things as they came up and everyone more or less taking a turn at helping. Finally, in 8% of the families, the elderly parent made the decisions about which adult child was to do what, asking particular children to do particular tasks. What is most interesting about this last 8% of cases is the implication that in 92% of the families, the adult children appeared to make decisions in relation to the parent's care without input from the parent.

The final question posed to study participants about siblings' caregiving contributions asked how the siblings would go about making decisions for parents who could no longer make their own. Responses revealed several degrees of sibling participation in the decision. In 57% of the families, all the siblings discussed the issue in person or by telephone to arrive at a consensus decision. In another 8% of the families, all the siblings discussed the issue but the principal caregiver felt that she would have the greatest influence in the decision making. In 14% of the cases, one or two siblings would make the decision and solicit the approval of the others, and in another 19%, one or two siblings simply would make the decision without involving the others. Finally, 2% of the respondents indicated that to attempt to bring siblings into any decision regarding the parent would involve a family fight. Fortunately, in the majority of the families studied, the siblings were able to reach some sort of agreement about decisions affecting the parents.

Brody (1990) has noted that when a principal caregiver shared caregiving decision making with siblings, the siblings (especially sisters) seemed to be very appreciative. Since sisters tended to feel guilty that they were not providing more help to the parent, inclusion in the decision-making process helped them feel that their efforts were approved by the principal caregiver and that they were accepted despite their inability to give more help. When decision making was not shared with geographically distant siblings, they felt uninformed and excluded. Clearly communication and cooperation between the adult children in the family is a prerequisite for optimal sibling sharing of caregiving responsibilities and caregiving decision making.

SIBLING HELPING PATTERNS IN RELATION TO AUTONOMY AND PATERNALISM BELIEFS AND CAREGIVING DECISION MAKING

The final questions to be considered in this chapter are concerned with the effect of siblings upon the principal caregivers' paternalism and autonomy beliefs and on caregiving decisions: What is the effect of sibling participation in caregiving? What is the effect of sibling gender?

Effect of Sibling Participation

To investigate the first question, the beliefs and decisions of two groups of caregivers were compared, with the groups based upon the patterns of sibling caregiving help that were identified earlier. The first group, called the "single helper" group, consisted of principal caregivers who provided all or the majority of help needed by their parents. The principal caregivers in this group received either no help from siblings or received from them amounts of help that were small in comparison to their own efforts. The second group, called the "shared help" group, consisted of study participants who reported an approximately equal division of caregiving tasks with their siblings or who reported an unequal division of tasks with the siblings but with no one providing more than half of the help required.

When the two groups were compared, no significant difference was found between them on mean scores for beliefs in Paternalism, Independent Autonomy, or Shared Autonomy. Thus daughters with stronger beliefs in Paternalism do not appear more likely to be self-selected (or designated by others) for a principal caregiver's role than daughters with weaker beliefs in Paternalism.

Next, the two groups were compared on the measures of caregiving decision making. (Respondents were asked to indicate who made the decisions in 40 common caregiving areas.) Caregivers in the single caregiver group ($M = 6.14$) made significantly more paternalistic decisions for the parent than caregivers in the shared help group ($M = 2.14$). Conversely, elderly mothers of the daughters in the shared help group ($M = 30.79$) made significantly more autonomous decisions than mothers of daughters in the single caregiver group ($M = 24.15$). No difference was found between the two groups in shared decision making.

It is puzzling that the two groups showed no significant difference on beliefs but then differed in regard to paternalistic and autonomous decision making. One would have expected a relationship between beliefs and decision making. Perhaps siblings influence such a relationship in a way not yet understood.

Since some investigations (e.g., Brody, 1990) have found that help from the principal caregivers' siblings decreases as parents become more impaired, it is possible that the observed differences between the single caregiver and the shared help groups on the measures of decision making reflected greater degrees of impairment among the mothers of the single caregiver group than among the shared help group. When the number of hours of care provided by the principal caregiver and ratings of the parent's health were used as covariates in the analysis, the observed differences in decision making between the two groups were still significant.

Effect of Sibling Gender

To determine whether sibling gender had any effects upon the principal caregivers' beliefs or decision making, the method used by Coward and Dwyer (1990) was used. The sample was subdivided into those principal caregivers who had brothers only, those who had sisters only, and those who had both brothers and sisters. In analyses of variance with the belief measures and decision-making variables as dependent variables, a significant difference was found between the three groups on the Paternalism measure. Those caregivers who had brothers only ($M = 101.00$) had stronger beliefs in paternalism than those who had both brothers and sisters ($M = 94.65$) and those who had sisters only ($M = 87.47$). Differences on the Independent Autonomy and Shared Autonomy measures were not significant. No significant differences were found between the three sibling gender groups on the measures of decision making. In this case, a difference in belief but no difference in decision making was found.

SOME OVERALL CONCLUSIONS

The literature on sibling participation in parent caregiving activities is rather sparse and suffers from the typical deficiencies of exploratory research in a new area. Samples tend to be small and selective, measures tend to be qualitative or experimental, many pertinent variables are uncontrolled, and so on. Nonetheless, some conclusions are tentatively advanced:

First, the weight of the evidence available thus far indicates that in most families, siblings of a principal caregiver also participate to some degree in provision of care to an elderly parent. In the majority of families, a principal caregiver provides the bulk of the care, but in a minority of families sibling help is sufficient to result in a more equitable distribution of caregiving responsibility.

Second, sisters tend to provide more care than do brothers, although brothers take on more caregiving tasks when no sisters are available.

Third, sisters tend to share helping tasks more equally than do brothers.

Fourth, despite their unequal caregiving contributions, the majority of the principal caregivers studied feel that the division of caregiving responsibilities with their siblings is essentially fair, given the circumstances of all involved. Most feel that they understand their siblings' situations in relation to their willingness and ability to help with parent care.

Fifth, in the majority of families, the siblings do manage some degree of coordination of their caregiving activities and feel that they could work together to provide for their parents' care. The principal caregiver and the other siblings tend to discuss questions relating to the parent's care to arrive at a consensus decision, at least with regard to major concerns.

Sixth, the degree of sibling participation in caregiving appears to have little effect upon the principal caregivers' beliefs in independent autonomy, shared autonomy, and paternalism. (Having at least one brother seems to be related to a stronger belief in paternalism among daughters who are principal caregivers.)

Seventh, when siblings share the parent care tasks more evenly, fewer paternalistic decisions are made by the caregiver and more decisions are made by the elderly parent than when a single caregiver provides most of the care. The implication is that siblings acting as a group to provide care may be more respecting of an elderly parent's exercise of autonomy than a single adult child acting independently as a principal caregiver. When a principal caregiver is responsible for all or most of a parent's care, the pressures of caregiving tasks themselves may lead to paternalistic decisions based upon expediency quite apart from any other considerations.

PART FOUR

Conclusions

TWELVE

Summary and Concluding Remarks

This final chapter is written in the hope of helping the reader gain some further understanding and integration of findings about autonomy and paternalism in family caregiving decision making.

JUSTIFICATION OF THE RESEARCH STRATEGY

Family caregiving for the elderly depends upon either explicit or implicit decision making, with decisions made to determine the type and amount of help provided to an aging family member. Effective decision making takes place when goals of both the caregiver and care receiver are attained and the quality of the relationship of the individuals involved in the decision making is maintained or enhanced. Effective decision making may depend in part upon whether the elder is an autonomous decisionmaker or the caregiver is a paternalistic decisionmaker. In attempting to predict the agent of decision making (*who* makes the decisions), I really am attempting to identify the dyad members' choice of a given type of decisionmaker, not the subsequent decision about a caregiving task itself. (Interest in the latter exists only as an indicator to infer the identity of the decisionmaker). Knowing whether the caregiving decision situation involves an autonomous or paternalistic decisionmaker may help one evaluate whether subsequent decision making regarding caregiving tasks will lead to beneficial or harmful outcomes.

The family is often defined as a system, that is, a set of component parts that are interacting and influencing each other. In this book, a *family caregiving decision-making system* is defined as a hierarchical and semiautonomous system. Hierarchical means that all the component parts interact but do not necessarily have the same impact on each other—they do not influence each other equally. Some component parts have a greater impact than others throughout the whole system. Also, some of the component parts are more central to the survival of the system. For example, if the brain as a component of the neural subsystem is destroyed, then the total bodily system would collapse, whereas the system can survive the loss of other parts. For certain purposes, one may conceive of dyadic units existing within systems or subsystems. For example, conceptualizing the heart and lungs as a dyadic unit may lead to the study of how such a unit works in itself, as well as its impact upon the effective and efficient functioning of the total bodily system.

The family caregiving system being semiautonomous means that at times certain component parts may have little or no effect upon the total system. For example, loss of one kidney may have minimal impact upon the total bodily system. Should illness occur, however, it could have a great impact.

Applying this mode of thinking to the family, I identified the adult daughter-elderly mother relationship as a basic dyadic unit of the total family caregiving decision-making system. This is the primary caregiving unit, as demonstrated in many empirical studies (e.g., Brody, 1990; Tennstedt & McKinlay, 1989). This dyadic unit has the greatest impact upon the effective and efficient functioning of the total caregiving decision-making system. This functioning, however, does not prevent other family members from having an impact as well, interacting and influencing both caregiving and decision making. Husbands, brothers, female siblings, and other kin are all part of the total system, but their impact or influence is secondary (less than that of the primary dyadic unit).

Semiautonomy of a dyad occurs when other family members have little or no interaction with the dyad, and hence no impact. This situation may vary at different time periods. For example, husbands may have a significant impact until they themselves become frail. Or, brothers may participate in caregiving or decision making in a crisis situation but not participate at all in later routine decisions. At that point in time, they would have no impact; the caregiving dyad would be semiautonomous relative to the total system. The occurrence of semiautonomous portions of the family system lends further justification to the research strategy of studying the adult child-elderly parent dyadic unit.

Such a view of the family system permits me to focus upon the adult daughter-elderly mother as the primary caregiving decision-making dyad, temporarily studying it as an isolated unit for greater understanding. Many times, before applying a systems analysis to interacting parts, the researcher might do better to explore the internal aspects of the component parts of the system. This method does not dispute the value of viewing the family as a system. (Also, in working with a component dyadic part of the total system, one may feel justified in using a linear sequence strategy to search for antecedents of outcomes of interest. An analytic and systems approach may be complementary rather than mutually exclusive).

This concept of the aging family system not only led me to select the daughter-mother dyad as the basic caregiving decision-making unit, but guided my search for antecedent factors influencing autonomous and paternalistic decision making within that unit. Obviously, many possible antecedent factors of autonomous and paternalistic decision making by the mother or daughter go beyond the dyad, such as restrictions imposed by other family members for the common good of the family, or rules and regulations of institutions in society. If dyads can be semiautonomous, however, one can justify studying the dyad not only as an entity relatively independent of the family system of which it is a part, but also as relatively independent of larger systems external to the family. The characteristics of the daughter and mother themselves can be studied to determine whether they are antecedents of autonomous and paternalistic decision making. Aside from the decisional incapacity of the care receiver, characteristics of the dyad members have not been seriously explored previously as predictors of the agent of decision making.

Finally, an obvious point must be made explicit. This study was correlational, not experimental. Any reference to causal relationships on the basis of the correlational findings is based upon logical inferences to the degree that such inference is possible. Sometimes, the temporal characteristics of the situation itself can dictate drawing such logical inferences.

SUMMARY AND FURTHER
INTERPRETATION OF FINDINGS

In exploring questions of autonomy and paternalism in the family caregiving setting, three content domains were investigated: (a) predicting the agent of decision making from characteristics of daughters and mothers in a caregiving situation, (b) demonstrating a relationship between the agent of decision making and the characteristics of a multi-dyadic caregiving group of the daughter's siblings, and (c) comparing the intergenerational congruence and differences in autonomy and paternalism between daughters and mothers in the dyadic caregiving relationship.

Predicting the Agent of Decision Making

The findings presented in Chapter 10 demonstrated a definite relationship between beliefs about autonomy and paternalism and the agent of decision making. In considering beliefs and decision making from the daughters' perspective (using data collected from the daughters), I found that the stronger a daughter's belief in independent autonomy, the greater the frequency of the mother's autonomous decision making; the stronger a daughter's belief in shared autonomy, the greater the frequency of shared decision making; and the stronger a daughter's belief in paternalism, the greater the frequency of her paternalistic decision making.

Contrary to my expectations, perceived dependency of the mothers did not predict the agent of decision making; this finding may have been due to the limited range of dependency existing among the mothers in the study.

In terms of background characteristics, the younger the mother and the weaker the daughter's negative attitude toward elderly people in general, the greater the number of the mother's autonomous decisions. On the other hand, the older the mother and the stronger the daughter's negative attitude toward elders, the greater the number of the daughter's paternalistic decisions. No background variables predicted shared autonomy.

Some of the background variables had an indirect effect upon determining the agent of decision making through their effect upon beliefs. The weaker the daughters' affective feelings for their mothers and the less their negative attitude toward elderly people in general, the stronger their belief in independent autonomy (and, in turn, the greater the mothers' autonomous decision making). No indirect effects regarding shared decision making were found. The greater the daughters' affection for their mothers, the more negative their attitudes toward elderly people in general, the less their education, and the older their mothers, then the stronger their belief in paternalism (and, in turn, the greater the daughters' paternalistic decision making).

When comparing the background variables versus beliefs as predictors of the mother's autonomous decision making, the predictive power of the two types of variables was approximately equivalent. From knowledge of the daughter's profile of beliefs, one can predict the mother's autonomous decision making about as well as predicting from knowledge of the daughter's age and negative attitudes toward elderly people in general. Similarly, one can predict the daughter's paternalistic decision making about as well from knowledge of the daughter's profile of beliefs as from knowledge of the daughter's education and negative attitudes toward elders. Similarly, one also can predict shared decision making from knowledge of beliefs, although no antecedent variables as predictors were found.

It seems that certain key variables are common predictors in these various relationships. If the daughters have a less negative attitude toward elderly people in general, if they have a weaker attachment to their mothers, if they have a higher level of education, and if they have younger mothers, then there is a greater tendency for mothers to make autonomous decisions. On the other hand, if daughters have a more negative attitude toward elderly people in general, a greater attachment to their mothers, a lower level of education, and older mothers, then there is a greater tendency for daughters to make paternalistic decisions.

In considering beliefs and decision making from the mothers' perspective (using data collected from mothers), beliefs were found also to be related to the agent of decision making. Background variables were stronger predictors of mothers' autonomous decisions and daughters' paternalistic decisions than were mothers' autonomy and paternalism beliefs. In general, the relationships of beliefs to the agent of decision making were not as strong for mothers as they were for daughters, suggesting that daughters' views may predominate over those of their mothers in determining who will make caregiving decisions.

The observed relationships can be interpreted in terms of cultural and socialization factors. Despite recent efforts to promote a more positive image of older people, prejudice or discrimination toward elderly people may be still quite pervasive in our society and may even involve adult children's attitudes toward their own elderly parents, as well as attitudes among the elderly themselves. Members of older families and those with less education tend to hold such negative attitudes more frequently. Their origins may be found in the ideology of the traditional authoritarian family. Regardless of the cause, prejudice and negative attitudes toward elderly people in general tend to lead to paternalistic decision making when daughters provide care to elderly mothers.

In light of these results, the theory of the agent of decision making presented in Chapter 4 can be refined to include specifically these key background factors that directly and indirectly influence selection of the agent of decision making.

Further research needs to be done with longitudinal data to determine changes over time. Also, further studies should look at the input of dyad members' characteristics on dyadic interaction during the decision-making process, and the relationship of the latter to determining the agent of decision making.

From a practical standpoint, it is important to understand the autonomy and paternalism beliefs of adult children and elderly parents as a basis for attempting to modify these beliefs in order to promote the autonomy of older people who are receiving family care. One way in which beliefs (and underlying attitudes) might be modified is through further education of caregiving daughters, both in regard to general topics and more specifically in regard to understanding of the abilities and strengths of older people.

Practitioners working with mothers and daughters in a family caregiving situation should be sensitive to differences in autonomy and paternalism beliefs as a possible source of conflict between them.

The availability of instruments to assess beliefs in respect for autonomy and paternalism suggests possible uses in an applied setting. Practitioners are cautioned that the reliabilities of the Independent Autonomy and Shared Autonomy scales are of a magnitude that restricts their use to group comparisons. Although the reliability of the Total Paternalism instrument suggests that it could be used for conclusions about individuals, as well as for group comparisons, it is recommended that all three measures be used conservatively.

The scales might be used in a heuristic way by counselors for situations in which family conflict about caregiving is involved. Identifying underlying beliefs could be a focal point of counseling to resolve caregiving conflicts, to negotiate differences, and to accept compromises. The scales might be of value also in programs for the training of family caregivers to maximize the elderly parent's exercise of autonomy and minimize the adult child's exercise of paternalism. Assessment of caregivers could in itself increase their awareness and sensitivity to the existence of their beliefs and the implications of their decisions, as well as provide a baseline for any desired modification of beliefs in training programs.

(Although findings from use of the instrument are not reported in this book, the Autonomy/Paternalism Diagnostic Measure also developed in this project is presented in Appendix C. The instrument may be useful to practitioners seeking to identify the modal type of decision making preferred by daughters and mothers in dyadic family caregiving situations. It may help alert practitioners to conflicts that may exist between daughter and mother regarding the mode of decision making, or the degree to which they reinforce each other's views. In either case, counseling or working with such dyad could be facilitated by having such knowledge.)

From a standpoint of policy, a concerted effort should be made to educate families (particularly family caregivers) about elderly people in order to reduce prejudice and discrimination in regard to older people and to enhance their autonomy in later years.

Comparison of Multidyadic Sibling Caregiving to
Parent-Child Dyadic Caregiving

Although dyadic family caregiving was the main focus of this book, I felt that it would be fruitful to stray beyond this topic to gain some idea of how sibling participation in shared caregiving tasks for their elderly mothers affects autonomy and paternalism beliefs and caregiving decision making.

Apparently the degree of sibling participation in caregiving has little relationship to the principal caregiver's beliefs in independent autonomy, shared autonomy, and paternalism. Having at least one brother, however, seems to be related to a stronger belief in paternalism among daughters who are principal caregivers.

More important, when siblings share the responsibility of parent caregiving tasks more evenly, then fewer paternalistic decisions are made by the caregiver and more autonomous decisions are made by the elderly parent than when a single caregiver provides most of the care. The implication is that siblings acting as a group to provide care may be more respecting of an elderly parent's exercise of autonomy than a single adult child acting independently as a principal caregiver. When a principal caregiver is responsible for all or most of a parent's care, the pressures of caregiving tasks themselves may lead to paternalistic decisions based upon expediency quite apart from any other considerations. Further studies are needed to clarify these initial findings regarding the effects of sibling caregiving participation upon beliefs and decision making.

Given present-day trends toward increased longevity of elderly parents (particularly elderly widows), limitations on the formal care system, smaller siblingship sizes, larger numbers of women in the work force, and larger numbers of divorced and never-married adult children, it is likely that increased sibling cooperation in parent caregiving will occur in the future. All adult siblings, including brothers, will need to regard parent caregiving as a team function (Felder, 1990), to assume more equitable shares of caregiving duties, and to become more flexible in performing a variety of caregiving tasks. Daughters who traditionally would assume a principal caregiver's role will need to learn to shift to supporting roles as the situation demands. Women need to learn to delegate caregiving assignments to their siblings (including brothers) and to train and guide their brothers in taking on routine caregiving tasks. A happy by-product of this increased sibling cooperation would appear to be a greater respect for the elderly parent's exercise of autonomy in decision making.

Intergenerational Comparisons
on Autonomy and Paternalism

Intergenerational congruence is the degree of agreement between a pair of individuals separated by a generation, such as a mother and daughter. Thus congruence exists when there is agreement between mothers and daughters regarding beliefs in respect for autonomy and/or paternalism (e.g., if mothers are high on these beliefs, then their daughters also will be high).

When one is considering delegated or surrogate autonomy, then congruence in beliefs regarding autonomy and paternalism becomes important. In regard to surrogate autonomy, if the elderly person desires to have a family member make some future decision regarding care according to what the family member judges to be best, then no problem exists regarding congruence of views. But if the elderly person desires to have the family member make a choice as the elderly person would have wished, then a problem could exist. As shown in Chapter 6, congruence between family members on various topics related to decision making is only moderate at best. Thus family members may not be able to make accurate substituted judgments conveying an older person's wishes. Even in instances when family members are accurate in their knowledge of the older person's wishes, or when they simply feel that they know the older person's wishes, they may decide in terms of what they think is best for the elderly person (paternalism) despite their knowledge of the elder's desires.

One can only conclude that if elderly parents desire to have adult children carry out their wishes should they become incapacitated, then better communication is necessary. Parents should make their wishes known clearly to the adult children well in advance.

Parents' choice of the adult children as surrogates seems to be based upon trust and confidence that the parents and children have the same beliefs and values. Thus elderly parents seem to be more concerned that trusted, responsible adult children make decisions for them in case of future incapacity, regardless of whether the decisions are made according to the parents' wishes or according to what the children think is best for them. In either case, the quality of the relationship seems to have priority over the content of the decision; when the relationship is of high quality, the parents can feel secure that their well-being will be protected. Nevertheless, facilitating congruence between parents and their children in a caregiving situation is important in order to avoid conflict and promote greater willingness to work together.

If parent-child congruence can be explained by genetic similarity and/or family transmission of views through socialization, the lack of congruence may indicate that universal or common socialization across families is more difficult in today's world. Perhaps existing incongruence can be accounted for in terms of discontinuity in socialization between generations.

An intergenerational difference is the mean difference between pairs of adult daughters and elderly mothers on a given topic or variable. When intergenerational differences occur regarding beliefs in autonomy or paternalism, the average difference between mothers' and daughters' beliefs is appreciable, regardless of the degree of congruence among pair members.

In determining whether differences existed between the views of the generation of elderly parents and those of adult children about who should make decisions for elderly parents, I found that the two generations had similar beliefs regarding independent and shared autonomy but that the older generation had much stronger beliefs in paternalism. Belief in paternalism seemed to be preferred if it ensured the welfare, health, and safety of the elderly.

Although the majority of mothers and daughters felt that mothers should make their own decisions, a good-sized minority of mothers feel that the daughters should become involved in decision making. Both daughters and mothers felt that mothers should make their own decisions to a greater extent in the domain of everyday living than in the health or financial domains. Both adult daughters and elderly mothers agreed that paternalism is warranted when the mother is mentally incompetent but, in general, the adult daughter seems more reluctant to make paternalistic decisions than the elderly mother is ready to submit to such paternalistic decision making. This finding might be accounted for in terms of cultural or generational differences leading to discontinuity in socialization, or in terms of developmental changes within an individual's life span.

A FINAL THOUGHT

The initial aim of my work was to find antecedents of autonomous and paternalistic decision making that could be manipulated to promote the autonomy of the elderly in family caregiving situations and to avoid premature, unnecessary, or excessive paternalism.

The results of this investigation indicate the importance of education in such an effort, as one central theme stands out in the findings. Attitudes of prejudice exist toward the elderly in general, and apparently some adult children direct such attitudes toward their own elderly parents. These negative attitudes are reflected in the children's stronger beliefs in paternalism and in their making of a greater number of paternalistic decisions.

Such prejudice could arise from the transmission of the older generation's traditional authoritarian family culture from parents to children, as well as from other sources. Since better educated families tend to develop a more democratic family style, however, it is important for people to become more educated in general and, more specifically, to gain more knowledge of the elderly person in our culture. Optimistically, such knowledge could lead to a general view that the elderly still can remedy some defects, continue to grow, or at least make more decisions for themselves than family caregivers may be allowing them to do at present.

Limitations of Independent Autonomy

As much as one might wish to promote independent autonomy among the elderly, one must be realistic about its limitations or its value in a modern technological society.

Autonomous decision making in itself may be unrealistic if one continues to include rational or deliberated decisions as part of the definition. Many decisions in life are based upon rationalization, impulse, the existence of intense need, and so on. Yet what seems important is that one feels free to make the decision according to one's own needs and values. Perhaps the illusion that one has made freely a rational choice that leads to a beneficial outcome is a more important attribute of autonomy than actually being truly rational or deliberated. In dyadic decision making, the dyadic interaction itself plays a role in determining decisions above and beyond any internal process in the individuals. This situation may reduce further the rationality of the decision making.

Generally speaking, other limitations have more significance in the modern world. One must consider not only the decisional capacity of the care receiver but also the fluctuation of this capacity (Moody, 1985). One must not ignore the existence of alien values or goals in the individual, the degree of harm to self or society resulting from the decision, or the degree of selfishness involved in autonomous decision making that may jeopardize the common good of the family, the norms of society, or the rules and regulations of certain institutions. Perhaps the most challenging obstacle to independent autonomy in the modern world is the need for ever greater amounts of highly technical information as a basis for reasoned decisions leading to beneficial outcomes. A single individual no longer can hope to have the knowledge and expertise needed to make certain decisions. In a complex society, that person may lose forever the individualistic freedom of true independent autonomy.

Shared Autonomy

In this book, the term *shared autonomy* refers to the participation in some form of one or more other people in an individual's decision making. As discussed in Chapter 2, shared autonomy may include joint, delegated, and surrogate autonomy. In each case, the individual no longer makes his or her own decisions; a sharing of the decision occurs in some degree.

Perhaps instead of advocating independent autonomy, it is more realistic to think in terms of advocating shared autonomy or such ideas as paternalistic promotion of autonomy and negotiated autonomy (Moody, 1985). Perhaps, in a modern technological society, shared decision making might be a better ethical ideal. Shared autonomy would allow autonomy to exist, maximizing its positive side while drawing on the expertise of other family members to limit its negative consequences.

An emerging view about developmental gender differences may further justify shared autonomy as an ethical ideal. Humans need each other for their mutual development; they interact, communicate, and participate in various activities to form relationships that bind them together over time. They are involved in each other's lives, influencing each other in many areas (including decision making). Gilligan (1982, 1988) has concluded that important gender differences are found in interpersonal relationships. Men desire more privacy and independent autonomy, while women's basic need is for connectedness. Simply put, women have a greater need to relate to others. If this is true, then women would have a greater tendency than men for shared autonomy in decision making. In a modern, technological society, mature men (in contrast to the adolescents studied by Gilligan) also may have a need for connectedness. In other words, there may be a developmental change over time resulting in little gender difference in the need for connectedness in adulthood. If such a hypothesis were true, then the need for shared autonomy and for the cultivation of conditions for its occurrence among connected individuals would be great.

It was disappointing that in this study I found no anteced-ents of shared decision making other than belief in shared autonomy. Since the identification of a belief in shared auton-omy was itself an unexpected result of this work, I failed to include relevant antecedents in the study. One clue to a pos-sible antecedent of shared autonomy emerges from the review of previous literature in Chapter 4. Delegated and surrogate autonomy seem to depend more upon trust and confidence between family members than on any other factor. In other words, perhaps the best way to promote shared autonomy is to do so indirectly by enhancing the quality of the relationship between family members. Certainly, this is an important area for further research.

Appendix A

RESPECT FOR AUTONOMY SCALE

Each of the following statements concerns an elderly parent and an adult child. Please tell how much you agree or disagree with each statement: strongly agree (SA), agree (A), undecided (U), disagree (D), or strongly disagree (SD).

1. If an elderly parent of sound mind decides not to see the doctor about a chronic condition, the adult child should support the parent's decision.
2. If an elderly parent who is emotionally unstable wants to donate money to charity, the adult child should help the parent decide how much to give.
3. If an elderly parent of sound mind is away and a broken refrigerator must be replaced, the adult child should try to decide in the way the parent would.
4. If an elderly parent of sound mind must decide whether to have a series of difficult physical therapy treatments, the adult child and the parent should discuss the treatments, but the parent should decide what is to be done.
5. When an elderly parent who is forgetful asks an adult child to make decisions about regular living expenses, the adult child should try to decide things in the way that the parent would.
6. If an elderly parent who is of sound mind decides to drive alone across the country, the adult child should not interfere.

7. When an elderly parent who knows little about health matters must decide about having a heart operation, the adult child and the parent should decide together.

8. If an elderly parent is too physically ill to make decisions about paying household bills, the adult child should make such decisions but try to decide as the parent would.

9. If an elderly parent of sound mind is considering installing safety handbars in the house to prevent falls, an adult child should give his or her opinions about it but let the parent decide what to do.

10. When a mentally confused parent asks an adult child whether he or she should go to the hospital about leg pains, the child should put himself or herself in the parent's place when making the decision.

11. When an elderly parent of sound mind decides to invest a large part of his or her life savings in a very risky business venture, the adult child should not interfere.

12. When an elderly parent is mentally confused, the adult child and parent should decide together what visitors and social activities the parent should have.

13. When an elderly parent is too mentally confused to decide about having minor surgery, the adult child should put himself or herself in the parent's place before making the decision for the parent.

14. If an elderly parent of sound mind needs to decide about an insurance policy, the adult child should discuss the pros and cons of the policy with the parent but not try to influence the parent's decision.

15. If an elderly parent who is becoming forgetful asks an adult child to make decisions about household repairs, the adult child should do so but try to decide as the parent would.

16. Even when an elderly parent is mentally confused, the adult child still should respect the parent's decision not to take needed medicine that has unpleasant side effects.

17. If an elderly parent of sound mind asks an adult child to help decide how much money to leave various relatives in a will, the adult child should do so but try to keep in mind the wishes of the parent.

18. If an elderly parent is too mentally confused to make decisions about day-to-day personal care, the adult child should decide these things but do so in the way the parent would want them done.

19. If an elderly parent of sound mind is uncertain how to deal with a stomach problem, he or she may discuss this with the

adult child, but the parent should make the final decision regarding any treatment.

20. If an elderly parent of sound mind asks an adult child to handle banking decisions, the adult child should do so but make the decisions as the parent would want.

21. When an elderly parent who is very forgetful decides that he or she would be happier living alone in his or her own home no matter what the risk to his or her safety, the adult child should respect that decision.

22. When an elderly parent of sound mind needs to decide whether to go on a weight-reducing diet, the adult child and the parent should decide together what to do.

23. If an elderly parent is away on a long trip and cannot be reached for a needed decision about some property, the adult child should make the decision as he or she thinks the parent would have done.

24. If an elderly parent is somewhat mentally confused, the adult child and parent may discuss the parent's needs for new clothing, but the parent should decide what will be bought.

25. If an elderly parent of sound mind asks an adult child whether to see a doctor about headaches, the adult child should make a decision that fits in with the parent's views on medical treatment.

26. If an elderly parent who is mentally confused decides to buy more clothes than he or she needs, the adult child should not interfere.

27. If an elderly parent of sound mind needs to decide where to live in later years, the adult child and elderly parent together should reach a decision that best fits the parent's needs and values.

28. If an elderly parent of sound mind ignores the need to make a decision about having medical tests to find the cause of fainting spells, the adult child should try to see things from the parent's point of view in deciding whether the parent should take the medical tests.

29. If an elderly parent who no longer can think clearly needs to budget money for living expenses, the adult child should discuss the budget with the parent, but the parent should make the actual decisions about what to spend.

30. When an elderly parent of sound mind asks an adult child to make decisions about his or her diet, the adult child should do so but remember the parent's likes and dislikes.

PATERNALISM SCALE

Each of the following statements concerns an elderly parent and an adult child. Please tell how much you agree or disagree with each statement: strongly agree (SA), agree (A), undecided (U), disagree (D), or strongly disagree (SD).

1. No matter how much an elderly parent objects, the adult child should do whatever he or she thinks is best in the long run for the parent's health.
2. When an adult child knows more than an elderly parent about how to manage money, the child should take charge of the parent's spending but explain to the parent why it is necessary to do so.
3. When an elderly parent can no longer take care of himself or herself, he or she no longer has any say in how an adult child takes care of him or her.
4. If an adult child decides it is best for an elderly parent's health, he or she should slip needed medicine into the parent's food so that the parent has no chance to object.
5. If an elderly parent decides to risk a great deal of money in a business opportunity that is likely to fail, the adult child should forbid it.
6. If an elderly parent pays no attention to getting a proper diet, the adult child should decide what the parent will eat.
7. When necessary, an adult child should force an elderly parent to stick to a treatment the doctor ordered but also explain to the parent the need to do so.
8. Regardless of what the parent thinks should be done, if the parent is too confused to handle money anymore, the adult child should decide how to spend the money for the parent's benefit.
9. If it is for the elderly parent's own good, the adult child should do whatever is needed for day-to-day care of the parent regardless of what the parent thinks should be done.
10. An adult child should let an elderly parent try whatever treatments the parent thinks best for an illness but should stop the parent from doing so if the child thinks the parent would be harmed.
11. When an elderly parent pays no attention to things like paying bills or paying taxes, the adult child should take over and manage the parent's money.

12. When an elderly parent has decided to keep an electrical appliance that the adult child judges to be unsafe, the child should do something secretly to keep the appliance from working to be sure the parent will not use it.

13. When an elderly parent is senile, the adult child should do what he or she thinks is best for the parent's health, even if the parent has been against it all of his or her life.

14. It is all right for the adult child to force an elderly parent to agree to a financial arrangement for the older person's own good, even when the parent has decided against it.

15. It is all right for an adult child to force an elderly parent to change his or her daily routine as long as the adult child talks to the parent about it and explains why it is best.

16. When an elderly parent does not want to talk or think about an obvious health problem, the adult child should insist upon taking the parent to the doctor.

17. If an adult child decides that an elderly parent needs insurance that the parent feels is unnecessary, the adult child should arrange it without telling the parent.

18. An adult child should insist upon making changes in an elderly parent's living environment when something is harmful or unsafe for the elderly parent.

19. When an elderly parent must decide between treatments for an illness, the adult child should insist that the parent choose the treatment that will be best in the long run.

20. When an elderly parent becomes forgetful about financial matters, the adult child should take over and run things as he or she thinks best.

21. When an adult child decides that visits from certain friends are upsetting to the parent, the child should stop the friends from visiting without letting the parent know.

22. When an elderly parent has decided against having an operation that will prolong his or her life, the adult child should insist that the parent have the operation.

23. When an adult child decides that an elderly parent should be saving more money for an emergency, the child secretly should put some of the parent's money into a savings account each month.

24. If an elderly parent is mentally confused, the adult child should make whatever changes in the parent's daily routine that he or she judges to be best for the parent, even when the parent has lived that way for many years.

25. If an adult child can explain why a certain diet is best for the parent's health, the adult child should insist that the elderly parent follow the diet.

26. When the adult child knows a great deal more about managing finances than the elderly parent, the adult child should take charge of the parent's money matters.

27. An adult child should make whatever decisions are needed about a parent's daily living when the elderly parent does not seem to care what is done.

28. If an elderly parent ignores his or her own health, the adult child should make all decisions about medical treatments.

29. When an elderly parent has decided to spend a lot of money on an insurance policy that an adult child regards as worthless, the adult child should prevent the parent from doing so.

30. The adult child should make whatever decisions about the parent's daily care that he or she thinks will be best for the parent but should be sure to tell the parent why it is best.

Appendix B

Table B.1 Means and Standard Deviations of Independent
Autonomy Scores for Various Groups of
Adult Children and Elderly

Group	N	Mean	SD
Adult children from Lafayette, IN	147	36.66	5.95
Males	38	36.82	5.04
Females	109	36.57	6.28
Age < 52	63	37.94	6.67
Age > 52	84	35.70	5.19
High School education	34	36.59	7.34
Education past High School	113	36.69	5.51
Employed	97	36.23	6.21
Not employed	50	37.50	5.38
Adult children from Lafayette, IN	62	37.37	5.62
Adult children from Charlotte, NC	34	35.71	6.94
Elderly parents from Lafayette, IN	81	36.67	5.37
Males	17	37.94	6.80
Females	64	36.33	4.93
Age < 81	39	38.05	5.89
Age > 81	42	35.38	4.53
High School education	39	37.41	6.27
Education past High School	42	35.98	4.34
Married	32	37.44	5.96
Widowed	49	36.16	4.95
Elderly parents from Lafayette, IN	62	36.87	5.30
Elderly parents in senior housing in Lafayette, IN	15	35.20	3.05

Table B.2 Means and Standard Deviations of Shared Autonomy
Scores for Various Groups of Adult Children
and Elderly

Group	N	Mean	SD
Adult children from Lafayette, IN	147	69.33	6.51
Males	38	68.53	6.40
Females	109	69.55	6.60
Age < 52	63	68.02	7.98
Age > 52	84	70.30	4.97
High School education	34	70.91	7.36
Education past High School	113	68.85	6.19
Employed	97	69.04	6.93
Not employed	50	69.88	5.63
Adult children from Lafayette, IN	62	69.55	7.41
Adult children from Charlotte, NC	34	69.21	8.17
Elderly parents from Lafayette, IN	81	69.98	4.19
Males	17	71.00	5.11
Females	64	69.70	3.91
Age < 81	39	70.00	5.14
Age > 81	42	69.95	3.12
High School education	39	70.82	4.52
Education past High School	42	79.19	3.72
Married	32	70.09	4.54
Widowed	49	69.90	3.99
Elderly parents from Lafayette, IN	62	69.87	5.50
Elderly parents in senior housing in Lafayette, IN	15	69.13	1.77

Table B.3 Means and Standard Deviations of Paternalism Scores for Various Groups of Adult Children and Elderly

Group	N	Mean	SD
Adult children from Lafayette, IN	147	95.07	17.02
Males	38	99.05	16.50
Females	109	93.58	17.18
Age < 52	63	89.52	19.92
Age > 52	84	99.23	13.13
High School education	34	105.94	14.51
Education past High School	113	91.80	16.40
Employed	97	95.91	17.04
Not employed	50	93.44	17.05
Adult children from Lafayette, IN	62	89.87	16.84
Adult children from Charlotte, NC	34	97.29	17.67
Elderly parents from Lafayette, IN	81	98.43	14.91
Males	17	96.47	16.49
Females	64	98.95	14.56
Age < 81	39	96.13	18.17
Age > 81	42	100.57	10.87
High School education	39	99.95	18.43
Education past High School	42	97.02	10.71
Married	32	95.34	17.34
Widowed	49	100.44	12.88
Elderly parents from Lafayette, IN	62	103.68	12.96
Elderly parents in senior housing in Lafayette, IN	15	98.93	9.03

Appendix C

ETHICAL BELIEF SITUATION TEST

For each of the following situations, indicate who you think has the right to decide what should be done, parent or child. Then indicate why you think so.

Situation 1. Mrs. C is a 78-year-old widow. She lives alone but has poor vision and arthritis, which make her dependent upon her son for help. Her husband made all the decisions for her when he was alive, and now she relies upon the son for decisions.

Mrs. C developed a malignant ovarian tumor, and the doctor recommended surgery and chemotherapy. She told her son to talk to the doctor and to decide what was best. The son decided in favor of the surgery and chemotherapy, and Mrs. C signed the consent form.

After the surgery, Mrs. C began the chemotherapy, but she experienced extreme nausea and weakness. Suddenly, she refused to continue with the treatment. Mrs. C said, "I've never been so sick. If the cancer comes back, I'll deal with it." The doctor tells her that without the chemotherapy the cancer may come back.

The son feels that his mother is being unreasonable. He knows that if he pressures her, she will give in and continue with the treatments.

Who has the right to decide what should be done, mother or son?

Why do you feel the (mother, son) has the right to make the decision in this case?

Situation 2. Charles L is 77 years old. He lives alone but near his daughter. He has lived there for the past 15 years, managing on his Social Security. He has a strong sense of independence. Within the past 2 years, however, he has grown increasingly frail and has begun to show signs of memory loss. On one occasion he lost his way about a mile from his house and had to call his daughter to bring him home.

One evening, Mr. L fell on the stairs of his house and suffered a concussion and fractured foot. Fortunately, his daughter came over and found him. At the hospital, tests showed that he also had diabetes and was poorly nourished.

Mr. L's daughter feels that he should not live alone any longer and that he should come to live with her after he is discharged from the hospital. Mr. L is furious at the thought and insists that he should go back to his own home. He says that he can take care of himself and that he would be happier living there. He says he will take the risk of another accident in order to be independent.

Who has the right to decide what should be done, daughter or father?

Why do you feel the (daughter, father) has the right to make the decision in this case?

Situation 3. John M, 82 years old, lives with his son. He is alert, relatively vigorous, and active. He has diabetes, however, and has developed a gangrenous condition in his right foot. The doctor, after tests and consultations with specialists, recommends that the foot be amputated.

Mr. M says that he does not want to undergo the pain and risk of amputation surgery, especially at age 82. "I don't want to live with only one foot and be stuck in a wheelchair. I'll take a chance with this infection, even if it means the end."

His son attempts to change Mr. M's mind, explaining that without the amputation the condition will lead to great pain, immobilization, and possibly death. Mr. M sticks by his decision, saying that such an infection can get better and if it does not . . . he cannot live forever anyway.

The son feels that Mr. M's decision is unreasonable. He thinks perhaps he should force his father to get the amputation, even if it means having the father declared incompetent.

Who has the right to decide what should be done, father or son?

Why do you feel the (father, son) has the right to make the decision in this case?

Situation 4. Sarah F is in her late seventies and has been living with her daughter and her family for 9 months. Four months ago, Mrs. F had a case of pneumonia and was left too weak to get around on her own, so the daughter got a wheelchair for her. Although Mrs. F now appears to have recovered, she does not think so and does not want to leave her wheelchair. Medical tests show that nothing is wrong, but Mrs. F insists that the pneumonia has damaged her legs. She refuses to do any physical therapy sessions to strengthen her legs and is uncooperative with her daughter and other family members.

Mrs. F's daughter feels that perhaps she should remove the wheelchair in order to force her mother to try to walk. When she mentions that to her mother, Mrs. F says that she will just sit in her room if she does not have her wheelchair. She says she cannot use her legs no matter what anyone else says.

Who has the right to decide what should be done, daughter or mother?

Why do you feel the (daughter, mother) has the right to make the decision in this case?

Situation 5. Louise P is a 71-year-old widow who lives in her own home not far from her daughter. Although she has a few chronic complaints, she is in relatively good health. She has been active in her church for many years and is a strong believer in her faith.

Recently Mrs. P announced to her daughter that she wishes to make a large donation to help finance an educational center for the children of her church. To do so, she plans to sell her house and move into a small, inexpensive apartment near the church. The daughter feels that since Mrs. P has no assets other than her house, a small pension, and Social Security, making such a large gift to the church would leave her with nothing to fall back on in later years. Further, she says that the kind of apartment her mother could afford would not be adequate for the needs of an older person. Mrs. P argues that her needs are few now, that she does not need to have a house, and that she wants to do something that will provide the children of the church with a good start in life. Besides, it is her money to spend as she pleases, and the future will take care of itself.

Who has the right to decide what should be done, daughter or mother?

Why do you feel the (daughter, mother) has the right to make the decision in this case?

Situation 6. Thomas R is 84 years old and has lived next door to his son's family for the past 2 years. He has been confined to a wheelchair since a fall 3 years earlier and depends upon his son and daughter-in-law for help. Each month when he gets his Social Security check, he pays a taxicab driver to buy liquor and bring it to his house.

Within the past few months, Mr. R's monthly drinking episodes have become a problem as he has become hostile and verbally abusive to his son and daughter-in-law. On one occasion he attempted to hit his daughter-in-law when she tried to keep him from drinking too much. Mr. R's son and his wife feel that the father's drinking is not good for him and that perhaps they should stop the taxi driver from bringing him alcohol. Mr. R is angry at the thought of such a thing. He says that life in a wheelchair is very hard and that a little drinking once a month is a pleasure he does not want to give up. He says that since he pays his own expenses, he has a right to spend his money any way he wants.

Who has the right to decide what should be done, father or son?

Why do you feel the (father, son) has the right to make the decision in this case?

Situation 7. Mrs. D is a 69-year-old widow who lives alone in the same city as her son. She has always worked, and over the course of her life she has operated successfully a variety of small businesses. She and her husband had accumulated enough of a nest egg to allow them to live comfortably in their later years, but Mrs. D has become bored with retirement living since her husband's death. Mrs. D wants to use a large portion of her nest egg to open a gift shop in a new mall in their city. She says the challenge would be good for her, and she feels sure that she could make a go of it. Anyway, she says it is her decision and her risk.

Mrs. D's son works in the loan department at the local bank. He feels that the business his mother wants to start would be a bad risk and she is likely to lose the money she puts into it. He is worried that she no longer has the energy she thinks she has and would not be able to take on the long hours of the business. Also, he has noticed that she is occasionally forgetful and is afraid that she could not manage the business details. He wonders whether to use his influence at the bank to keep his mother from getting the lease for the shop at the mall.

Who has the right to decide what should be done, mother or son?

Why do you feel the (mother, son) has the right to make the decision in this case?

Situation 8. Raymond N is 73 years old and somewhat frail. He lives with his daughter and her husband and has been recuperating from a recent hip fracture. He spends most of the day in a wheelchair, although he can take a few halting steps on his own. A physical therapist visits every day, and Mr. N is making a little progress in his ability to walk.

One evening Mr. N fell while trying to get from his wheelchair to the bed. He wasn't hurt, but he fell again a few days later and bruised his arm. His daughter asked him not to try to get out of the wheelchair without her help, but he persisted in his little trips out of the wheelchair. Two weeks later, he fell again and was badly bruised.

His daughter has decided to tie him in the wheelchair for his own protection. She says, "I know you are having a difficult time now, but I think that you should think of what is best in the long run. If you fall again, you could really hurt yourself and be worse off than you are now." Mr. N is angry and demands to be untied, saying, "Life isn't worth living tied down like this. If I can't get up and try to walk a little, I'll never be able to walk again. Anyway, I may be dead tomorrow of something else."

Who has the right to decide what should be done, daughter or father?

Why do you feel the (daughter, father) has the right to make the decision in this case?

Situation 9. Mary T is 80 years old and has been widowed for many years. She lives in a small apartment near her married daughter and manages to remain independent. She is still in relatively good health but is beginning to get a little frail and forgetful.

Mrs. T has always enjoyed going shopping and likes to buy unexpected gifts for her daughter and grandchildren. Recently, she has shopped more than ever.

Mrs. T's daughter finds a stack of unpaid bills while visiting one day and a letter from her mother's landlord threatening eviction if the rent is not paid. She knows that her mother's income is enough to allow her to live comfortably and wonders if her mother is still able to manage her money in a responsible way.

The daughter confronts Mrs. T and says that she should take charge of her mother's money, paying the bills and doling out a weekly allowance. She feels that if Mrs. T goes on spending her money so foolishly, she no longer will be able to live on her own. Mrs. T says she does not want her daughter treating her like a child. She says she has been busy and has not got around to taking care of her bills. Mrs. T tells her daughter, "I haven't lost my mind yet. I know I've been a little extravagant lately, but life's not worth living if I can't buy something I like once in a while."

Who has the right to decide what should be done, daughter or mother?

Why do you feel the (daughter, mother) has the right to make the decision in this case?

Situation 10. Philip M, a widowed 83-year-old man, lives alone in the small house that he and his wife bought 60 years earlier. Mr. M has always taken great pride in his home and still keeps it in good repair.

However, the neighborhood has gone downhill, and there has been a good deal of crime lately. Mr. M's house was broken into once when he was out, although only a few small items were taken. Recently, he was mugged on the way to the store and his wallet taken. When a neighbor was beaten to death right across the street, Mr. M's son said, "That's enough, Dad! You must move out of this neighborhood right away. I don't want to see you dead too, or in the hospital."

Mr. M said, "I want to stay right here. I love this house. All my memories of the happy years with your mother are here. I know the neighborhood is not as good as it used to be, but I still have friends nearby. I don't keep much money around, and I don't go out at night. Anyway, at my age I don't have too much longer to live, and I want to be where I am happy." The son said, "I think you're too old to see the danger you're in. I'll move you out by force if I have to."

Who has the right to decide what should be done, son or father?

Why do you feel the (son, father) has the right to make the decision in this case?

Situation 11. Donald T, age 71, has been retired for 4 years. His wife died 2 years ago, and he lives alone. In addition to a small Social Security check each month, he has been living on the interest income from his life savings, which he has had invested in CDs at a local bank. Lately, Mr. T has grown very worried over world economic conditions. One day, he buys a safe and tells his son that he is going to take his money out of the bank and keep it in the safe at home, using it as needed. He says, "I'm worried that if things get worse, the banks will fail again the way they did in 1929. My father lost everything he had then."

The son says, "If you do that, your savings will be gone long before you die. You need the interest on your savings to have enough money to live on. The government insures bank savings, so you don't have to worry. Besides, you might get robbed at home. If you won't listen to reason, I'll have to take legal action to see that you don't do something foolish." Mr. T answers, "I worked hard all those years to save that money, and I'm not going to take any chances of losing it now."

Who has the right to decide what should be done, son or father?

Why do you feel the (son, father) has the right to make the decision in this case?

Situation 12. Anna P, age 74, is widowed. She has become quite forgetful and now lives with her married daughter. For many years, she has had severe arthritis in her shoulder joint, with pain and difficulty in moving her arm. At her last checkup, the doctor told Mrs. P that the joint was getting worse and recommended surgery. He said that he could clean out the joint and after 8 or 9 months of rehabilitation exercises, she would regain full movement in her shoulder.

Mrs. P doesn't want to have the operation, saying that she doesn't know if she could stand to go through the surgery and all those months of rehabilitation. She says, "I've lived with that bum shoulder all these years and can go on living with it. Besides, there's no guarantee that the shoulder will be better after I go through all that."

Mrs. P's daughter strongly urges her to go ahead with the surgery, saying, "If you don't do it, you could completely lose the use of that arm in the years ahead. Then you wouldn't be able to do most the things you can do now." Mrs. P says, "I'm too old to worry about the years ahead. Nobody in my family has lived past 80. I'm likely to go before my arm does."

Since Mrs. P is otherwise in good health, her daughter continues to press her to have the surgery.

Who has the right to decide what should be done, daughter or mother?

Why do you feel the (daughter, mother) has the right to make the decision in this case?

Scoring. Of the 12 decision situations presented above, 6 (#1, 2, 3, 4, 6, 8) were adapted from the work of Collopy (1986); the remaining 6 situations were original. Each response that the parent should make the decision is scored 1 point; the total autonomy score is the number of such autonomy-respecting decisions. The possible range of scores is 0-12.

(If so desired, the instrument might be scored for paternalistic decisions by scoring each response that the adult child should make the decision as 1 point; the total paternalism score is the number of such paternalistic decisions. The possible range of scores is 0-12. The reader should note that an autonomy-respecting decision and a paternalistic decision are mutually exclusive choices in this instrument; thus use of more than one of the scores would be redundant.)

AUTONOMY/PATERNALISM
DIAGNOSTIC MEASURES

For each of the following statements, select the alternative that you feel is the way the adult child should act in this situation.

1. If an elderly parent of sound mind is wondering whether to see a doctor when a chronic condition flares up, the adult child should
   a. not interfere with the parent's decision

   b. discuss the issue with the parent but let the parent decide
   c. reach a decision together with the parent
   d. make the decision if the parent cannot decide but do so the way he or she thinks the parent would
   e. make the decision the way he or she thinks the parent would but do so only if asked
   f. make the decision that he or she thinks would be best for the parent, regardless of the parent's views

2. When an elderly parent who has become forgetful needs to make decisions about regular living expenses, the adult child should

   a. not interfere with the parent's decision
   b. discuss the issue with the parent but let the parent decide
   c. reach a decision together with the parent
   d. make the decision if the parent cannot decide but do so the way he or she thinks the parent would
   e. make the decision the way he or she thinks the parent would but do so only if asked
   f. make the decision that he or she thinks would be best for the parent, regardless of the parent's views

3. When the elderly parent of sound mind needs to make a decision about where to live, the adult child should

   a. not interfere with the parent's decision
   b. discuss the issue with the parent but let the parent decide
   c. reach a decision together with the parent
   d. make the decision if the parent cannot decide but do so the way he or she thinks the parent would
   e. make the decision the way he or she thinks the parent would but do so only if asked
   f. make the decision that he or she thinks would be best for the parent, regardless of the parent's views

4. When an elderly parent who is somewhat confused is considering a decision about changing doctors, the adult child should

   a. not interfere with the parent's decision
   b. discuss the issue with the parent but let the parent decide
   c. reach a decision together with the parent
   d. make the decision if the parent cannot decide but do so the way he or she thinks the parent would
   e. make the decision the way he or she thinks the parent would but do so only if asked
   f. make the decision that he or she thinks would be best for the parent, regardless of the parent's views

5. When an elderly parent of sound mind is considering investing most of his or her life savings in a very risky business venture, the adult child should

   a. not interfere with the parent's decision
   b. discuss the issue with the parent but let the parent decide
   c. reach a decision together with the parent
   d. make the decision if the parent cannot decide but do so the way he or she thinks the parent would
   e. make the decision the way he or she thinks the parent would but do so only if asked
   f. make the decision that he or she thinks would be best for the parent, regardless of the parent's views

6. When an elderly parent is too confused to make a decision about his or her day-to-day personal care, the adult child should

   a. not interfere with the parent's decision
   b. discuss the issue with the parent but let the parent decide
   c. reach a decision together with the parent
   d. make the decision if the parent cannot decide but do so the way he or she thinks the parent would
   e. make the decision the way he or she thinks the parent would but do so only if asked
   f. make the decision that he or she thinks would be best for the parent, regardless of the parent's views

7. When an elderly parent of sound mind ignores the need to make a decision about having medical tests to find the cause of fainting spells, the adult child should

   a. not interfere with the parent's decision
   b. discuss the issue with the parent but let the parent decide
   c. reach a decision together with the parent
   d. make the decision if the parent cannot decide but do so the way he or she thinks the parent would
   e. make the decision the way he or she thinks the parent would but do so only if asked
   f. make the decision that he or she thinks would be best for the parent, regardless of the parent's views

8. When an elderly parent is no longer able to think clearly but needs to decide how to budget money to pay for living expenses, the adult child should

   a. not interfere with the parent's decision
   b. discuss the issue with the parent but let the parent decide
   c. reach a decision together with the parent

    d. make the decision if the parent cannot decide but do so the way he or she thinks the parent would

    e. make the decision the way he or she thinks the parent would but do so only if asked

    f. make the decision that he or she thinks would be best for the parent, regardless of the parent's views

9. When an elderly parent who is of sound mind is trying to decide whether to take a lengthy trip out of the country, the adult child should

    a. not interfere with the parent's decision

    b. discuss the issue with the parent but let the parent decide

    c. reach a decision together with the parent

    d. make the decision if the parent cannot decide but do so the way he or she thinks the parent would

    e. make the decision the way he or she thinks the parent would but do so only if asked

    f. make the decision that he or she thinks would be best for the parent, regardless of the parent's views

10. When an elderly parent is mentally confused but a decision must be made about a heart operation that could extend the parent's life, the adult child should

    a. not interfere with the parent's decision

    b. discuss the issue with the parent but let the parent decide

    c. reach a decision together with the parent

    d. make the decision if the parent cannot decide but do so the way he or she thinks the parent would

    e. make the decision the way he or she thinks the parent would but do so only if asked

    f. make the decision that he or she thinks would be best for the parent, regardless of the parent's views

11. When an elderly who is of sound mind needs to make a decision about an insurance policy, the adult child should

    a. not interfere with the parent's decision

    b. discuss the issue with the parent but let the parent decide

    c. reach a decision together with the parent

    d. make the decision if the parent cannot decide but do so the way he or she thinks the parent would

    e. make the decision the way he or she thinks the parent would but do so only if asked

    f. make the decision that he or she thinks would be best for the parent, regardless of the parent's views

12. When an elderly who is very forgetful needs to decide whether to continue living alone in his or her own home, the adult child should

   a. not interfere with the parent's decision
   b. discuss the issue with the parent but let the parent decide
   c. reach a decision together with the parent
   d. make the decision if the parent cannot decide but do so the way he or she thinks the parent would
   e. make the decision the way he or she thinks the parent would but do so only if asked
   f. make the decision that he or she thinks would be best for the parent, regardless of the parent's views

13. When an elderly parent of sound mind must decide whether to have a lengthy and difficult series of physical therapy treatments to allow him or her to walk again, the adult child should

   a. not interfere with the parent's decision
   b. discuss the issue with the parent but let the parent decide
   c. reach a decision together with the parent
   d. make the decision if the parent cannot decide but do so the way he or she thinks the parent would
   e. make the decision the way he or she thinks the parent would but do so only if asked
   f. make the decision that he or she thinks would be best for the parent, regardless of the parent's views

14. When an elderly parent who is becoming confused mentally is thinking about buying a lot of new clothes, the adult child should

   a. not interfere with the parent's decision
   b. discuss the issue with the parent but let the parent decide
   c. reach a decision together with the parent
   d. make the decision if the parent cannot decide but do so the way he or she thinks the parent would
   e. make the decision the way he or she thinks the parent would but do so only if asked
   f. make the decision that he or she thinks would be best for the parent, regardless of the parent's views

15. When an elderly parent of sound mind needs to make decisions about meal planning and preparation, the adult child should

   a. not interfere with the parent's decision
   b. discuss the issue with the parent but let the parent decide
   c. reach a decision together with the parent

d. make the decision if the parent cannot decide but do so the way he or she thinks the parent would
e. make the decision the way he or she thinks the parent would but do so only if asked
f. make the decision that he or she thinks would be best for the parent, regardless of the parent's views

Scoring. The response alternatives represent each of the five subtypes of autonomy, as well as paternalism

a. direct autonomy
b. consultive autonomy
c. joint autonomy
d. surrogate autonomy
e. delegated autonomy
f. paternalism

Scores for each of the subtypes of autonomy and paternalism can be obtained indicating the total number of times each response alternative is used over the entire 15 items, with a possible score ranging of 0-15 in each case. Although a forced-choice format was used, the large number of alternatives makes these scores relatively independent of each other.

Appendix D

Table D.1 Summary of Regression Analyses Predicting Mothers'
Autonomous Decisions from Background
Characteristics (Daughters' Data)

Variable	B	SE B	Beta	R	R^2
Attitude toward elders	−0.30	0.15	−.28*		
Affective feelings	−0.43	0.38	−.15		
Daughter's education	0.11	0.80	.05		
Mother's age	−0.46	0.19	−.35*	.52*	.27

*$p < .05$.

Table D.2 Summary of Regression Analyses Predicting
Shared Decisions from Background
Characteristics (Daughters' Data)

Variable	B	SE B	Beta	R	R^2
Attitude toward elders	−0.04	0.11	−.07		
Affective feelings	0.07	0.26	.04		
Daughter's education	−0.07	0.76	−.02		
Mother's age	0.09	0.12	.13	.13	.02

*$p < .05$.

Table D.3 Summary of Regression Analyses Predicting Daughters'
Paternalistic Decisions from Background
Characteristics (Daughters' Data)

Variable	B	SE B	Beta	R	R^2
Attitude toward elders	0.21	0.10	−29*		
Affective feelings	−0.01	0.29	.00		
Daughter's education	−1.59	0.81	−.29*		
Mother's age	0.11	0.14	.12	.48*	.23

*$p < .05$.

Table D.4 Summary of Regression Analysis for Variables Predicting the Mothers' Autonomous Decisions (Daughters' Data)

Variable	Step	B	SE B	Beta	R	R^2
Independent autonomy	1	0.81	0.27	.42*		
Shared autonomy	1	−0.35	0.18	−.28*	.45*	.20
Independent autonomy	2	0.63	0.27	.33*		
Shared autonomy	2	−0.33	0.18	−.26		
Attitude toward elders	2	−0.33	0.15	−.31*		
Affective feelings	2	−0.38	0.40	−.13		
Daughter's education	2	0.02	0.82	.02	.54*	.29

*$p < .05$.

Table D.5 Summary of Regression Analysis for Variables Predicting Shared Decisions (Daughters' Data)

Variable	Step	B	SE B	Beta	R	R^2
Shared autonomy	1	0.20	0.10	.30*	.30*	.09
Shared autonomy	2	0.22	0.11	.32*		
Attitude toward elders	2	−0.04	0.10	−.06		
Affective feelings	2	0.19	0.25	.12		
Daughter's education	2	0.01	0.73	.01		
Mother's age	2	0.05	0.12	.06	.33	.11

*$p < .05$.

Table D.6 Summary of Regression Analysis for Variables Predicting the Daughters' Paternalistic Decisions (Daughters' Data)

Variable	Step	B	SE B	Beta	R	R^2
Paternalism	1	0.14	0.06	.35*	.35*	.12
Paternalism	2	0.04	0.08	.09		
Attitude toward elders	2	0.16	0.14	.22		
Affective feelings	2	−0.06	0.32	−.03		
Daughter's education	2	−1.49	0.89	−.26		
Mother's age	2	0.10	0.14	.11	.49*	.24

*$p < .05$.

Table D.7 Summary of Regression Analysis for Variables Predicting
Adult Daughters' Belief in Independent Autonomy
($n = 46$)

Variable	Step	B	SE B	Beta	R	R^2
Daughter's education	1	0.67	0.62	.16		
Mother's age	1	−0.16	0.10	−.23	.29	.08
Daughter's education	2	0.59	0.64	.14		
Mother's age	2	−0.13	0.10	−.19		
Attitude toward elders	2	−0.20	0.10	−.35*		
Affective feelings	2	−0.45	0.22	−.31*	.53*	.28

*$p < .05$.

Table D.8 Summary of Regression Analysis for Variables Predicting
Adult Daughters' Belief in Paternalism ($n = 46$)

Variable	Step	B	SE B	Beta	R	R^2
Daughter's education	1	−5.89	1.93	−.41*		
Mother's age	1	0.67	0.31	.21*	.51*	.26
Daughter's education	2	−3.08	1.78	−.21		
Mother's age	2	0.31	0.28	.14		
Attitude toward elders	2	1.02	0.25	.52*		
Affective feelings	2	1.49	0.59	.31*	.71*	.51

*$p < .05$.

Table D.9 Summary of Regression Analyses Predicting Mothers'
Autonomous Decisions from Background
Characteristics (Mothers' Data)

Variable	B	SE B	Beta	R	R^2
Attitude toward elders	−0.07	0.10	−.01		
Affective feelings	−0.57	0.45	−.18		
Daughter's education	0.30	0.64	.11		
Mother's age	−0.46	0.18	−.39*	.45*	.20

*$p < .05$.

Table D.10 Summary of Regression Analyses Predicting Shared
Decisions from Background Characteristics
(Mothers' Data)

Variable	B	SE B	Beta	R	R^2
Attitude toward elders	0.08	0.06	.21		
Affective feelings	0.28	0.28	.16		
Daughter's education	0.24	0.65	.06		
Mother's age	−0.01	0.11	−.01	.27	.07

Table D.11 Summary of Regression Analyses Predicting Daughters'
Paternalistic Decisions from Background
Characteristics (Mothers' Data)

Variable	B	SE B	Beta	R	R^2
Attitude toward elders	−0.07	0.06	−.17		
Affective feelings	0.32	0.28	.15		
Daughter's education	−1.99	0.65	−.42*		
Mother's age	0.23	0.11	.31*	.52*	.27

*$p < .05$.

References

Aldous, J. (1987). New views on the family life of the elderly and the near-elderly. *Journal of Marriage and the Family, 49,* 227-234.

Aristotle (1925). *Ethica Nicomachia* (W. D. Ross, Trans.). London: Oxford University Press.

Beauchamp, T. L., & Childress, J. J. (1983). *Principles of biomedical ethics* (2nd ed.). New York: Oxford University Press.

Bengtson, V. L., Cutler, N. E., Mangen, D. J., & Marshall, V. W. (1985). Generations, cohorts, and relations between age groups. In R. H. Binstock & E. Shanas (Eds.), *Handbook of aging and the social sciences* (2nd ed.) (pp. 304-338). New York: Van Nostrand Reinhold.

Bennett, R., & Eckman, J. (1973). Attitudes toward aging: A critical examination of recent literature and implications for future research. In C. Eisdorfer & M. P. Lawton (Eds.), *The psychology of aging* (pp. 575-597). Washington, DC: American Psychological Association.

Biegel, D. E., & Blum, A. (1990). Introduction. In D. E. Biegel & A. Blum (Eds.), *Aging and caregiving: Theory, research, and policy* (pp. 9-24). Newbury Park, CA: Sage.

Blenkner, M. (1965). Social work and family relationships in later life with some thoughts on filial maturity. In E. Shanas & G. F. Streib (Eds.), *Social structure and the family: Generational relations* (pp. 46-59). Englewood Cliffs, NJ: Prentice-Hall.

Bowlby, J. (1979). *The making and breaking of affectional bonds.* London: Tavistock.

Bowlby, J. (1980). *Attachment and loss. Vol. 3. Loss, sadness, and depression.* New York: Basic Books.

Braiker, H., & Kelley, H. (1979). Conflict in the development of close relationships. In R. Burgess & T. Huston (Eds.), *Social exchange in developing relationships* (pp. 135-168). New York: Academic Press.

Brinberg, D., & Jaccard, J. (1989). Multiple perspectives on dyadic decision-making. In D. Brinberg & J. Jaccard (Eds.), *Dyadic decision making* (pp. 313-333). New York: Springer Verlag.

Brody, E. M. (1978). The aging of the family. *The Annals of the American Academy, 438*, 13-27.

Brody, E. M. (1985). Parent caring as a normative family stress. *The Gerontologist, 25*, 19-25.

Brody, E. M. (1990). *Women in the middle: Their parent care years.* New York: Springer.

Brody, E. M., Hoffman, C., Kleban, M. H., & Schoonover, C. B. (1989). Caregiving daughters and their local siblings: Perceptions, strains, and interactions. *The Gerontologist, 29*, 529-538.

Brody, E. M., Kleban, M. H., Hoffman, C., & Schoonover, C. B. (1988). Adult daughters and parent care: A comparison of one-, two-, and three-generation households. *Home Health Care Services Quarterly, 9*, 19-45.

Brody, H. (1978). The role of the family in medical decisions. *Theoretical Medicine, 8*, 253-257.

Byrne, D., & Kelley, K. (1981). *An introduction to personality* (3rd ed.). Englewood Cliffs, NJ: Prentice-Hall.

Callahan, D. (1984). Autonomy: A moral good, not a moral obsession. *Hastings Center Report, 14*, 40-42.

Cantor, M. H. (1975). Life space and the social support system of inner city elderly of New York. *The Gerontologist, 15*, 23-27.

Cantor, M. H. (1985). Families: A basic source of long-term care for the elderly. *Aging, 349*, 8-13.

Cassel, C. K. (1988). Ethical issues in the conduct of research in long term care. *The Gerontologist, 28*(Suppl.), 90-96.

Cassel, C. K., & Zweibel, N. R. (1987). Attitudes regarding life-extending medical care among the elderly and their children [Special Issue]. *The Gerontologist, 27*, 229A-230A.

Cherry, F., & Byrne, D. (1977). Authoritarianism. In T. Blass (Ed.), *Personality variables in social behavior* (pp. 109-133). Hillsdale, NJ: Erlbaum.

Cicirelli, V. G. (1980, December). *Adult children's views on providing services to elderly parents.* Report to the NRTA-AARP Andrus Foundation, Purdue University, Department of Psychological Sciences, West Lafayette, IN.

Cicirelli, V. G. (1981). *Helping elderly parents: The role of adult children.* Boston: Auburn House.

Cicirelli, V. G. (1983a). Adult children's attachment and helping behavior to elderly parents: A path model. *Journal of Marriage and the Family, 45*, 815-822.

Cicirelli, V. G. (1983b, August). *Agreement of elderly parent and adult child views on health.* Paper presented at the 91st Annual Convention of the American Psychological Association, Anaheim, CA.

Cicirelli, V. G. (1984). Marital disruption and adult children's perception of their siblings' help to elderly parents. *Family Relations, 33*, 613-621.

Cicirelli, V. G. (1988). A measure of filial anxiety regarding anticipated care of elderly parents. *The Gerontologist, 28*, 478-482.

Cicirelli, V. G. (1989, December). *A measure of family members' belief in autonomy and paternalism in relation to caregiving practices toward elderly parents* (Final report to the Retirement Research Foundation). West Lafayette, IN: Purdue University, Department of Psychological Sciences.

Cicirelli, V. G. (in press). Attachment theory in old age: Protection of the attached figure. In K. Pillemer & K. McCartney (Eds.), *Parent-child relations across the life span*. Hillsdale, NJ: Erlbaum.

Cole, T. R. (1985). Aging & meaning. *Generations, 10*(2), 49-52.

Cole, T. R. (1987). Class, culture, & coercion. *Generations, 11*(4), 9-15.

Collopy, B. J. (1986, December). *The conceptually problematic status of autonomy*. New York: Fordham University.

Collopy, B. J. (1988). Autonomy in long-term care: Some crucial distinctions. *The Gerontologist, 28*(Suppl.), 10-17.

Coulton, C. J., Dunkle, R. E., Chow, J. C., Haug, M., & Vielhaber, D. P. (1988). Dimensions of post-hospital care decision-making: A factor analytic study. *The Gerontologist, 28*, 218-223.

Coulton, C. J., Dunkle, R. E., Haug, M., Chow, J., & Vielhaber, D. P. (1989). Locus of control and decision making for posthospital care. *The Gerontologist, 29*, 627-632.

Coward, R. T., & Dwyer, J. W. (1990). The association of gender, sibling network composition, and patterns of parent care by adult children. *Research on Aging, 12*, 158-181.

Crowne, D. P., & Marlow, D. (1960). A new scale of social desirability independent of psychopathology. *Journal of Consulting Psychology, 24*, 349-354.

Dengiz, A., Rakowski, W., & Hickey, T. (1982, November). *A study of congruence between the elderly and their primary care providers*. Paper presented at the annual meeting of the Gerontological Society, Boston, MA.

Doty, P. (1986). Family care of the elderly: The role of public policy. *Milbank Memorial Fund Quarterly, 64*, 34-75.

Dreitzel, H. P. (1984). Generational conflict from the point of view of civilization theory. In V. Garms-Homolova, E. M. Hoerning, & D. Schaeffer (Eds.), *Intergenerational relationships* (pp. 17-26). Lewiston, NY: C. J. Hogrefe.

Dubler, N. N. (1990). Legal issues. In W. B. Abrams & R. Berkow (Eds.), *Merck Manual of Geriatrics* (p. 1147). Rahway, NJ: Merck Sharp & Dohme Research Laboratories.

Dworkin, G. (1988). *The theory and practice of autonomy*. New York: Cambridge University Press.

Ehrlich, H. J. (1978). Dogmatism. In H. London & J. E. Exner (Eds.), *Dimensions of personality* (pp. 129-164). New York: John Wiley.

Elias, N. (1982). *The civilizing process. Vol. II: Power and Civility*. New York: Urizon.

Feinman, S., & Lewis, M. (1984). Is there social life beyond the dyad? In M. Lewis (Ed.), *Beyond the dyad* (pp. 13-41). New York: Plenum.

Felder, L. (1990). *When a loved one is ill*. New York: New American Library.

Fincham, J. E., & Wertheimer, A. I. (1985). Using the health belief model to predict drug therapy defaulting. *Social Science & Medicine, 20*, 101-105.

Fishbein, M., & Ajzen, I. (1975). *Belief, attitude, intention and behavior*. Reading, MA: Addison-Wesley.

Fromm, E. (1941). *Escape from freedom*. New York: Rinehart.

Gadow, S. (1980a). Existential advocacy: Philosophical foundation in nursing. In S. F. Spicker & S. Gadow (Eds.), *Nursing images and ideals* (pp. 79-101). New York: Springer.

Gadow, S. (1980b). Medicine, ethics, and the elderly. *The Gerontologist, 20,* 680-685.

Gert, B., & Culver, C. M. (1979). The justification of paternalism. In W. L. Robison & M. S. Pritchard (Eds.), *Medical responsibility* (pp. 1-14). Clifton, NJ: Humana Press.

Gilligan, C. (1982). *In a different voice: Psychological theory and women's development.* Cambridge, MA: Harvard University Press.

Gilligan, C. (1988). Remapping the moral domain: New images of the self in relationship. In C. Gilligan, J. V. Ward, & J. M. Taylor (Eds.), *Mapping the moral domain* (pp. 3-19). Cambridge, MA: Harvard University Press.

Gilliland, N., & Havir, L. (1990). Public opinion and long-term care policy. In D. E. Biegel & A. Blum (Eds.), *Aging and caregiving: Theory, research, and policy* (pp. 242-253). Newbury Park, CA: Sage.

Gillon, R. (1985). Autonomy and consent. In M. Lockwood (Ed.), *Moral dilemmas in modern medicine* (pp. 111-125). New York: Oxford University Press.

Goetting, A. (1986). The developmental tasks of siblingship over the life cycle. *Journal of Marriage and the Family, 48,* 703-714.

Goodnow, J. J. (1990). Shared activity: Its nature and norms. *Newsletter: International Society for the Study of Behavioural Development,* (No. 1, Serial No. 17), pp. 1-2.

Gronvold, R. L. (1988). Measuring affectual solidarity. In D. J. Mangen, V. L. Bengtson, & P. H. Landry, Jr. (Eds.), *Measurement of intergenerational relations* (pp. 74-97). Newbury Park, CA: Sage.

Gubrium, J. F. (1991). *The mosaic of care: Frail elderly and their families in the real world.* New York: Springer.

Hagemann-White, C. (1984). The societal context of women's role in family relationships and responsibilities. In V. Garms-Homolova, E. M. Hoerning, & D. Schaeffer (Eds.), *Intergenerational relationships* (pp. 133-142). Lewiston, NY: C. J. Hogrefe.

Halper, T. (1980). The double-edged sword: Paternalism as a policy in the problems of aging. *Milbank Memorial Fund Quarterly/Health and Society, 58,* 472-499.

Hansson, R. O., Nelson, R. E., Carver, M. D., NeeSmith, D. H., Dowling, E. M., Fletcher, W. L., & Suhr, P. (1990). Adult children with frail elderly parents: When to intervene? *Family Relations, 39,* 153-158.

Held, T. (1984). Intergenerational co-residence and the transfer of authority: Some illustrations from Austrian household listings. In V. Garms-Homolowa, E. M. Hoerning, & D. Schaeffer (Eds.), *Intergenerational relationships* (pp. 41-52). Lewiston, NY: C. J. Hogrefe.

High, D. M. (1987). Planning for decisional incapacity: A neglected area in ethics and aging. *Journal of the American Geriatrics Society, 35,* 814-820.

High, D. M. (1988). All in the family: Extended autonomy and expectations in surrogate health care decision-making. *The Gerontologist, 28* (Suppl.), 46-51.

High, D. M. (1989a). Caring for decisionally incapacitated elderly. *Theoretical Medicine, 10,* 83-96.

High, D. M. (1989b). Standards for surrogate decision making: What the elderly want. *The Journal of Long-Term Care Administration, 17*(2), 8-13.

High, D. M. (1990a). Old and alone: Surrogate health care decision-making for the elderly without families. *Journal of Aging Studies, 4,* 277-288.

High, D. M. (1990b). Who will make health care decisions for me when I can't? *Journal of Aging and Health, 2,* 291-309.

High, D. M., & Turner, H. B. (1987). Surrogate decision-making: The elderly's familial expectations. *Theoretical Medicine, 8,* 303-320.

Hinde, R. A. (1989). Reconciling the family systems and the relationship approaches to child development. In K. Kreppner & R. M. Lerner (Eds.), *Family systems and life-span development* (pp. 149-163). Hillsdale, NJ: Erlbaum.

Hofland, B. F. (1988). Autonomy in long term care: Background issues and a programmatic response. *The Gerontologist, 28,*(Suppl.), 3-9.

Hollingshead, A. B. (1957). *Two-factor index of social position.* New Haven, CT: Author.

Horowitz, A., & Dobrof, R. (1982, May). *The role of families in providing long-term care to the frail and chronically ill elderly living in the community.* New York: Brookdale Center on Aging of Hunter College.

Horowitz, A., & Reinhardt, J. (1988, November). *Issues concerning personal autonomy within family caregiving relationships.* Paper presented at the 41st Annual Scientific Meeting of the Gerontological Society of America, San Francisco, CA.

Horowitz, A., Silverstone, B. M., & Reinhardt, J. P. (in press). A conceptual and empirical exploration of personal autonomy issues within family caregiving relationships. *The Gerontologist.*

Huber, O. (1989). Information-processing operators in decision making. In H. Montgomery & O. Svenson (Eds.), *Process and structure in human decision making* (pp. 3-21). New York: John Wiley.

Hummert, M. L. (1990). Multiple stereotypes of elderly and young adults: A comparison of structure and evaluations. *Psychology and Aging, 5,* 182-193.

Jaccard, J., Brinberg, D., & Dittus, P. (1989). Couple decision making: Individual and dyadic-level analysis. In D. Brinberg & J. Jaccard (Eds.), *Dyadic decision making* (pp. 81-103). New York: Springer Verlag.

Jecker, N. S. (1990). The role of intimate others in medical decision making. *The Gerontologist, 30,* 65-71.

Johnson, C. (1983). Dyadic family relations and social support. *The Gerontologist, 23,* 377-383.

Johnson, C. L., & Catalano, D. J. (1981). Childless elderly and their family supports. *The Gerontologist, 21,* 610-618.

Kahana, E., & Young, R. (1990). Clarifying the caregiving paradigm. In D. E. Biegel & A. Blum (Eds.), *Aging and caregiving: Theory, research, and policy* (pp. 76-97). Newbury Park, CA: Sage.

Kane, R. A., Illston, L. H., Eustis, N. N., & Kane, R. L. (1990). *Quality of home care: Concepts and measures* (Contract No. 500-89-0056). Minneapolis, MN: University of Minnesota, School of Public Health.

Kane, R. A., & Kane, R. L. (1982). *Long-term care: Principles, programs and policies.* New York: Springer.

Kant, I. (1964). *Groundwork of the metaphysics of morals* (H. J. Paton, Trans.). New York: Harper & Row.

Keith, P. M. (1983). Patterns of assistance among parents and the childless in very old age: Implications for practice. *Journal of Gerontological Social Work, 6*(1), 49-59.

Kenny, D. A., & Acitelli, L. K. (1989). The role of the relationship in marital decision making. In D. Brinberg & J. Jaccard (Eds.), *Dyadic decision making* (pp. 51-62). New York: Springer Verlag.

Kite, M. E., & Johnson, B. T. (1988). Attitudes toward older and younger adults: A meta-analysis. *Psychology and Aging, 3,* 233-244.

Kogan, N. (1961). Attitudes toward old people: the development of a scale and an examination of correlates. *Journal of Abnormal and Social Psychology, 62,* 44-54.

Lachman, M., & McArthur, L. (1986). Adulthood age differences in causal attributions for cognitive, physical, and social performance. *Psychology and Aging, 2,* 127-132.

Levin, W. C. (1988). Age stereotyping. *Research on Aging, 10,* 134-148.

Larzelere, R. E., & Huston, T. L. (1980). The Dyadic Trust Scale: Toward understanding interpersonal trust in close relationships. *Journal of Marriage and the Family, 42,* 595-604.

Linn, B. G., Linn, M. W., & Knopka, P. (1978). The very old patient in ambulatory care. *Medical Care, 16,* 604-610.

Livingston, M. (1987). How illness affects patients' families. *British Journal of Medicine, 38,* 51-53.

Maddox, G. L., & Douglas, E. B. (1973). Self-assessment of health: A longitudinal study. *Journal of Health and Social Behavior, 14,* 87-93.

Mancini, J. A., Thompson, L., Blieszner, R., & Travis, S. S. (1985, November). *Measurement of affection and antagonism in aged parent-adult child relations.* Paper presented at the annual meeting of the National Council on Family Relations, Dallas, TX.

Mangen, D. J., & Westbrook, G. J. (1988). Measuring intergenerational norms. In D. J. Mangen, V. L. Bengtson, & P. H. Landry, Jr. (Eds.), *Measurement of intergenerational relations* (pp. 187-206). Newbury Park, CA: Sage.

Marshall, V. W. (1981). Physician characteristics and relationships with older patients. In M. R. Haug (Ed.), *Elderly patients and their doctors* (pp. 94-118). New York: Springer.

Maslow, A. H. (1967). A theory of metamotivation: The biological rooting of the value-life. *Journal of Humanistic Psychology, 7,* 93-127.

Matthews, S. H. (1987). Provision of care to old parents: Division of care among adult children. *Research on Aging, 9,* 45-60.

Matthews, S. H. (1988, October). *Gender and the division of filial responsibility.* Paper presented at the Conference on Gender Roles through the Life Course, Ball State University, Muncie, IN.

Matthews, S. H., Delaney, P. J., & Adamek, M. E. (1989). Male kinship ties: Bonds between adult brothers. *American Behavioral Scientist, 33,* 58-69.

Matthews, S. H., & Rosner, T. T. (1988). Shared filial responsibility: The family as primary caregiver. *Journal of Marriage and the Family, 50,* 185-195.

Matthews, S. H., & Sprey, J. (1989). Older family systems: Intra- and intergenerational relations. In J. A. Mancini (Ed.), *Aging parents and adult children* (pp. 63-67). Lexington, MA: D. C. Heath.

Mill, J. S. (1926). *On liberty and other essays.* New York: Macmillan.

Montada, L., & Bierhoff, H. W. (in press). Studying prosocial behavior in social systems. In L. Montada & H. W. Bierhoff (Eds.), *Altruism in social systems* (pp. 1-26). Toronto: Hogrefe.

Montada, L., Schmitt, M., & Dalbert, C. (in press). Prosocial commitments in the family: Situational, personality, and systemic factors. In L. Montada & H. W. Bierhoff (Eds.), *Altruism in social systems* (pp. 177-203). Toronto: Hogrefe.

Montgomery, R. J. V., & Kamo, Y. (1989). Parent care by sons and daughters. In J. A. Mancini (Ed.), *Aging parents and their adult children* (pp. 213-230). Lexington, MA: Lexington.

Moody, H. R. (1985). Ethics and aging: Old answers, new questions. *Generations, 10*(2), 4-7.

Moody, H. R. (1987). Ethical dilemmas in nursing home placement. *Generations, 11*(4), 16-23.

Noelker, L. S., & Townsend, A. L. (1987). The impact of parental impairment, community resources, and caregiver characteristics. In T. H. Brubaker (Ed.), *Aging, health and family: Long-term care* (pp. 58-79). Beverly Hills, CA: Sage.

Nunnally, J. C. (1967). *Psychometric theory*. New York: McGraw-Hill.

Nye, F. I., & Berardo, F. M. (1973). *The family: Its structure and interaction*. New York: Macmillan.

Phillips, L. R., & Rempusheski, V. F. (1985, November). *Validating an instrument to measure beliefs about caregiving*. Paper presented at the 38th Annual Scientific Meeting of the Gerontological Society of America, New Orleans, LA.

Pines, H. (1973). Locus of control orientation and informational dependence. *Journal of Personality and Social Psychology, 26*, 262-272.

Poole, M. S., & Billingsley, J. (1989). The structuring of dyadic decisions. In D. Brinberg & J. Jaccard (Eds.), *Dyadic decision making* (pp. 216-248). New York: Springer Verlag.

Pratt, C. C., Jones, L. L., Shin, H. Y., & Walker, A. J. (1989). Autonomy and decision-making among single older women and their caregiving daughters. *The Gerontologist, 29*, 792-797.

Pratt, C., Schmall, V., & Wright, S. (1987). Ethical concerns of family caregivers to dementia patients. *The Gerontologist, 27*, 632-638.

Pruitt, D. G. (1981). *Negotiation behavior*. New York: Academic Press.

Rakowski, W., & Hickey, T. (1979, November). *Family resource persons and geriatric clinic outpatients: Examining congruence of health beliefs and temporal perspective*. Paper presented at the 107th Annual Meeting of the American Public Health Association, New York.

Rakowski, W., & Hickey, T. (1983). Older adult patients and family resource persons: Examining congruence of health beliefs and temporal perspective. *Interdisciplinary Topics in Gerontology, 17*, 1-9.

Rand McNally & Co. (1987). *Road Atlas: United States-Canada-Mexico*. Chicago: Rand McNally.

Ransom, D. C., Fisher, L., Phillips, S., Kokes, R. F., & Weiss, R. (1990). In T. W. Draper & A. C. Marcos (Eds.), *Family variables: Conceptualization, measurement, and use* (pp. 48-63). Newbury Park, CA: Sage.

Raush, H. L., Barry, W. A., Hertel, R. K., & Swain, M. A. (1974). *Communication and conflict in marriage*. San Francisco: Jossey-Bass.

Raveis, V. H., Siegel, K., & Sudit, M. (1990). Psychological impact of caregiving on the caregiver: Critical review of methodologies. In D. E. Biegel & A. Blum (Eds.), *Aging and caregiving: Theory, research, and policy* (pp. 53-75). Newbury Park, CA: Sage.

Reid, D. W. (1984). Participatory control and the chronic illness adjustment process. In H. M. Lefcourt (Ed.), *Research with the locus of control concept: Vol. 3, Extensions and limitations* (pp. 361-389). Orlando, FL: Academic Press.

Reid, D. W., Haas, G., & Hawkings, D. (1977). Locus of desired control and positive self-concept of the elderly. *Journal of Gerontology, 32,* 441-450.

Rhoden, N. (1988). Litigating life and death. *Harvard Law Review, 102,* 375-446.

Rogers, C. R. (1963). Actualizing tendency in relation to "motives" and to consciousness. In M. R. Jones (Ed.), *Nebraska symposium on motivation.* Lincoln, NE: University of Nebraska Press.

Rokeach, M. (1960). *The open and closed mind: Investigations into the nature of belief systems and personality systems.* New York: Basic Books.

Roscowe, I. (1981). Coalition in geriatric medicine. In M. R. Haug (Ed.), *Elderly patients and their doctors* (pp. 137-146). New York: Springer.

Rosenberg, M. (1965). *Society and the adolescent self-image.* Princeton, NJ: Princeton University Press.

Rothbaum, R., Weisz, J. R., & Snyder, S. S. (1982). Changing the world and changing the self: A two process model of perceived control. *Journal of Personality and Social Psychology, 42,* 5-37.

Rotter, J. B. (1966). Generalized expectancies for internal versus external control of reinforcement. *Psychological Monographs, 80*(1), 1-28.

Rotter, J. B. (1971). Generalized expectancies for interpersonal trust. *American Psychologist, 26,* 443-452.

Scanzoni, J. (1989). Joint-decision making in the contemporary sexually based primary relationship. In D. Brinberg & J. Jaccard (Eds.), *Dyadic decision making* (pp. 251-267). New York: Springer Verlag.

Schlesinger, M. R., Tobin, S. S., & Kulys, R. (1980). The responsible child and parental well-being. *Journal of Gerontological Social Work, 3*(2), 3-16.

Schulz, R. (1986). Successful aging: Balancing primary and secondary control. *Adult Development and Aging News, 13*(3), 2-4.

Schulz, R. (1990). Theoretical perspectives on caregiving: Concepts, variables, and methods. In D. E. Biegel & A. Blum (Eds.), *Aging and caregiving: Theory, research, and policy* (pp. 27-49). Newbury Park, CA: Sage.

Shanas, E. (1979). The family as a social support system in old age. *The Gerontologist, 19,* 169-174.

Shanas, E. (1980). Older people and their families: The new pioneers. *Journal of Marriage and the Family, 42,* 9-15.

Sigel, I. E. (1985). A conceptual analysis of beliefs. In I. E. Sigel (Ed.), *Parental belief systems: The psychological consequences for children* (pp. 345-372). Hillsdale, NJ: Erlbaum.

Sillars, A., & Kalblesch, P. J. (1989). Implicit and explicit decision-making styles in couples. In D. Brinberg & J. Jaccard (Eds.), *Dyadic decision making* (pp. 179-201). New York: Springer Verlag.

Spitze, G., & Logan, J. (1990). Sons, daughters, and intergenerational social support. *Journal of Marriage and the Family, 47,* 335-348.

Stanley, B., Stanley, M., Guido, J., & Garvin, L. (1988). The functional capacity of elderly at risk. *The Gerontologist, 28*(Suppl.), 53-58.

Steiner, I. D. (1972). *Group process and productivity.* New York: Academic Press.

Steinmetz, S. K., & Amsden, D. J. (1983). Dependent elders, family stress, and abuse. In T. H. Brubaker (Ed.), *Family relationships in later life* (pp. 173-192). Beverly Hills, CA: Sage.

Stinnett, N., & Walters, J. (1977). *Relationships in marriage and family.* New York: Macmillan.

Stoller, E. P. (1990). Males as helpers: The roles of sons, relatives, and friends. *The Gerontologist, 30,* 228-235.

Stoller, E. P., & Earl, L. L. (1983). Help with activities of everyday life: Sources of support for institutionalized elderly. *The Gerontologist, 23,* 64-70.

Stone, R., Cafferata, G., & Sangl, J. (1987). Caregivers of the frail elderly: A national profile. *The Gerontologist, 27,* 616-626.

Tennstedt, S. L., & McKinlay, J. B. (1989). Informal care for frail older persons. In M. G. Ory & K. Bond (Eds.), *Aging and health care* (pp. 145-165). New York: Routledge.

Tennstedt, S. L., McKinlay, J. B., & Sullivan, L. M. (1989). Informal care for frail elders: The role of secondary caregivers. *The Gerontologist, 29,* 677-683.

Thompson, E. (1990). Two into one: Structural models of couple behavior. In T. W. Draper & A. C. Marcos (Eds.), *Family variables: Conceptualization, measurement, and use* (pp. 129-142). Newbury Park, CA: Sage.

Tomlinson, T., Howe, K., Notman, M., & Rossmiller, D. (1990). An empirical study of proxy consent for elderly persons. *The Gerontologist, 30,* 54-64.

Tonti, M. (1988). Relationships among adult siblings who care for their aged parents. In M. D. Kahn & K. G. Lewis (Eds.), *Siblings in therapy: Life span and clinical issues* (pp. 417-434). New York: Norton.

Townsend, A. L., & Poulshock, S. W. (1986). Intergenerational perspectives on impaired elders' support networks. *Journal of Gerontology, 41,* 101-109.

Treas, J. (1977). Family support systems for the aged: Some demographic and social considerations. *The Gerontologist, 17,* 486-491.

Troll, L. E. (1971). The family of later life: A decade review. *Journal of Marriage and the Family, 33,* 263-290.

Uhlmann, R. F., Pearlman, R. A., & Cain, K. C. (1988). Physicians' and spouses' predictions of elderly patients' resuscitation preferences. *Journal of Gerontology: Medical Sciences, 43,* M115-121.

von Winterfeldt, D. V., & Edwards, W. (1986). *Decision analysis and behavioral research.* London: Cambridge University Press.

Warren, J. W., Sobal, J., Tenney, J. H., Hoopes, J. M., Damron, D., Levenson, S., DeForge, B. R., & Muncie, H. L., Jr. (1986). Informed consent by proxy: An issue in research with elderly patients. *The New England Journal of Medicine, 315,* 1124-1128.

Wetle, T. (1985). Ethical issues in long term care of the aged. *Journal of Geriatric Psychiatry, 18,* 63-73.

Wheeler, R., & Davis, J. M. (1979). Decision-making as a function of locus of control and cognitive dissonance. *Psychological Reports, 44,* 499-502.

White, D. L. (1989). Addressing critical issues in care of the elderly. In M. D. Peterson & D. L. White (Eds.), *Health care of the elderly: An information sourcebook* (pp. 11-25). Newbury Park, CA: Sage.

Wolk, S. (1976). Situational constraint as a moderator of the locus of control-adjustment relationship. *Journal of Consulting and Clinical Psychology, 44,* 420-427.

Woodward, N. J., & Wallston, B. S. (1987). Age and health care beliefs: Self-efficacy as a mediator of low desire for control. *Psychology and Aging, 2,* 3-8.

Young, R. (1986). *Personal autonomy: Beyond negative and positive liberty.* New York: St. Martin's.

Zarit, S. H., Reever, K. E., & Bach-Peterson, J. (1980). Relatives of the impaired elderly: Correlates of feelings of burden. *The Gerontologist, 26,* 260-266.

Ziegler, M., & Reid, D. W. (1979). Correlates of locus of desired control in two samples of elderly persons: Community residents and hospitalized patients. *Journal of Consulting and Clinical Psychology, 47,* 977-979.

Zweibel, N. R., & Cassel, C. K. (1989). Treatment choices at the end of life: Comparison of decisions by older patients and their physician-selected proxies. *The Gerontologist, 29,* 615-621.

Zweibel, N. R., & Lydens, L. A. (1990). Incongruent perceptions of older adult/caregiver dyads. *Family Relations, 39,* 63-67.

Author Index

Subject Index

249

About the Author

Victor G. Cicirelli is Professor of Developmental and Aging Psychology in the Department of Psychological Sciences at Purdue University in West Lafayette, Indiana, where he has been since 1970. He received a Ph.D. in educational psychology from the University of Michigan in 1964 and a Ph.D. in developmental psychology from Michigan State University in 1971. In addition, he holds a master's degree in philosophy from the University of Illinois. He is a Fellow of the American Psychological Association and of the Gerontological Society of America. Currently he serves on the editorial board of the *Journal of Marriage and the Family*. He has been a Postdoctoral Fellow at both the Institute for Cognitive Learning at the University of Wisconsin and the Andrus Gerontology Center of the University of Southern California. In the spring of 1991, he held a Visiting Research Fellowship at the Center for Psychology and Human Development of the Max Planck Institute for Human Development and Education in Berlin. In addition to his teaching activities in gerontological psychology, his research interests include parent-child relationships in later life, sibling relationships, and family support of the elderly. Most recently, he has directed a research project investigating family members' beliefs in autonomy and paternalism in relation to care of the elderly. In addition to the present volume, he is the author of *Helping Elderly Parents: Role of Adult Children*, as well as numerous articles and book chapters.